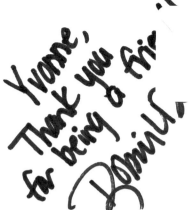

Yvonne,
Thank you
for being a frie...
Bonnie...

MW00939478

Steel Town Girl

By

Robin Donnelly

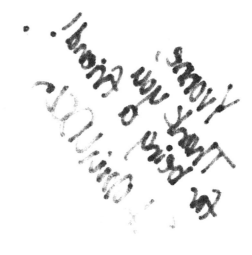

Dedication

For Robin Lynn,
I'm sorry it took me so long to come back for you.
I hope you can forgive me for leaving you behind
without a voice for your pain.
I see you now and I hear you loud and clear.
Be free, little one.

Acknowledgements

The most special thank you goes to my husband, Jeff, whose love, support, and the space he provided me to wrestle demons helped me bring this book to life. I love you and will forever be grateful for you.

And to my sons, Cody and Dylan,

Don't let society tell you that big boys don't cry or that your feelings don't matter. Feel all your feelings no matter how *over them* you think you should be and if there ever comes a time when life gets too difficult to manage alone, please promise me you'll reach out for help and if necessary, go to counseling. There is no shame in needing help. Your strength will always be there but will get buried beneath the weight of life at times, and sometimes we need someone else to help us find our strength and our light again. Please know, I love you both more than I could ever express and will always do whatever it takes to be there for you whenever you need me.

A special thank you to my original therapist, Susan, who picked up on my newly exacerbated symptoms as C/PTSD and encouraged me to continue with no contact from those who had abused and discarded me, and recommended huge amounts of self-love as treatment for overcoming the pain of narcissistic abuse. Thank you for recommending further research and reading. It all makes perfect sense now.

Special thanks to my therapist, Lanny, for pointing out the ways in which I was allowing myself to still be abused as a result of childhood conditioning and for helping me dig deeper in the cesspool of garbage I had to wade through to get to the other side of this bridge. Without my weekly appointments, where I raged, ranted, sobbed, cussed and shook with all the feelings I had suppressed for so long, I don't think I could have made it to the other side.

You both taught me that trusting my feelings and intuitions, regardless of what others say, is where I needed to start to find my strength again.

Thank you to my editor, Lauren Baratz-Logsted, for taking on the challenge of editing my manuscript while working feverishly to publish another of her own. Thank you for comforting me when I was afraid of being judged, but for being firm in explaining your job as editor as helping me walk the red carpet at the Academy Awards and how it was simply your job to make sure I looked as gorgeous as possible. — I feel beautiful! — And, look! My dress twirls!

And last, but not least, thank you to Carl Graves of *Extended Imagery* for designing the book cover for Steel Town Girl and hitting it out of the park; and Cheryl Perez of *You're Published* for all the hand-holding she did for me during the formatting process and for her expertise in formatting for Kindle, inside design, layout and for her spine and back cover design that brought it all home.

I am grateful and appreciative to you all.

"Someone I loved once gave me a box full of darkness. It took years to understand that this, too, was a gift."

~ Mary Oliver

Prologue

The rickety old bridge was the stuff nightmares were made of. The two-lane bridge with a pedestrian sidewalk to one side was a huge silver steel contraption marred with rust streaks and black skid marks down its insides. It was the Steubenville Bridge and you had to cross it to get from Ohio to the northern panhandle of West Virginia. It was an industrial town whose main source of industry was steel and was where I mainly grew up as a kid.

If you got caught at the red light at the end of the bridge, there was a sign that said, "Welcome to Wild, Wonderful West Virginia." I can't tell you how many times in my life I looked at that sign as we sat and waited for the light to turn green and wondered, "What the hell makes this place so wonderful?"

The see-through metal slats that formed the bottom of the bridge pulled your tires back and forth making a humming noise as you drove. You had to steer with both hands, and the slight back-and-forth motion from the pulling of the tires made it look like the overly dramatic steering you see in movies.

My mom told me that once, when she was a young girl, my grandma Edith, who was four foot nine, misjudged her car and scraped the side of her big gray Oldsmobile down the entire length of bridge, metal screeching and sparks flying the whole way on the passenger side where my mom sat.

If you look out the window and over the side, you see the murky brown water below. If you are unlucky enough to get stopped by the light that sends you out onto Route 2, you sit feeling the bridge swaying back and forth. I swear the timing of the light was just long enough to let you conjure up the notion that at any moment you'd go over the edge, hit the cold, brown water like a rock, never to be heard from again.

I'd cross this bridge so many times with my parents and later alone as I learned to drive myself, and each time I still had the same reaction to it. Trepidation. Wonderment.

When I was little and asked about the movement of the bridge my dad would say not to worry, that bridges needed to sway to stay strong. He pointed out, that if it were rigid, the bridge would collapse under the pressure of the water and cars.

If you turned left off the bridge, coming from Ohio, you headed toward Weirton. If you turned right off the bridge and followed Route 2, you snaked along the Ohio River that divides Ohio from West Virginia.

First up, the city of Follansbee. You'll know you're there when you see the coke plants off to your right. The tall smokestacks billow large white clouds into the air that make the area smell like rotten eggs and covers everything in a thin dusting of gray powder. They have a Dairy Owl, a baseball field, gas station, a middle school and three traffic lights.

When the street becomes a four-lane highway again, you're on your way to the city of Wellsburg. And although I moved a lot, it's the city in which I grew up the most until my mid teens. At the time, there was Kroger's grocery store, a drugstore called Super X that sat in the same plaza, the tail end of Rabbit Hill, a gas station, the West Virginia State Highway Patrol, and the dirt patch where the carnival was held each summer and the start of Washington Pike to your left.

When I was twelve, we finally got a Pizza Hut, and the town about shit itself with excitement. But, if you go past Washington Pike, there on the right, you'll see DiCarlo's Pizza, home of the hot pizza with cold toppings you can buy by the slice for just a few cents. It's still the same pizza joint it was in the '70s and they still use the same old pay phone attached to the wall to take incoming orders for pizza. It's the best damn pizza you will ever eat.

If you take this book with you the next time you visit, you'll see that with the exception of a few dollar stores, and a Dairy Queen now, my description of the city and the surrounding areas haven't changed much and is why the place is referred to as, "the town that time forgot."

I learned to drive up and down Washington Pike and Rabbit Hill like all kids did. We didn't have Driver's Ed in school; our parents had to teach us. And because my dad was my dad, he was giving me the keys to the Nova at age fourteen to drive out to pay his bill at the water department located in the little white building that still exists at the end of Manner Ridge Road today.

If you learned to navigate the roads without going over a hill, you easily passed your driver's test given by the West Virginia State Highway Patrol in downtown Wellsburg. At age sixteen, a state trooper, or a "Mountie," as my Dad called them, sat in the passenger seat of your car in their intimidating gray uniform, and large black-brimmed hat, while you parallel parked next to where they held the carnival every August. How any of us passed with that kind of intimidation is beyond me now, but we did.

I practiced for weeks leading up to my test. Practice made perfect, my dad said. I got so good at parallel parking that I could do it in less than thirty seconds from start to finish. I know, because my dad timed me. And because I was already so used to using the car, I remember at least once during my test, the Mountie reaching for the dash, telling me that I could take my time and reminding me that there were no deductions for going slowly.

I can remember when they handed me my new license. It was still warm from the laminating machine. There it was, a shiny plastic card that meant I had graduated from maneuvering a fifteen-pound ten-speed to handling a three-thousand-pound car around West Virginia's mountainous terrain. I opened my blue Velcro wallet that had a rainbow cloud design on the front so many times to admire it, that I nearly wore the Velcro right off.

I was sixteen in the summer of 1983, and I drove my dad's '79 silver Nova. The burgundy red plastic interior got scorching hot in the summer and would burn the faux weaved pattern of the seats into the back of your legs if you wore shorts. Sometimes, we'd pad the seats with our wet towels from the swimming pool and wear just our bathing suits while driving around town. Our hair would blow wildly around our faces in the fresh mountain air that was occasionally laced with the strong scent of fresh lilacs, honeysuckle and wild onions that grew off roadsides.

We were all dolled up, smoking, laughing and singing to the radio, not a care in the world on our way to the Fort Steuben Mall that day.

It was my friend Annie who spotted the police car behind us.

She tapped me on my shoulder to look in the rearview mirror. I turned down the radio and pulled to the side of the road in front of Follansbee Middle School and we both mashed out our cigarettes in the ashtray. My heart was in my throat as I reached for my purse, doing everything my dad taught me to do in case I was ever pulled over.

The gray uniform and big hat appeared at my window.

"Where ya goin in such a hurry?" he said as he bent over to talk to me in the window.

"Um, nowhere special, just to the mall," I said as I handed over my license and registration.

"I clocked you going 52 miles an hour in a 35, young lady," he said.

He scanned the documents and looked back at me.

"Um, I'm really sorry, officer... I didn't realize —"

"You sit tight and I'll be back in a minute," he interrupted.

I could see him in my rearview mirror talk on his police radio. We didn't move a muscle or say a word.

After a few minutes he reappeared at my window.

"You Harland Jessup's daughter?" he asked.

"Yes, sir, I am. Why?" I asked.

"Uh... no reason... uh... you go on and git outta here, but beeeee careful. You're a new driver and you both know what happens to a lot to new drivers around here if they're not careful, don't ya?"

We knew.

We'd hear the adults talking about how some new driver got seriously injured or even killed in a car accident on those dangerous roads that these damn kids just weren't experienced with enough yet.

"Yes, sir, thank you, sir," I said excitedly.

I waited for him to pull out from behind me and drive away. Then I did the same. I was careful to use my turn signal and keep a close eye on the speedometer. Annie and I didn't say a word to each other for what seemed like forever.

And then she spoke.

"Oh my God, I felt so bad for you back there, but you handled yourself like a champ!" she said as she slapped at my shoulder.

"Thanks," I said as I laughed, "but I was sooooo scared!"

"You sure didn't show it! I would have cried, I just know I would have!" she said. "And," she added, "he didn't even give you a ticket!"

"Yeah, I know! I guess it pays to grow up the daughter of one of the most hated, feared men in town," I said. "If I can handle living with my dad, I can handle a god-damned West Virginia State Trooper."

We quickly fished our mangled cigarettes from the ashtray, straightened and re-lit them. I turned up the radio and we sang to the top of our lungs "Shock the Monkey" by Peter Gabriel as we approached the Steubenville Bridge. And with a racing heart and sweaty palms I drove us across the bridge that nightmares were made of, and made our way to the mall.

Like nothing ever happened.

Part 1

Marland Heights

Weirton, West Virginia

Chapter 1

Richard Nixon was president and our house was filled with the sounds of Ricky Nelson singing "Garden Party" on the radio in the daisy-filled kitchen when I lived in the large green house with white trim. I was five years old and wore my hair in pigtails on the side of my head when I had my first memories of being in this world. My mom was twenty-one and my dad was twenty-three.

There was a long, steep driveway that wrapped around the back of the house and a small cement porch in the front with black wrought-iron handrails on each side of the two steps. We had a silver tin box on the porch where the milkman delivered milk in a glass bottle and eggs every few days. I'd hear the tin lid hit the box early in the morning from underneath my window upstairs and hurry downstairs for cereal and cartoons.

When you walked in the front door and stood on the square piece of linoleum that made up the foyer, the dining room was to the right. It held the much larger than needed, clunky Early American dining room furniture that we never used. Big gold coin decor imprinted with Early American figures were on the walls and the table held the large glass grapes in purple and green that reminded me of clackers older kids played with but I was not allowed to have.

The living room had its '70s type couch that barely had any cushion on it and the back of the couch, with its large fabric-covered buttons, dug into your back as you sat. A recliner sat in front of the large picture window facing one of our two television sets. Our metal TV trays were folded up behind the chair to the left. The steps leading upstairs were directly in front of the linoleum square patch we called a foyer. We said, "*foy-er*," not "*foy-ay*." Foy-ay was for highfalutin people, my mom said, and we were not that.

At the top of the steps there was a pink tiled bathroom. Goldfish decor spurting bubbles from their mouths hung on the wall. My parents room was to the left; my room was to the right. I had white furniture trimmed in gold. My tall white bed had a pink, purple and white-checkered canopy over the top of it with a large ruffled bed skirt and pillows that matched.

The ceiling of my room was slanted on the left and the room itself was long and narrow, running the length of the house. In the front section of the room, where the ceiling was straight again, was my desk, chalkboard and school area I created. There, I taught my dolls, bears and other toys their ABC's, how to write and read basic words.

"C-A-T. CAT!" I would say as I pointed to them.

"Can everyone say cat?" I would ask my dolls and teddy bears.

And apparently they said cat because I said, "Good, very good. You're all such good students."

"Now, class, turn to page 5."

Downstairs I could hear the fighting, things hitting up against the walls, the shattering of glass, my mom crying.

"You no good fuckin' whore! Get this fucking shit cleaned up or else!" he'd scream.

I'd try to go back to teaching, but jump at the sounds and hurry to my dolls to protect them as I heard doors slamming and things breaking.

If you stood in the doorway of my room, to the left was a small walk-in closet with four wooden shelves inside. I'd sit in that closet with my toys and books with the door closed for hours when they fought like that, playing and imagining. Feeling safe.

I'd look at the pictures in books before I could read and later read fairy tales about Cinderella, and Snow White. But I never wanted to be them waiting on a prince to come. I was a tomboy, my mom said, that still liked to play with dolls. I had one doll whose hair grew by pulling on it and whose eyes turned four different colors, including pink. I fed my Baby Tender Love doll her pink gooey food while she sat in her high chair and changed her diapers when she wet them and had a white Barbie tote full of Barbie dolls, clothing and shoes to mix and match.

When it got too loud, eventually, I'd cover my ears and begin to cry.

I'd sit alone, knees pulled to my chin, rocking myself. I was scared and nervous and my nails were always "bitten down to the quick to prove it," my mom would say.

I always felt better when I'd hear the car screech out of the driveway and see my dad leaving from my window when he was like that. I knew my mom would be crying and upset and I was glad he'd be gone.

I'd slink down the steps to the kitchen to check on her.

"M...om. Where are you?"

I heard her sobbing in the daisy-filled kitchen, where she sat with her head in her hands at the Formica table. The kitchen was bright and cheerful. My mom had decorated it with daisy decor and they were everywhere: the toaster cover, bowls, clock, dishes and place mats. But, she was sad and blue. She lifted her head and I could see she had a red mark on the side of her face, near her eye.

"Oh, Mommy... why does Daddy do that?" I'd say.

"It's o.k, she'd say as I handed her a tissue. "Don't you worry about anything, you just go back up to your room and play."

"But —"

"No, don't but me... you do what I say now, ya hear?"

"But — "

"You heard me, young lady. Do this for Mommy."

Anything for her, so I'd go.

I had a friend named Archie who lived next door. He was a dark, curly-haired boy who wasn't shy about walking into my house and asking my mom what there was to eat. On hot summer days my mom would fix us peanut butter and jelly sandwiches and deliver them to us on a paper plate, one on top of the other, to the front steps we sat on.

"Hey, you gonna eat the rest of that?" he'd say.

"No, you can have it," I said.

We'd sit on my front porch and eat with only a few words spoken between us.

"Your dad home?" he'd finally ask.

"No, he's at work, why?"

"I don't know... well... he kinda scares me," he said.

"Yeah, he does me too," I admitted.

When I was allowed to be further away from the house, Archie and I would wander into the nearby woods.

Our feet were submerged up to our ankles. It was hot and humid and my hair stuck to my sweaty face that was streaked with dirt. I'd softly run my fingers over the brown and green slimy moss-covered rocks that waved under the water at me, while watching minnows streak through the water like silver swooshes. I caught tadpoles for our coffee can and an occasional salamander or two.

"Oh… so pretty," I'd say to the salamander. "So pretty!"

Archie would be nearby but out wading up to his knees.

"Awww… come here, little guy," I'd say. "Come here, little one, I'm gonna take you home with me." And in the can I'd put him. We'd spend hours in the water, looking under every rock, and when we had enough tadpoles to split between my utility tub and Archie's, we'd go walking home. On our way, we ate sour grass by the handfuls and smelled so many dandelions we'd have yellow noses by the time we got home.

I knew better than to enter the house with a coffee can full of tadpoles, so I went in the house through the basement. I carefully and quietly added my new catches of the day to the utility tub in the basement, then I'd stand and watch them all meet each other.

I walked up the basement steps to the kitchen that was the room next to the dining room we never used.

"Wash up for dinner," my mom said.

"Okay. But you gotta SEE the baby tadpoles I caught today!" I said.

"I don't know why you even bother with those stinky things — gross!" she said.

"I know, but you just have to see them, they're so cute!"

"I will, I promise, right after supper," she'd say.

I washed my hands as I looked in the mirror. I was smiling, excited my mom agreed to go say hi to the baby tadpoles. I'd get up close in the mirror and try to pick the green grass from my little Chiclet teeth.

"Don't forgot to wash your face!" she yelled just as I was washing the dirt streak off my face.

"Okay!" I yelled back.

I turned the light off in the downstairs powder-blue-tiled bathroom and turned left to go to the kitchen.

I didn't want to upset her and have her not come see my tadpole friends later, so I tried to eat and be quiet. Something was wrong. She ate without looking up from her plate. I twisted in my seat, uncomfortable.

"Sit still, Robin Lynn. You're always fidgeting. Always gotta be into something, skippin' along, always singin', hoppin' all over the place like a damn rabbit... drive me crazy," she said.

Chapter 2

My dad worked at Weirton Steel. The steel mill was known as the most advanced in the world then and was called the "showcase of the steel industry." And my dad was one proud employee. When he was in a good mood, I loved to watch him get ready for work. He'd lather his face with the shave cake that sat inside the thick ceramic Steelers mug that was rimmed in gold that sat on the side of the sink. He'd wet the brush, then rub in a whisking motion inside the cup and create foam. I'd sit and talk to him while he shaved and await a tap of the brush that left behind a dollop of shave cream on the end of my nose.

"So, what're you gonna do today, squirt," he'd say as he lifted his chin to the light to see better.

"Probably just play outside with Archie," I said.

"He's a nice kid, that Archie," he'd say.

"He is. Guess what?" I'd say.

"I don't know, what?" he'd say.

"We found a nest of baby rabbits on the side of the house yesterday and they're over his house in a box."

"Is that so?" he said.

"I'll probably go over and play with them," I said.

"Do they talk like Bugs Bunny?" he'd say as he launched into talking in his Bugs Bunny impersonation.

"Eh, What's Up Doc!" he said.

I'd giggle.

"Boop!" he'd say with the brush to my button nose.

And I giggled some more as I looked at it in the mirror.

When he was done shaving, he would splash on Old Spice cologne after a shower with the green and white Irish Spring soap that was just for him.

I loved the smell of my daddy.

He carried a white cloth canvas bag to work my grandma sewed for him that held extra clothing and clean socks and a black metal lunch box that clipped shut. And my mom would fill his large green thermos with hot coffee before he left.

Sometimes I had to be quiet during the day because he was getting his sleep from working night shift. Sometimes, my mom and I were home alone at night and I never liked that. And every few weeks his schedule would change.

One day in December 1972, nineteen of my dad's co-workers were killed and eight seriously injured in a series of explosions at the mill. The destruction from the blasts left twisted metal girders and sheet metal pinning most of those killed under the debris. A major blast happened in the battery basement that day. People said the "blasts were so powerful, the men killed never had a chance." It was later reported that men could be seen staggering out of the smoke carrying two men at a time on their backs and debris flew far and wide. They reported that one man had been severely injured in the first blast, but went back in to save someone else, only to lose his life in the third and final blast. I don't know if my dad was off that day, worked a later shift, or was in another part of the mill altogether, but I remember overhearing talk of just how dangerous steel work could be and it worried me. A lot.

I loved my daddy even though he scared me sometimes and was mean to my mom. I was glad he was o.k. He was my friend and he called me "buddy," "kiddo," and "squirt."

Chapter 3

In the summertime when Archie and his family were away and there was no one to play with, I went to the basement to play alone. It was cooler down there with its thick cement block walls and concrete floor. I had a swing down there attached to the rafters by rope my dad hooked up for me and an old-time rocking horse from when I was a baby, stuffed in the corner. In the attached garage that was next to the basement was where my dad kept the model airplanes we built and flew together. I even had a kite in there. We stood on the slope going down in our back yard on windy days and flew the kite high above the apartment building's rooftop behind our home.

When my dad worked day shift, he called it "day turn," I waited by the garage door coming inside the basement with a smile at precisely 3:20 p.m., hoping he'd be in a good mood and had enough energy to play with me.

He bought us a racetrack and set it up in the den. The tracks glowed in the dark and each car had real working headlights. We'd race for hours in there while our black cat Fluffy watched the track intently as we laughed and played. We laughed harder when Fluffy would move closer to the track studying it, moving her head in tight fast circles, mesmerized, and wide-eyed at the rapid movement. We even had motorcycles for the racetrack. And

I always chose the bike that had Evel Knievel on it while my dad's had some unknown rider. We watched Evel Knievel do his death-defying jumps every weekend on TV in the den as we played with my racetrack or watched the Harlem Globetrotters and ate Pringles.

My dad would eventually get tired and lay down on the couch.

"Dad? You asleep?" I asked.

"Nope. Just checking my eyelids for holes," he'd say as he laughed.

I'd get my light blue nurse's kit with the red cross on the front and bandage him up as he slept. I'd put bandages and gauze wraps all over him and listen to his heart with my red plastic stethoscope.

"Daddy, open your mouth, I have your medicine," I'd say.

Eyes still closed, he'd open his mouth and I'd plop in a round piece of candy I pulled off of a waxed paper roll. He would move his mouth around, swallow loudly and say, "Oh, I feel better already," as he opened one eye to look at me.

I loved him so much. I especially loved his big white teeth that looked like large Chiclet gum, his hearty laugh and his big bushy eyebrows that reminded me of the caterpillars I played with outside. He could move them up and down and make them dance as he sang songs. I loved when he sang "Disco Duck" in the sound of Donald Duck's voice and he could do Fat Albert's "Hey, Hey, Hey!"

He made a homemade jump for me with old boards on top of cement blocks. I'd jump over it in my Big Wheel that I later learned he made my mom go buy for me, even after she reported they had only sixty-three dollars left in the account until his next pay. He let me eat Oreos by the dozens when Mom wasn't around and he loved Pringles in the can as much as I did. I'd sit as close to him as I could get. He'd pass the can of chips to me as he ate, my small arm disappearing down inside the greasy tube as we watched TV together. I loved when my dad made lips with his chips, one up and one down, and made a quacking noise.

"Quack, quack!" he'd say. And I'd giggle.

Then he'd talk in the voice of Donald Duck some more, "Where's my chips, little girl?" as I acted like I was eating them all.

"Oh, no," he'd say in Donald Duck's voice. "Bring me my chips!"

And I'd giggle as I'd fall to the floor, him tickling me in my sides with my mouth full of chips.

"Stop it. She's gonna choke to death with her mouth full like that!" my mom said as she came in the room.

"Party's over, kiddo…" Dad would say with an animated sad face and bottom lip purposely pushed out.

"Awwwwwwwwwwww, but Dad!" I'd say, standing up and catching my breath.

"I know, I know… but it's late. Why don't you go get ready for bed now, o.k, and we can play again tomorrow?" he'd say.

"Okay. Thanks for playing, Dad. Love you."

"Love you too, squirt," he'd say as he tapped me on my behind to get moving upstairs.

My mom would come in and bathe me. And each night my mom would scrub my head clean then rake through it with a comb. It was heavy and thick and down to my butt once, but she cut it off herself after I got bubblegum stuck in the side of it. But, even short, it was still a tangled rat's nest, she would say. She'd sit me in front of her while she sat on the toilet and spray No More Tears spray to detangle it. I would wince and whine about the pulling and tugging of it every single night. She said if I wasn't so into dirt and grime most of the time, we could go without washing it so much, but that never stopped me from getting filthy dirty. I was more like a boy than any girl she'd ever known, she said. I was a tomboy, with short brown, bubble-headed hair. I still loved dresses, though, but they had to twirl when I turned around in the mirror or I wouldn't wear them. It was apparently my rule before I knew I had rules about such things.

I'd overhear my mom on the phone talking to my aunt about me.

"Never in my life have I seen such a girl as her," she'd say. "Climbs trees like a monkey, skins her knees like a boy but throws an absolute fit to wear a dress to school everyday — even if there's snow up to her ass."

She'd look at me from a side-glance and chuckle, and then tell me to get outside and play.

I didn't see what the big deal was to like dresses and climb trees. "Why can't I do both?" I'd ask as I was putting on yet another new Band-Aid. I loved Band-Aids and if my mom would have allowed it, I would have gone through an entire box a week. And it took things forever to heal, because I was a big scab picker too, just to use another Band-Aid, my mom would say.

One day my dad took me fishing with him at Tappan Lake. We planned a few days before and the night before our trip we packed a big tackle box full of our purple and pink jelly worms and bobbers and stopped on the little pier to buy live worms on the way. My mom packed us a cooler that morning. For me, a few Orange Slice pops, and two peanut butter and jelly sandwiches. For my dad, a few Iron

City beers and salami with mustard sandwiches for him. And a can of Pringles to share.

"O.k., squirt, you throw the line out there like this," he'd say as he demonstrated.

I'd pick up my pole and do the same thing.

"Now just be quiet and listen. When you see little round circles coming up around the line in the water, that means there's a fish about to bite and you just yank the line like I showed you, 'k?"

"OK, Dad," I said.

"But, remember," he added, "not so hard you break the line."

He pushed the little boat out a few feet and walked back to the sandy beach to set up the beach towels and cooler, while I sat in the boat quietly watching for circles.

When you sit and stare at an invisible fishing line in the water, your eyes can play tricks on you. Did it just move? Did I feel a nibble? Do I yank the line now? I wanted to catch something to make my dad proud and I didn't want to make him mad, but I just felt there was something nibbling at that line.

I waited, though. More circles floated up and faster they came around the barely visible line. I jerked the line, but was careful enough not to jerk too hard. Then I paddled our little boat over to the line still in the water and got my net ready.

My dad came flying off the little beach and into water that was only as high as his hips to help me.

"Woohooo! You did it, kiddo!" he yelled. "Your mom's going to be cooking fish for dinner tonight! Robin's catch of the day!" he said, so happy and excited.

He grabbed the net from my hands and swooped down deep into the dark water.

And there, at the other end of the line, scooped up in the net staring up at us both, was a huge bullfrog with bulbous eyes that sat right on top of his big fat head.

"A frog!" I yelled. "Daddy, I caught a frog!"

"You sure did, you sure did!" he yelled as he laughed.

"I stand corrected!" he said. "Your mom will be making frog legs for dinner tonight," he said.

I was too caught up in the moment of my dad's happiness to say I didn't want to eat the legs off a frog for dinner, so I just went with it.

"O.k., paddle us back to shore, little one, I have Mr. Jeremiah the Bullfrog held tight here in this bucket," he said.

Once to shore, we scurried out of our boat and sat the bucket in the sand with the net over it.

"You sit right here and don't take your eyes off that bucket," he said. "I'll be right back. I have to run to the car for something." He left the tiny beach singing "Jeremiah was a Bullfrog" by Three Dog Night.

There was sea glass, shells, rocks of all kinds and twigs. To pass the time, I collected the things I liked the most and put them in a pile. These beautiful things would find their way into my top dresser drawer where I placed all my most valuable things.

"O.k., so, let's put Mr. Jeremiah in this," he said as he returned, "with just enough water in it so he's comfortable for the ride home." My dad held up a larger bucket that had a lid. "What the — " he said as he turned to look at the bucket on the beach.

I turned around and the net was off the bucket. The frog was gone. We scanned the beach area quickly and then turned our attention out to the dark water.

And there in the middle of the lake were two bulbous eyes looking back at us.

"Oh no, I'm sorry, Dad, he must have – " I started to explain.

He dropped his shoulders.

"Man oh man. That's too bad. No one's gonna believe the size of that thing," he said.

"Are you mad?" I asked.

"No, just disappointed," he said.

I was glad he wasn't mad. And I was certainly glad that I didn't have to eat frog's legs for dinner that night.

As we packed up and drove around the lake to go home that evening, I looked back out over the still water. I smirked at the thought of that fat old bullfrog getting away and going back to be with his frog family.

"I'm glad you got away," I said to the old frog in my mind.

"Those rocks stink!" my mom would say. "Take those downstairs! I better not find those in your drawer, I'm not even kidding."

I had some rock collection too. Silvery flat rocks, square ones that had sparkles in them, rocks shaped like hearts, some that had swirls in them and some that had another piece of stone in them. I had a large round piece of green glass that was beautiful when you held it up to the light, but my all-time favorites were the large glossy black stones.

We called them Black Beauty's, after the horse and in my overalls pocket they would go, bound for my dresser drawer. But, only after I washed them sparkling clean with soap and water. I'd sniff them to make sure the smell was gone. There were some marbles in my drawer because I liked those, too, with their colorful swirls inside and my mom would remind me, as I admired them, not to put those goddamned things in my mouth or I'd choke to death. I didn't care; I did anyway when she wasn't looking. I'd roll them around my mouth, listening to them clank against my teeny tiny Chiclet teeth and put them in my cheeks and make squirrel faces in the mirror. My mom said I was my own best friend because I could spend hours alone laughing and playing and never really needed a playmate.

My mom would say, "Admit it, you have sticks in your dresser drawers too." I didn't know what the big deal was to admit I had sticks in my dresser.

"O.k., I admit it. There are sticks in there too," I'd say back to her. Like anyone cared.

When I went down to the basement to add my washed rocks to the utility tub that held my tadpoles, it was empty. The tub was wet and suds were slowly cracking as they disappeared from the bottom of the tub. Encrusted in the bubbles along the top of the tub that had long been dried to the sides, were the smallest of tadpoles, dead.

My mom had done laundry.

Instead of moving the C-curved hose that came from the washer into the other tub so I could keep my tadpoles, she left the hose in the tub and took the plug out.

Chapter 4

From the time I woke up in the morning in the soft pink light of day that caught my canopy bed, till the time I fell into bed at night all bathed and warm, I was mostly outside playing. Sometimes I played with Archie next door, but I had a few more friends too. Some my age, some older than me, and some my mom said were imaginary. But I knew they weren't.

There was a much older boy down the street, named Jeb, who used to walk me to the store to get candy. He walked with a limp. People said he was a little slow, but I thought he walked just fine. He was funny and kind and would even lift me up on his shoulders and carry me if we were gone too long and I was too tired to walk. He made sounds as he walked when he carried me on his shoulders, exaggerating his down steps, acting like he might drop me to make me giggle.

He didn't seem to have friends his age and only watched the boys at the park play ball from a distance. I think I may have been his only friend. The thing was, though, he was a man, not a boy. He was eighteen at the time and I was six. They said he functioned at a much younger age than eighteen. My mom and his mom were friends and she said there was no other boy in the world she'd trust me with more than him. Jeb was a "good boy and wouldn't hurt a fly," she said.

When my dad was in one of his moods, my dad was nice to his face, but called him a fucking retard behind his back.

Mom would say, "Harland, Shhhhh! No, he isn't! Don't say that!" and he'd laugh, throwing his head back in the air as if he just told the funniest joke.

Jeb would come to the front door and peer through the glass with his hands formed in parentheses around his coke-bottle-thick eyeglasses.

"Hey, Mr. Jessup, is Robin here?"

"Yeah, hold on a minute," he said. "Robin, your retard friend is here,"

"Daddy stop it, he is not. Stop saying that. He's nice to me," I said.

"Oh, good for him. He's nice to you. Whoopity do," he'd say.

I didn't like my dad much when he acted like this so when I sensed it, I tried to stay away from him as much as I could.

Jeb's mother said he was injured at birth. Something about his air being cut off too long and this made him walk the way he did. Said something about he may be in a wheelchair someday but for now all he liked to do was walk and walk. And that's all we did. We walked all over town. We'd go to the park, the playground, and corner store, through the neighborhoods, to the ice cream store and even through the far-away woods that I wasn't supposed to go into by myself.

And my mom was right. He never hurt me, or a fly.

That night, I'd be scrubbed clean and pink again, the water dingy gray and dirty. And again, my mom would be annoyed.

"Jesus Christ!" my mom would say as she scrubbed at or combed out my rat's nest of a head of hair.

She raked through my hair as I admired the Prell bottle with the pearl at the bottom, which sat in the corner of the powder blue tub. I wanted that pearl but knew enough to keep the lid on. Every time you'd tip the bottle over, the pearl would go back up inside the bottle in a big fat glob of a bubble. I would sit and play with it, watching it tumble around inside. It was like the lava lamp my parents had in the den, except not hot.

"Don't you dare let me see you smearing with that, Robin Lynn, leave the lid on it," she said.

"I'm just looking at it, Mommy. Isn't it pretty?" I'd say.

"Just another one of your goddamn messes to clean up, damn it," she'd say as she left to fold down my bed in my room next to the bathroom.

I dried quickly, put my Holly Hobbie nightgown on over my head with the paisley print and ruffle at the bottom, and put my days-of-the-week underwear on underneath. Mom gave me Wednesday but it was Saturday. It was something else I apparently had a rule about; wearing the correct day's underwear. Before I could complain, she said, "Don't even start, it doesn't matter. No one should be looking at your underwear except you anyway."

"O.K.," I said, as I rubbed my nose up with the palm of my hand, "but why else would they be labeled if you were just going to wear the wrong day?"

Every night I made sure to plug in my Lite Brite I used as my nightlight. I was scared to death of the dark. I'd plug it in then take a running leap for my bed, arms sprawled out wide, feet flailing behind me, and jump in the bed and get under the covers pulled up tight up over my head. I folded them down neatly at my chest for my goodnight kiss and hug from my mom.

"Night, love you," she said.

"Love you too," I said back, hugging her tight around her neck, making a "Mmmmmm!" sound letting her know it was a good hug.

She giggled. "Come on, let go, time for sleep," she said.

She closed the door behind her.

I could hear her cleaning up the water I got all over the bathroom and wondered if she was crying. The fighting was worse. It was more frequent and I'd pretend not to hear a lot of it until my dad was gone.

I got situated and cozy in bed then rolled to my side to gaze at my Lite Brite from my bed. I'd admire the rainbow of colors that beamed out the back of it and up the walls and onto the ceiling. But this night I wrote "You are Loved" inside a red heart using only yellow pegs for the words. I heard my dad watching the 700-Club one day on TV and they were selling pins for God for a small donation. The pins were blue hearts with silver words in them that said, "You Are Loved" and my dad wanted one. When he got it in the mail I wanted it too. When he caught me eyeing it, he placed it in his jewelry box so I couldn't take it, so I made my own sign.

How silly to make hearts blue, I thought. Red is love, not blue. And, "You Are Loved" should be gold not silver. I had specific ideas about how things were supposed to be even as a child, I'd hear my mom telling someone on the phone.

A "self-soother," she bragged.

When I woke the next morning, the curtains were blowing softly in the breeze coming through my window. A soft pink-yellow light warmed my room and bounced off the walls. In the distance, I heard a dog barking, and the milkman drop the tin lid down on the box as he delivered that day's groceries. And somehow my Lite Brite would be magically unplugged. I remember thinking how I wanted to catch a glimpse of this milkman my dad joked I might belong to, but I never did. He was as elusive as Santa and the Easter Bunny, but not nearly as exciting.

My eyes were still lazily opening. I rolled to my back and gazed up at the ruffly pink, purple and white checked canopy bed moving back and forth with the movement of the bed. I stretched and yawned; feeling like the princess my mom said would own a bed like this. I loved this room.

I slid down from my bed, which seemed stories higher than me, and opened my bedroom door. My parents bedroom door was still closed. I went to the bathroom quietly to brush my teeth and wash my face. I had sleep marks on my face from the sheets. My mom said that happened when you don't move a muscle all night and sleep as soundly as I did.

Now I had a shag haircut. I wasn't sure how I felt about it yet. I fell asleep with gum in my mouth one night and got a wad of pink bubble gum stuck on the side of my head. I liked that my mom didn't pull it into ponytail holders shaped like an eight with two hard plastic balls on the end now. I admired myself in the mirror and practiced smiling. I looked good, I thought, all except for the missing front tooth. But, no matter how I tried to smile though, I showed teeth. I decided a grin just wasn't my style and so there I was in my school pictures smiling widely minus my front right tooth.

I tiptoed past my mom and dad's door and grabbed the handrail to go down stairs but as I took the first step, I heard crying. I stepped back up and moved down the small hall. I walked slowly up to their door and pressed my ear against it and I could hear my mom crying. I tried to call to her but nothing would come out. I could hear my heartbeat pounding in my ears and my throat was dry. There was no spit in my mouth to swallow.

"Mommy?" I finally said.

No answer. But the crying stopped.

"Mommy? You in there?" I said.

"Go away. Go downstairs and get your cereal," she said.

"Mom, what's wrong? What happened?" I tried to turn the doorknob but it was locked.

"Nothing's wrong, everything's fine," she said.

Some mornings my mom would be so happy she'd start singing as she opened the blinds in my room. On good days like today, she'd sing "Happiest Girl in the Whole U.S.A." by Donna Fargo.

"You know there's snow up to your butt out there, right?"

"Yeah, Mom."

"You sure you want to wear that skirt... it's gonna be mighty cold with nothing covering your legs underneath," she said.

"It's picture day and I want to wear a dress," I said.

"You know pictures only show from your shoulders up, right?"

"Yeah, I just like to wear a skirt on picture day," I said.

"You sure you don't want to wear tights or long johns under it?"

"No, Mom… I'm fine," I said.

"O.k. then, have fun at school today and smile nice, I'm not buying pictures that you don't smile in," she said.

"Mom, I always smile," I said as I flashed her my holey smile.

"Yes, I guess you're right, you do, don't ya? You're about the only one who ever radiates true happiness in photos now that I think about it," she said as she laughed.

My mom started singing again.

Out the door to the bus stop I went, wearing a knee-length skirt with my brown-wedged Buster Brown boots and tan knee length coat with white furry collar. I got to the bus stop, which was directly across the street from our house, and turned around to see my mom watching out the window.

We heard the bus chugging all the way up the hill long before it got to us. The chains they put on the bus's tires made a clinking sound that reminded me of Christmas bells as the yellow bus trudged through the deep snow.

Archie would start throwing snowballs at people, but when he got to me, I'd look him square in the face. He never did throw one at me. We played together all the time and I think he knew I was tough enough to thump him a good one.

Knowing our stop was next, I'd wave to my mom who stood in the window before the big yellow bus blocked her from my view. Then, I'd find a seat on that side of the bus to wave good-bye one more time. She'd wave and blow me a kiss, I'd blow one back.

I'd slide down in my seat alone and sing quietly as I looked out the window, the ending of "The Happiest Girl."

I knew I wasn't the happiest girl in the whole U.S.A., but if I smiled in my school pictures, no one would ever know I wasn't. If I acted happy, I would be the happiest girl. I just would.

Winter turned to summer again and Archie and I were back to gallivanting all over the neighborhood, my mom called it. Soon we'd have another utility tub full of tadpoles in all different stages of becoming frogs.

I walked into my house and found my mom sitting at the Formica table, with the avocado green and daisy printed plastic chairs, talking on the phone. She looked like she'd been crying but quickly acted as if she hadn't when she saw me walk in the kitchen.

"Hi Mom, what's wrong?" I asked.

"Oh, nothing, I was just on the phone with your aunt Della talking..." she said trying to sound upbeat. "How was your day?"

"Good," I said wondering if she really cared.

"What'd you do in school today?" she asked.

And without missing a beat, I started to tell her.

"It was really cool, Mom, the teacher took a dried lima bean last week and placed it between two wet paper towels, we kept watering the towels and today the lima bean grew a sprout!" I said. "Isn't that neat?"

"Sure is, honey," she said. "Are you and Archie going to go play?"

"Yeah, he's gonna come get me after he eats supper."

"Supper..." she said. "Yeah, I gotta get some supper in my growing girl, don't I? "What do you want?" she asked as she clasped her hands together waiting for my request.

"How about a Hungry Man TV dinner?" I said. "I like the one with Salisbury steak, mashed potatoes and corn and chocolate cake for dessert, the best."

"O.k. but it'll take about 45 minutes after I preheat the oven," she said.

"That's o.k.," I said and I was off.

Later, I ate my foil-lined supper in front of the TV on a metal folding table with a faux wooden surface. My dad would eat on them too when he watched the Steelers football games.

I guzzled the last sip of red Kool-Aid from my Pillsbury Doughboy plastic cup, rinsed my cup, put it in the sink, and threw the tin foil tray in the garbage. I wiped my red Kool-Aid mustache on the back of my arm. I went upstairs to my room and changed out of my school clothes for play clothes, and made sure to take my book order form out of my book bag and take it down to my mom.

"You done already?" she said.

"Yeah... Mom, can I get some books? Here's what I want, circled... and we have to turn in the order slip by Wednesday of next week. Can I, huh?" I asked not waiting for an answer. "Bye, Mom. I'll be outside playing with Archie."

"O.k. Be in before the street lights come on," she said.

Chapter 5

"Yeah," she said into the receiver, "I think someone's in the basement," as she patted her index finger against her lips for me not to say a word.

"Yeah, I'm not quite sure but I think I heard something fall over… Yeah, I know, but…" She got a little louder. "I'm too scared to go down into the basement, Della," she said as she winked at me.

We both knew it was my dad down there. He would pretend to go to work, park his car somewhere down the street and walk back to the house late at night and break in to scare my mother.

My mom, who was tired of his antics, propped a shampoo bottle up near the basement door he had to walk through, knowing that if she placed it close enough to the door she'd hear the bottle fall over and know he was in the house.

"Oh, Robin Lynn is so scared, she's just attached to my leg here," she would say.

She continued on. "I know, maybe I should go call Harland at work and have him come home," she said a little louder. "Yeah, yeah, I'll do that and I'll call you back," she said to my aunt on the other end of the phone.

She hung up and whispered to me with widened eyes, "Your dad's in the basement but don't let on you know it's him, o.k.?"

I'd nod yes.

She released the metal cradle piece with her finger as she held the phone to her ear with her shoulder, and redialed the avocado green phone attached to the wall. The sound of the circular clear plastic dial swiveling back into its place, after every number dialed, intensified my nervousness.

She'd propped herself up against the wall with one foot and twisted the cord around her finger as she waited for the phone to ring at my dad's work.

She knew he could hear every word she was saying though the floor down into the basement.

"Yes, hello, can you please get a message to my husband Harland Jessup? Can you please tell him to come home... This is an emergency. Tell him I think someone's broken into our house. Yes. His wife, Starlah, yes, thanks," she said.

A bit later, we heard my dad's big work boots coming up the basement steps. He acted as if he was coming in from the message he received at work.

"It's me!" he yelled up the steps. "No need to be scared, I ran the guy off," he assured us.

"There was a guy down there?" my mom asked, playing along.

"Yeah. Some punk kid trying to break into people's basements, probably to see what he can steal or they're after our model planes," he said.

And even though I knew it was my dad in our basement trying to scare us, I still pleaded with him not to go back to work.

"Dad, I'm so scared!" I said. "Please don't go back to work tonight, please!"

"It's fine, really. I gotta get back to work, everything should be fine now, but if you hear anything else, anything at all, you have my permission to call the police," he said.

He left and my mom called my aunt back.

"Yeah, the asshole pretended to chase away an intruder. Said it was some punk trying to break in and steal," she reiterated to my aunt. "Yeah, she just played along," she said looking at me proudly. "Hold on Della." She held her hand over the receiver's mouthpiece, "It's about your bedtime, go on up to your room and get ready for bed."

"Mom, I'm scared," I said.

"Honey, you and I both know it was your dad that was in the basement," she said.

"I know, but it still scares me," I said.

"There's nothing to be scared about, really. I'll go up with you and help you get ready for bed." Then she said into the phone, "I'll have to call you back, Della."

We collected my clean pajamas from my canopied room and went into the bathroom that was at the top of the steps with pink tiles. She ran the bathwater and added the pink Mr. Bubble.

I was older now, so I washed myself while my mom folded clothes, cleaned up in my room and folded down my bed. My room was so close to the bathroom we could talk.

"Mom. Why does Dad try to scare us?" I asked.

"Oh, honey, he's sneaking in, trying to catch me doing something I shouldn't be doing, I suppose," she said.

"Like what?" I asked.

"Oh, who knows… he's paranoid thinking I'll have someone here while he's working," she said.

"Mom. What's paranoid?" I asked.

"When someone suspects you of doing something you shouldn't be. It usually means they're doing it themselves," she said.

Upon entering the pink bathroom she became quiet, squinting to see something out the small bathroom window up high beside the toilet. She turned the light off saying she could see outside better that way.

"What's the matter, Mom?" I said.

"Nothing, just hurry up and get done," she said as she flipped the light back on.

I got out and dried off, put my toys back in their bucket, put my pajamas on and let the water out of the tub.

When she left the bathroom I got up on the toilet lid to look through the window.

Out behind our house in the apartment building down over the hill, you could see only the top row of apartments.

And there, in the last apartment on the right, was a window lit up with light. Inside that light was my dad, standing there kissing another girl.

I went to bed without another word and eavesdropped on the phone call to my aunt.

"He's at that whore's place tonight. He snuck home to scare us and then instead of going back to work, went over there," she said.

"Who knows," I heard her say, "I'm not sure if he's even scheduled tonight or not. I really don't care anymore. I'm leaving him and taking Robin Lynn," she said.

I sat in my bed with my knees tucked up under my nightgown softly rocking back and forth trying to console myself as I listened at the top of the steps. I never knew what was going to happen next, but usually when something like this happened my lips tingled and my hearing started to buzz.

The noise I made in the back of my throat soon developed into what my mom called a nervous tic, and soon I began to stutter. My dad made fun of me and would imitate me as he laughed.

"Bu, bu, but… Ro, Ro, Robin is ner, ner, nervous," he would mock.

I had bad nerves from the fighting but I also had bad nerves from the things I was hearing about. Like when I heard about the time my dad locked my mom out of the house in the middle of the night, naked, after cutting off all her hair in her sleep. I'm not sure if I was sound asleep or at my aunt's that night, but he left her outside to bang on the door until she ran a few houses down where Jeb's mother wrapped my mom in a blanket and called the police. She had also been raped. But she didn't call it that, instead she said, "He forced himself on her."

As day was breaking and the police arrived, they found my dad hanging in the hall coat closet with a rope around his neck. He was a pale, gray color, his lips were blue and he had dark circles around his glazed-over, half-opened eyes. His mouth had foam coming out one side.

My mom sat huddled at the kitchen table in the blanket crying while the police officers tried to console her as they radioed dispatch telling them there was no pulse, an obvious suicide, and to please send a hearse.

Drawn by the police cars and flashing lights, the neighbors were outside standing, staring, pointing and wondering what was going on.

Police cars, a fire truck and paramedics surrounded our home I was told.

The paramedics came into the house with their stretcher to collect my father's lifeless body that hung in our coat closet. Paramedics worked to free him from the rope he hung from, one cutting at it with a tool he retrieved from one of the firefighters and one holding the weight of my dad's limp body up to stop the pulling of the rope around his neck.

As the guy worked to free him and sawed back and forth at the rope, my dad started laughing hysterically. Mom said everyone screamed and jumped back not believing their eyes. She said she thought the young man trying to cut my dad loose was going to have a heart attack. They stood dazed and confused as he sprung to his feet saying that he had gotten them all. He laughed at them, saying they should all have seen the look on their faces and bragged about how he could slow his breathing and pulse down enough to fool even seasoned police officers and paramedics into thinking he was dead. He called them all idiots.

They reportedly told my mom they weren't sure how she lived like this and that she must be quite nuts herself, but eventually she convinced them she was fine, so they left and the hearse was sent away.

I remember being admitted to the hospital when I was seven years old for bad nerves. I had recurring urinary tract infections, which turned out to be from Mr. Bubble, constant stomachaches, I stuttered, had nightmares, and mysterious rashes that would creep up my neck when I was nervous and upset. My mom was in the hospital the same time I was, admitted to the adult ward one floor above mine for her nerves too.

I was put in the same room with a girl named Kelly who was constantly mean to me at school. She was a tall, big-boned girl with blond hair who seemed more like a boy to me, and for some strange reason, she was actually nice to me there. She read books about a red dog named Clifford and gave one of her books for me to keep when she was done with it. I don't remember what she was in the hospital for, but her parents visited her everyday bringing with them books, food, and toys. I was jealous. My dad didn't visit and since my mom was on the floor above mine, she didn't either.

I got to stay in bed and watch TV while people brought red Jell-O and pudding on trays to my room. At night, a grandma-type person with a gray bun on top of her head rolled a metal cart down the hall where we had our choice of coloring books, stickers and activity sheets. At night, she gave out your choice of peanut butter or cheese crackers and 7Up she poured into clear plastic cups she put on the overbed table for you before lights out. Most kids didn't like the hospital, but I felt comfortable there. Safe.

The first day I saw my dad was the day we were discharged to go home. He came with his big white smile ready, and presents in hand for us both. My mom got new pajamas and a matching robe with slippers all wrapped up in a box with pretty paper and a bow. I got an unwrapped plastic turtle and a Raggedy Ann and Andy radio from the hospital gift shop.

"Here ya go, kiddo," he said.

"Thanks, Dad."

"Dad?" he said quite shocked. You're getting too big to call me Daddy now?"

"I meant Daddy," I said.

He smiled.

"How ya been holdin' up in here, fun to be waited on hand and foot, huh?" he said.

"Good," I said. "Yeah, I like it pretty much, especially the books and red Jell-O."

"Well, you and I will make all the red Jell-O you want when we get home, sound good?" he said.

"Yep, sounds good."

"Now go get out of that hospital gown and get your regular clothes on so we can go home, o.k.?"

By this time Kelly had been discharged home and it was only the two of us in the room.

When I came out the bathroom from getting changed, the nurse had wheeled my mom into my room in a wheelchair. She had dark circles around her eyes that made her look hollow and she just sat there and stared forward.

I heard my mom on the phone talking to my aunt about a nervous breakdown and remember finding little yellow pills with the letter "V" on them in the medicine cabinet. Later, I remember finding out they were Valium.

"Here, I got these for you," he said as he handed her the wrapped presents.

She didn't reach for them. She didn't even look at him.

Without saying a word he laid the box in her lap. There was no effort anymore to make him happy.

She didn't try to smile, to answer him, to even try.

There was nothing.

I don't recall how soon after being discharged from the hospital it began again, but it wasn't long and they were back to the same routine. And there I was sitting at the table in the daisy-filled kitchen swinging my legs as I ate, acting like a happy kid.

She gave me a look.

"Sorry, Mommy." My smile was replaced with that nervous sound I made in the back of my throat again and I stopped swinging my legs. She hadn't made eye contact, so I was glad.

"This is good. I love your macaroni and cheese," I said to make her feel better.

She looked up from her plate. "Well, it's not like it's homemade or anything, it's from a box," she said.

"I know. But I still like it," I said shrugging my shoulders. I gave her a quick smile that crinkled my nose.

"Well, aren't you just all cute," she said.

"I'm not trying to be cute, Mommy. I just want you to feel better. What's wrong?" I said.

She butted her cigarette out in the large green glass ashtray at the dinner table and blew the smoke out the side of her mouth in the other direction.

"Well, if you must know, you're gonna have a baby brother or sister," she said. "But don't tell ANYONE, not yet," she said.

"I won't, Mommy. I won't," I said as I looked at my empty plate.

I looked at her again just to see if she appeared any different to me after learning this news.

She looked lost and sad.

Then I whispered to her across the table.

"A baby brother or sister?" I said.

I could barely contain my excitement. She nodded her head yes, then said, "Now go outside and play, I have to call your aunt Della.

As I waited for Archie to come over after dinner to get me, I stood on our front porch, swinging on the black wrought-iron banister, singing.

"My mom's gonna have a baby, my mom's gonna have a baby, I'm gonna be a sister, I'm gonna be a big sister."

"What're you singing about now?" Archie asked as he walked over to me.

"Oh nothing, just that my mom's gonna have a baby."

"Oh yeah? I remember when my mom told me I'd be a big brother," he said.

"Were you excited?"

"Yeah, I guess. But he's still too little to play with."

"Good thing you have me then," I said.

"Yeah, good thing." he said.

I remember hearing my mom on the phone talking about me and saying she wondered if I'd be jealous when the baby finally came. She said she was worried about me regressing because I had peed my pants in the car recently, but I clearly remember pleading with her from the back seat that I couldn't hold it any longer and could she please, please pull over, after I drank an entire bottle of pop.

But she wouldn't.

As far as jealousy, the thought never entered my mind. I was as excited as everyone else that the baby was coming and was happy to help as much as I could. I would be, "Mommy's Little Helper," she said.

When my baby brother finally arrived, he was tiny, red and shriveled. I have a picture etched in my mind of my dad holding him for a photo. My dad with his bushy caterpillar eyebrows, big white Chiclet teeth and thick '70s mustache he'd recently grew, was smiling widely and proudly at the picture taker who was my mother. He was holding my baby brother who was wearing a tiny football jersey with the number 55 on it. My dad had tilted him toward the camera for all to see while pulling him close into his chest as if to say, "see this, it's all mine."

Part 2

Highland Hills

Follansbee, West Virginia

Chapter 6

My brother was seven months old when we moved to Highland Hills in Follansbee. That's the town where the air is thick with smoke clouds that rise from the coke plants and make the area smell like rotten eggs and covers everything in a grayish white powder. But, don't worry, my dad said, our new neighborhood was located up high on a hilltop where the air became fresher the higher you drove up the mountain, and things came back into focus, and had color again. He breathed in deeply as he showed us the neighborhood.

We moved into a new neighborhood just under development and our house was a brown split-level home. My room was much smaller in this house and I didn't like it nearly as much as my old one. It was a small square room, with no slanted ceiling or classroom area, no walk-in closet to sit in, and I had to use my bed without the canopy on top of it in order to fit in the room. I didn't teach my dolls and bears anymore so my mom assured me that this was exactly the room made for the big girl I was becoming. Big girls didn't need canopies on their beds or a closet to sit in to read and play anymore, she said.

Things seemed calmer and happier now since my mom's breakdown and my dad's fake suicide attempt. My mom smiled while doing mom things, and my dad was happy to play with me while she was busy with my brother we'd nicknamed Doodle. They even went on dates together and hired a babysitter to watch us when they went out.

And as usual, when I couldn't find anyone to play with, I entertained myself. Sometimes I wore a blue and gold cheerleader outfit my mom bought me at Sears around the house. I did cartwheels and shook my pom-poms yelling cheers I made up as I went along. I overheard her telling someone on the phone that no matter what happened, I always seemed to bounce back to my cheerful, happy, self.

I remember my dad's parents visiting a lot around this time bringing with them housewarming gifts, flowers for my mom, trays of food covered in plastic wrap, Jell-O for me in the shape of a wiggly upside-down cone, but since it had fruit pieces suspended inside, I wanted nothing to do with it, and boxes of diapers for my baby brother.

I still played outside a lot, but sadly, I never did see Archie again. Now, I had friends that were girls. There were the identical twin girls with glasses, Holly and Molly, and my other two friends Sissy and Clare. I stayed overnight at each of their homes, but they never stayed at mine. Sleepovers and my Brownie troop were my life.

When I came home to tell my mom about how Holly and Molly's mom made pies with them out of the apples from the trees in their backyard, she said, for Christ's sake, why in the hell would anybody in their right mind do that when you can buy one already made down at Kroger's. When I told her that their parents ate wheat germ sprinkled on their cereal in the morning to stay healthy and asked if we could do the same, she shooed me off with her hand and a roll of her eyes.

I stayed with Clare a few times too until her mother decided she no longer wanted me around. Once, right in the middle of playing in her room, I remember being shooed at with a broom by her screaming mother to leave her house this instant. She swiped at me back and forth, right out the front door like she was screaming at a pest to leave her house. Because of that, Clare and I would sneak outside to play together instead.

When I stayed at Sissy's we sang to Elton John's "Yellow Brick Road" while standing on the end of her bed looking in her mirror. I wore the gold glitter star-framed glasses that had no lenses and she wore the red glitter heart-shaped ones. We both wore feather boas, mine yellow, hers red while I sang in the curling iron, her in the hairbrush.

Sissy's bedroom door opened.

"Hey, girls…" her mother whispered.

Sissy moved to turn the radio down.

"Hey, try to keep it down, Sissy… your dad's trying to go to sleep, o.k.?" her mom said. I knew what it was like to stay quiet for your dad's work. Her dad worked at the mill too. In fact most men in the area worked at the same mill.

"O.k., Mom. Sorry," she said.

"Yeah, sorry," I said, sitting down quickly and hugging the bed pillow tight to me.

Her mom would shut the door and we'd giggle.

Later, we'd practice kissing the boyfriends we'd have someday on our pillows.

"I'll kiss him like this," I'd say, and then demonstrate moving my head back and forth with my eyes closed and my tongue flailing all around.

"And I'll do it like this," Sissy would say and do the same.

We'd laugh and giggle as quietly as we could into the night about the thought of a boy's tongue in our mouths. Morning would be there before we knew it and we'd be greeted by the sun, the smell of breakfast cooking, and another full day to play outside.

We were the last of the new houses on the right then, at the start of the highest hill in the neighborhood where everyone went sled riding that winter. That hill was a bear to pull your sled up, but so fun to go down and the bottom ended right past our house in the neighbor's front yard. Sometimes my mom would sit with my baby brother in the window and watch as we slid by.

"O.k.," my dad said, "I'm gonna go down on my stomach, you lay on top of my back on your stomach. I'll steer and you just hold on, o.k.?"

"O.k., I will," I said as I rubbed the snot upwards with my gloved hand.

We'd wait until all the other kids got out of the way and he'd lay down on the wooden sled and then hold onto the frozen ground until I got on his back and held on tight.

When he let go, you could hear the steel blades of the sled cutting the thick, milky white ice below us. The wind was so cold in our faces it felt like a thousand tiny needles poking our skin. Swirling clouds of snow blew around the street in front of us as the wind whistled.

"Woohoooo!" Dad would yell.

I'd laugh and yell, "Weeeeee!"

And we'd laugh all the way down the hill.

The bottom seemed to get there quickly but the walk up took forever. We were usually the last to go home, because a Jessup could outdo any of those other dipshits out there, my dad reminded me.

And finally, he'd say out of breath, "Last time. Then we go in, o.k?"

And every time, I still said, "Awwwww."

"Yeah, we gotta eat and it's getting late," he said.

"Same thing," he said, "down on our bellies."

He got on the sled first, then I climbed on top of his back in my big puffy snowsuit. He'd let go of the ground. And down we'd go.

But halfway down I started to slide. I hung on for dear life trying not to topple off. But the slippery material of my coat against my dad's made it impossible to hold on so I let go completely.

"Woaaaah!" I yelled as I tumbled off.

I slid a bit then came to a stop facing down the hill as I watched my dad sliding farther and farther away.

I realized my face was burning. I took my mitten off, slid my hand over my right cheek and there was blood on my hand.

My dad got back to me as soon as he could.

"What the hell happened, squirt?"

I started to recap the story for him. How I let go when I felt we'd both topple if I didn't.

"You bleeding?" he asked as he bent to inspect my face.

"Yeah," I said as I showed him my cheek.

"Looks like some road and rock came through the snow to give you some road rash," he said. "You'll be o.k., you're tough. Let's go home."

He pulled the sled and I walked alongside him.

"What the hell happened to her? What'd you do?" my mom asked when she saw my face.

"I didn't do anything to her, she fell for Christ's sake," he said.

I started to cry because I knew they were going to fight.

My dad threw his hands up in the air as he removed his coat and gloves inside the front door.

"Fine, if you're going to be such a goddamn crybaby about it, getting your mom all upset and pissed, I'll never take you sled riding again."

"I just don't want you two to fight," I said.

"Ah, would you STOP with the not wanting us to fight thing all the time? I'm sick of hearing that from you. Go to your room. I'm sick of even trying with you."

We never did go sled riding again. And I tried to stay out of the house as much as I could when my parents were home together.

In the summer of 1975 we had what the adults were calling an Indian summer. I was now eight and my dad was twenty-seven. There was construction going on all around us and as our neighborhood grew, so did the neighbors' gardens.

"Hey, kiddo, you want to go with me to get some tomatoes?" my dad said.

"Yeah. Where?"

"The neighbor's house next door." He motioned with his head.

"But Dad… they're on vacation, they're not even home!"

He laughed hysterically, patting his leg.

"I know! That's the point. No sense in that garden over there goin' to waste while they're away now, is there?"

I didn't answer and looked down.

"Well, is there?"

"No, there's no point in that," I said.

"Well, come on then! Grab a bag and let's go!"

I grabbed a paper bag out of the cabinet and out the glass sliding door we went.

"Now, I know they're not home and all, but if they were, this is how you'd get tomatoes from their garden without getting caught," he said. "Watch and learn."

He bent way down as he walked and motioned with his index finger to his lips to "Shhh!" then made the 'get down' sign with his hand as he crouched down lower as he walked.

I got down low and started to walk. Then I started to giggle because it was like the duck walk we did at school in gym class.

"Shhhh! God damn it," he whispered loudly, "you're gonna bring attention to us."

I nodded and stopped laughing.

He picked as I bagged. Big red ones that seemed bigger than my head. And little ones that looked like cherries. Medium-sized ones, some oval instead of round and a few still-green ones for frying.

"Well, hell, since we're here," he said... "Let's grab some corn too..." and down he pulled a few corn stalks. He pulled out his knife and cut them off the stalk and threw them to me to add to the bag.

"O.k." He motioned with his head to turn around. "Go back to the house, quietly," he said.

I turned, bent down and walked through the large overgrown garden that no one was tending to at the moment.

I knew this was wrong, but it was fun and I was with my dad.

As we got nearer the house, he got ahead of me, laughing like a little kid. He threw open the glass sliding door and hurried me through with my paper bag full of garden tomatoes and corn.

"Starlah, look… dinner!" he announced proudly.

"Oh my gosh, what did you guys do?" she asked.

"We were gardening!" he proudly announced.

"Harland, you're teaching our daughter how to steal?"

"My ass, it's a garden! A garden! It's not like she's waltzing into Kroger's and stealing food, the goddamn neighbors aren't even fucking home! Can't we even have a little fun?" he asked.

She shot me a look as if to say she knew she'd better not provoke him and then acted all happy about it too. She started to laugh and said, "Well, looks like we're having corn and tomatoes with dinner tonight, huh?"

"Goddamn right we are. Good job, kiddo!" he said as he high-fived me. "You're somethin' else."

I smiled as he held me around the neck in a half a hug. He turned me around and walked me toward the bathroom to go wash my hands and face for dinner.

As we sat around the table for supper that evening, my dad raised his ear of corn to the ceiling and said, "Thank you, Lord, for this food you've so generously provided us this evening." He looked at me and winked.

"Amen," we said in unison. And we all ate our corn on the cob around and around, in circles, not back and forth like a typewriter.

One evening, that same Indian summer, as the sun was just about to set, and the sky was the color of pink and blue cotton candy, my best friend Sissy and I got into a fight about the proper way to collect and keep lightning bugs. She wanted to catch them and then smear their light with her foot to write her name on the pavement, or pull their light off and place it on her finger as a ring, and I was upset about it.

"No! Why would you do that?" I yelled.

"Because it's neat-o!" she said as she smeared one on the ground with her foot.

"That's terrible! Don't do that! They're so pretty!" I said.

She smeared another and soon, it was a screaming fight.

"My mom said you can't come over anymore," she said. "She doesn't like you or your family, you stupid jerk."

"Good, I don't want to come over anymore anyway."

"You're a bunghole," she said.

"No! YOU ARE!" I screamed.

"My mom said everyone in the neighborhood thinks your dad is a crazy pervert and your mom is a drunk," she said with her hands on her hips.

As I looked up, I could see the outline of my mother standing in the front window of our brown house looking out at us.

A crowd of kids was forming behind Sissy from the neighborhood as she walked closer to me with her fists clenched.

As she came closer, I retreated.

First to my yard, then the first step on the porch, then I opened the screen door, and then the main door. As I started to walk in, my mother appeared at the top of the steps glaring down at me.

"Robin Lynn…" She pointed outside. "You get your ass out there this instant and you defend yourself, do you hear me?"

"Whaaat?" I said. "Mom, I don't want to!"

"You heard me. Get your ass out there and stick up for yourself this instant."

I had no idea what I was going to do, but I went back outside.

I hesitated. But walked slowly to the edge of our yard. I looked back and there was my mother at the window again and this time she had the window opened.

"Go on now!" she yelled.

And with that, I started toward Sissy.

Soon fists were flying back and forth, you could hear hair ripping from the scalp and an occasional slap in someone's face. I had knocked her down on the ground and was sitting on top of her face to face like my dad did to my mom. The kids from the neighborhood cheering us on to fight, fight, fight!

"You god damn bitch! Don't you EVER talk about me or my family like that again or I'll beat you worse next time, you hear me?" I screamed in her face.

Sissy was crying.

"I'm gonna go home and tell my mom on you!" she said as she got up off the ground wiping the dirt from her face and fixing her clothes.

My mom chimed in from the window.

"You go home, Sissy, and when you tell on Robin for what she did to you, you tell her I said to mind her own goddamn business and if she has anything else she wants to say about us she can come up here and say it to my face. You got that?"

And with that, Sissy turned and ran down the street crying.

I went inside, sweaty and dirty, upset yet exhilarated at the same time.

"Go get ready for bed and take your shower," she said as she closed the window.

"But Mom..."

"Just go. We'll talk about it when you're done," she said.

As I was getting my clean pajamas and underwear on, my mom came into my room.

"Mom, why did you want me to fight her?" I asked.

She sat down on my bed.

"Honey, I want you to know if you start taking shit now, you'll take it for the rest of your life. You did the right thing by standing up for yourself and your family. Don't ever let people shit on you like that. You didn't do a thing to deserve how she treated you," she said.

"I don't get it, Mom, she was my best friend. I don't even know what happened."

"I know you don't. You'll find out soon enough what happened. Just know that none of any of this is your fault, o.k.?" she said.

I went to bed that night, staring at the ceiling and replayed the whole scenario out in my head. Long gone were the days of the protection I felt from falling asleep under a princess canopy and the Lite Brite to soothe me to sleep.

Life was becoming more difficult and harder to understand.

I turned to my side to watch the jar of lightning bugs I'd caught inside an empty mayonnaise jar. No matter how many holes I'd punch into the metal lid so they'd be able to breathe, in the morning they'd all be dead.

I walked to the bus stop the next day by myself where Sissy stood off to the side and behind her mother. I stood there in my Brownie uniform complete with hat and sash, just waiting to be provoked.

Around this time my dad started to disappear down to the basement more while listening to music. It seemed the older I got, the less interested in me he became but I just tried to remember, "it's not your fault."

"Dad, what're you doin' down here?"

"Just taping some music off the radio. Hold on a sec. Shhh!" he said as he pressed the record button after the DJ stopped talking.

"You wanna go outside and play with me when you're done?"

"Nah, squirt, I'm just gonna fill up this mix tape. Why don't you go out and play with some of your friends."

"I don't have any friends anymore," I said.

"Oh? Why not?"

"Sissy and I got in a fight. Her mom called Mom names and said some bad things about you."

"Really? Like what?"

"Um, I'd rather not say…" I said.

"You can tell me," he prodded.

"She said Mom was a drunk and you were a... I don't want to say it."

"Just say it."

"A crazy pervert. What's that even mean?" I asked.

He laughed like it was the funniest thing, ever.

"Well, I'll tell ya what, why don't you go over to Clare's house then?"

"Her mom said I couldn't come over anymore. She threw me out of the house the other day and told me not to come back."

"Oh? I didn't know that," he said. "Just remember, it's not your fault, o.k? Her mom's a witch. Doesn't like me, that's probably why."

I wondered how in the world he knew my friend's mother but didn't ask.

I entertained myself without my usual group of girlfriends at this point in the growing neighborhood because when one shooed you out of their house and another one didn't want you over, soon, no one did.

I played in the houses that were being built around ours. I played with the cement they left behind in big bags by pulling it out in handfuls and adding water from puddles. I made cement castles, drew my name with hearts in dirt piles and sawdust, collected nails that were laying on the ground, picked pieces of white foam off the floors, stacked leftover wood into shapes and mazes and went home smelling of the lumber that burned my eyes and made my nose run.

Soon, some of the newer kids in the neighborhood started to join me, mostly boys, except for one freckle-faced girl named Debbie who joined Brownies too. We'd plan on the bus ride home what house we'd play in that night and all meet there at a certain time.

We picked and ate blackberries as we walked in the woods near a swamp we were all told to stay away from as the boys told tales of swamp monsters trying to scare us. We kicked at dirt mounds as we lollygagged and finally decided since there was nothing to do, we'd all take turns telling stories. The storyteller sat up high on a hill as the others sat around them in a semi-circle, looking up at them. When it was my turn, I'd tell them how my dad taught me to raid a garden, how we got down and duck walked and ate corn and tomatoes for supper that night. They'd sit wide-eyed and interested and say how neat-o it would be to have a dad that taught them that.

I'd always be the last one outside when the streetlights came on at night; my group of new friends had long gone home hours before.

On my way home alone, I sang the Brownie Smile Song.

I walked around the back of the house to the garage and could hear my dad yelling and things crashing up against the walls. When I got inside, he was so enraged he was purple red in the face and I thought he might be having some kind of fit or was sick.

"Those cocksuckers!" he screamed at the top of his lungs, "I swear to Jesus Christ, when I die, I'm throwing God out of the heavens, and I'm taking over! Then, I'm coming back to torture and kill every last motherfucker who's ever crossed me! These son of a bitches are going to pay!" he screamed.

The crash I heard was the picture of Jesus' Last Supper we had over the fireplace. The glass and the wooden frame laid in pieces all over the floor and he had ripped the picture to shreds.

I snuck up the stairs and found my mother crying in the small bathroom holding my little brother.

"Mom, what is the matter? What is going on?" I cried as I ran to her.

"Honey, get in here," she said as she opened the bathroom door.

"He's upset because, well... remember the other day when Clare's mom shooed you out of her house?" she asked.

"Yes?" I said.

"Your dad's mad because Clare's mom is forbidding their daughter Cathy from seeing your father."

"Wait, what?"

"Honey, your dad and your friend Claire's sister have been having an affair."

"He's seeing my babysitter, Cathy?" I asked.

"Yes. That's why he's throwing a fit. I didn't want to tell you, but you're old enough to hear it now," she said.

My babysitter was sixteen. My dad was now twenty-nine.

We stayed in the bathroom huddled together in front of the tub listening to the destruction of the house from inside the bathroom.

"Mom?"

"Yeah, honey?" she said.

"Why isn't Daddy upset that *you* know?" I asked.

"Shhhhh," she said.

We didn't live in the brown split-level house before the big hill for very long after that. We were there just long enough for my dad to start sleeping with my babysitter, have her parents find out, and for the entire neighborhood to run us off like the pests that we were.

Part 3

Manner Ridge Road

Wellsburg, West Virginia

Chapter 7

There was a lot of talk in our house about being laid-off and out of work, making my parents fight a lot about money. My dad would say he spent all his time making it, while all my mom did was spend it. The stress in our house escalated during rumors of lay offs and cutbacks, and in 1976-77 Weirton Steel laid off seven hundred and eighty-one people.

My dad was not one of them.

I didn't know until I was much older, that my dad never really worried about money. My mom said Grandpap Jessup would always come to my dad's rescue financially. So, we moved to Manner Ridge Road, even though we barely lived in the new brown split-level house before the big hill because it was my grandfather who footed much of the bill.

I also didn't know until much later, that we moved so my dad wouldn't be around Cathy anymore. The move took him at least another thirty minutes away from her and was what my mom called her last-ditch effort to save their marriage. When I complained about the move, she said we needed to get out of the neighborhood where everyone was calling my dad a pervert and her a drunk and maybe without Cathy being so close, the temptation to run around behind her back would be gone.

My mom was always "wishin' in one hand, and shittin' in the other" that he'd change, my aunt said. "A leopard doesn't change its spots, Starlah Jean," she'd say.

Our new house was a tan brick ranch that sat up on a hill. The yard was so large we had fifty-nine trees in it. I know because I mowed around each one by hand. Later, my dad would chop down some of those trees we had in the back yard and have an aboveground pool put there. When I got older he bought a riding mower for me so mowing it didn't take all day long.

The middle of the house where the living room, dining room and kitchen were was built out of beautiful wooden beams and wooden walls. When my dad commented on how beautiful it was, the realtor told my parents an electrical fire from behind the refrigerator had broken out for the previous owners and when they rebuilt it, they used repurposed wood and wood beams from an old church that was being torn down. My mom said my father liked that story instantly.

Later, when we met our neighbors, we found out the wood and wood beams that rebuilt the middle of our new house were not from a church, they were from a Kingdom Hall. The previous owners of our house were Jehovah's Witnesses.

I'd hear my dad recount to many over the years of living there, the story of the old church instead. "Yeah," he'd say as he ran his hand over the wood beam in the living room. "Came from a very old church they were tearing down, ain't that a shame? It's like nothin's sacred anymore. Thought they'd go nicely in here." As if he did the work himself.

The dread would come over me like a gray thickness that started in the pit of my stomach and spread like wildfire to the rest of my body, until I thought I might be sick.

When first moving there, my aunt Diana and cousin Denny came over to pick us up to go roller-skating one Saturday afternoon as we had done so many times before. My mom and I were both getting our shoes on and about to leave when my dad came out of the bedroom.

"Go wait outside, Robin Lynn, I'll be out in a minute," my mom said.

I sensed a fight brewing between them immediately, so I went outside to sit with my aunt and cousin in the car and wait.

"What's going on in there, Robin?" my aunt asked.

"They're gonna fight again."

"How do you know that?" Denny asked.

"I can just feel it. I can feel it in my stomach. I hate it. I wish they would just get divorced already."

A few minutes passed and my mom came down to the car and said I had to get out of the car. Now.

"But why?" I asked.

"Just do it!" she ordered. "Not another word out of you, young lady, just move it!" she said as she scooted me up the hill from the driveway.

My aunt Diana and cousin Denny had gotten out and followed us up the hill and into the house. As we were entering the house, my dad squeezed passed us through the breezeway door on his way to work, not saying a word to anyone.

We all sat at the kitchen table.

"He just lost it, Diana, he said we weren't going anywhere and yanked me by my hair. Told me if I left he'd beat the shit out of me," she recounted.

My aunt was married to my dad's identical twin. And they were as different as night and day. From what I saw, my cousin Denny got day, I got night. Funny thing is, my uncle had a small area on his left ear that my dad didn't have, where the cartilage on the outer portion of the ear dips in. I have it and my cousin Denny doesn't.

I remember wondering if my uncle might be my dad instead. My mom would recount how when they were younger my dad and his brother would switch to try to stump their girlfriends to see if they noticed. My mom said she noticed every time because of that ear of his. My mom assured me yes, Robin Lynn, your father is your father. But with all the stories about my dad and uncle switching, and jokes about the milkman, it just made a kid wonder. And sometimes hope.

My mom made coffee and they sat and talked at the kitchen table.

"I'm so tired of this, Diana, I'm about to lose it. He just changes in the blink of an eye. Like Dr. Jekyll and Mr. Hyde and over the littlest things," she said.

"I'm sorry he hurt you, Mom," I said.

"It's o.k. I'll be alright," she said.

She was red around her eyes and her nose was pink from crying. Her hair had been done but now was all messed up. A large chunk of hair was ripped out of the back of her head.

"Mom, I hate him," I said as I clung to her side. "I want to leave here and live by ourselves," I added.

"Shhh! Don't say that, he could hear you," she said, paranoid that he was recording us or not completely gone.

"Mommy, why are we not allowed to go roller-skating?" I asked. "What's the big deal? We do it almost every Saturday," I said.

"You know. I'm just sick of the questions, just stop it," she said as she pushed me away from her and the kitchen table. "You're always asking questions and if it wasn't for you... always wantin' something —"

My aunt Diana chimed in and said, "Starlah, it's not her fault he hits you and it's only normal to ask what's the big deal when all of a sudden it's not o.k. to go," she explained.

"I just can't take it anymore," my mom said as she cradled her head in her hands at the table. "You'd better go now before he comes back and finds you still here and loses it even more," she said to Aunt Diana.

I started to cry at the thought of my only defender at the moment leaving me there with her. My aunt stood up to leave, and I went after her and asked her to please stay or at least take me with her.

My mother grabbed me by my arm and flung me to the floor. She was screaming at me how much of a little bitch I was and I wasn't going anywhere. "You're always gettin' everything you want, gettin' your way one way or another, cryin' around all the time, tryin' to make people feel sorry for you like you're somethin' special," she yelled as she was kicking at me on the floor.

Diana got up from the table with a shot and grabbed her arms. "Stop this! Stop this, now!" she demanded.

I started to run off to go to my room, but stopped. I sat crying with my knees pulled up to my chest just out of sight at the end of the hall. I still didn't want my aunt to leave. I couldn't trust anyone in this house. One minute they loved you and the next minute they were screaming everything was your fault. One day you could go roller-skating, the next day you couldn't. I never knew what to expect.

My mom took on a child-like demeanor when confronted about her behavior. She sat at the table and started to explain her actions to my aunt.

"You don't understand, Diana, you don't live with her," she started to defend.

"Starlah, she's a child. She's not the problem. Harland is the problem and you're taking it out on your daughter. Stop it and get a hold of yourself, right this minute!" she demanded. "Look at what you're doing here. You're take a beating from your husband and turning right around and taking out your frustrations on your child when he leaves for work. You have to see that," she pleaded.

My mom sat sobbing into her hands at the table, her shoulders and head shaking up and down in agreement with my aunt Diana.

After my aunt calmed her down, my mom looked over to see me sitting at the edge of the hall.

"Come here, Robin Lynn, I'm sorry," she said.

She motioned for me to come over to her and held out her arms in a hugging motion.

I reluctantly walked over, slowly at first then quickly fell into her arms crying.

"I'm sorry. I'm so, so, so, so sorry," she said into the top of my head as she pushed a kiss into my hair.

"It's o.k.," I said. "Please, Mom. Let's leave here and never come back."

She was nodding her head up and down, tears rolling down her face, lips pursed and red faced, looking at my aunt as if to say she knew it was just about time.

Only a few months after the roller-skating incident and not even a full year in the new house on Manner Ridge Road, my parents would be in the process of divorcing after eleven years of a marriage. The fight they had that day had been precipitated by the fact that Cathy had turned eighteen. She was legal and they had been seeing one another again, or had been all along, my mother never knew for sure. When my dad came home from work he said he wanted out of their marriage.

At first she cried not knowing what she'd do without him, they'd been together since they were teens. After she had a good talkin' to by my aunts and cousins, she eventually changed her tune and said she was happy to get on with the rest of her life and not have to live with abuse anymore.

So, we would be staying at Aunt Della's, until the divorce was settled.

Chapter 8

Way down Parson's Run Road, where my aunt Della lived, was at least ten degrees cooler, year round. The sun could be blazing and the humidity terrible and yet there it was comfortable. In winter, the main roads to get to her house would be covered with snow, yet the dirt road leading to my aunt's place would barely have a trace of white powder on it.

On the left side of the dirt road, that was slowly eroding away, was a lake that snaked around the side of the mountain. Part lake, part stagnant swamp. The lake was pretty but it was the swampy area that worried me, which was closest to the road. I remember worrying about going over the edge. In West Virginia, you don't have guardrails to protect you. You go over and you're never heard from again.

The thick, lush canopy of trees hung over the tube-like road leading to my aunt's house. In summertime, you'd occasionally find a hole in the canopy that hung over the road if you looked up to the sky and you could see birds circling slowly way up high.

The air down there smelled like rotten eggs too and you could hear the creek that ran alongside my aunt's house, running constantly. They called it a "crick" not a creek.

We'd sleep with the windows open. The fresh, dewy country air was like a sedative. The smell of lying on linens that were dried on a clothesline in the sweet sunshine of summer, and the smell of your earthy-scented hair from playing outside, was a signature scent I truly loved. I'd go to bed with dirty feet and I'd wake with a heaviness to my bones as if the nighttime air and morning dew settled somewhere deep inside and caused me to feel heavier, more rested than usual.

On dry days, I'd sit with my knees on the couch looking out the window and watch white smoke fly off the tires of passing cars as they barreled up the hill, waiting for my mom to come back for me. I especially liked when I heard horses being ridden up the road with the clipiddy-cloppitty sounds their hooves made against the dirt and their snorting. Their tails flipped in wild directions as they walked, batting off the flies that forever pestered them. Every sound magnified, and carried, right up to sit deep inside your ears, like you were right next to them.

On the mornings it rained was the best. I loved the sound the rain made when it hit the tin awning over my aunt's porch. The fast falling rain made the creek higher and run faster, turned it the color of chocolate milk, and diluted the stench of rotten eggs in the air. Early morning sounds were like a song. Crickets chirping, frogs singing and the rain made my mind wander.

She lived down in what was called the "holler." I think they called it that because it was like being down in a cool dark hole in the ground where no one could hear you holler.

My cousin Bernice was tall and wore a size three. Her long blond hair fell below her butt and when she wore the high-heeled clogs with her bell-bottomed pants, the extra height made her look like a fashion model. She was the youngest of her three sisters, almost ten years older than me, and I loved watching her get ready to go out. Most times she'd try to shoo me out of her room saying to leave her alone and find something else to do. Other times she'd let me stay if I promised to stay out of her way and just sit on the bed and be good.

Promising to be good, I'd lie across the bed and watch her put her makeup on. I'd watch the red, yellow, green and blue lights flicker from the speakers in the stereo/turntable console she had in her room. They changed with the beat of the music she played. And it was the first time I'd listened to The Steve Miller Band, the album with the horse's head on it, "Fly Light An Eagle" and "Dream Weaver."

She smoked her Salem Menthol 100s as she got ready, occasionally laying them in the old turtle shell she turned upside down and used as an ashtray. They'd burn while she brushed her long blond locks or while she carefully apply her blue powdery eye shadow and matching blue mascara. When she was all done, she'd stand and look at her reflection in the mirror on the back of her closet door and ask me, "How do I look?"

"You look SO pretty!" I'd say.

I thought she was beautiful and I wanted to be just like her when I grew up.

She wore short midriff tops that ended well above her navel on her flat tanned stomach and a suede vest with fringe. After flinging a purse that matched the fringed jacket over her shoulder and yelling bye, she'd be out the door with some friend waiting for her outside in their car. I'd run up to the couch and sit on my knees watching as the dirt flew off the tires as they drove up Parson's Run out of sight. I thought how cool it was to be older.

I wasn't involved in the divorce proceedings when my parents divorced and was never asked with whom I wanted to live. Before the divorce was final, my dad had a change of heart and did his fair share of trying to convince my mom to come back to him. I'd hear her on the phone at my aunt's.

"Oh, you always say that, Harland. I'm not going to sit here and listen to this nonsense anymore," she would say into the phone.

"Look, it's over," she would begin again. "I am going through with it this time. I can't and won't be beat anymore and I don't want my kids around it anymore. For Christ's sake, Harland, Robin Lynn is only nine and she's been hospitalized for her bad nerves already."

"Yeah, threaten to come beat my ass, that makes perfect sense. Your wife doesn't want to come back to you and you threaten to beat her ass? There's an offer I can't refuse!" and she'd break out laughing.

My aunt Della was in the background, doing the cut-off motion with her hand across her neck telling her to stop saying this stuff in front of me and to hang up the phone, but her efforts went unnoticed.

"Starlah Jean, just hang up. You're wasting your breath," she said.

Then pretty soon, you'd hear the receiver of the phone bang down on its cradle.

"He's crazy! He's threatening to come out here and beat my ass if I don't take him back!" my mom told everyone in the room.

"Starlah, just don't take his phone calls. It's that simple. And you have to start thinking about what you're saying in front of Robin Lynn," she said as she pushed her head out toward me. I was sitting in the corner soaking it all in, tears welling up in my eyes. Worried.

"Robin Lynn, stop. He's not going to come down here and do anything to me, don't you worry," she tried to comfort. But I knew she was scared. "Go back in your aunt's room and just color or something for awhile."

I went toward the bedroom but stopped short and stood in the hallway listening.

"I'm gonna have Mouse come out here just in case Harland wants to come out and start his shit," she said. Mouse was just one of her friends, she said.

I heard her pick up the phone and shortly thereafter hang up.

"He's on his way," I heard her say after she hung up the phone.

I didn't know it then, but Mouse was a guy my mom liked a little more than a friend and apparently he liked her enough to come out to my aunt's to protect her from the threat of my dad.

Soon enough I heard a car flying down the dirt road. It was Mouse. Like Mighty Mouse, he'd come to save the day.

Mouse was tall and lean. He had black, greased back hair, dark eyes, a neatly trimmed thinner mustache than my dad, and wore tight jeans that outlined the curve of his penis. He always wore cowboy boots and jeans and a leather jacket, even in the summertime. I had to admit, he was very handsome and he kind of acted like he already knew that.

I heard my mom open the door and when I peeked my head out she had slipped out onto the porch and quietly closed the door behind her. The door had small glass panels you could wind open to let the air in and I could hear every word.

"Shhhh!" my aunt said, "Voices carry in the country."

"Yeah, he's coming down here now to beat my ass," she said. "Robin Lynn's in the back bedroom with Doodle."

"It's going to be o.k, no one's going to touch you or those kids," he said as he hugged her and reassured her.

I kind of liked how he took my mom into his leathered chest holding her tight right there on the front porch. Her short blond hair bobbed up and down against the black leather, as she cried.

I wanted him to protect us. I wanted him to love my mom. I wanted him to care about us kids. I felt like everything was going to be fine with him around.

He came inside the house.

The rowdy, barking dogs settled enough to hear my aunt offer him a cup of coffee and I heard the murmuring of talking in the kitchen, catching only a few words.

Things were quiet, pleasantries exchanged, a few laughs were had, my aunt took a phone call and then hung up the phone. All was well.

I heard another vehicle coming down the gravel road and my heart jumped. I wondered if it was my dad. Pretty soon, I heard someone say, "No, it went by."

My chest was always tight and I was getting a rash up my neck from being worried. I knew that I had to calm myself and take deep breaths. I looked at myself in the mirror in my aunt's room. "It's going to be alright. Mouse is here and things will be fine. Heck, Dad's not even going to drive all the way down here," I assured my reflection.

I checked on my little brother; he was sleeping. I climbed up on the big tall bed and sank down in the huge comforter and situated the coloring book and crayons around me. Things were quiet, except for the sound in the back of my throat. I made that noise whenever I got nervous.

I could tell the next vehicle I heard coming down the road was a truck. My dad didn't have a truck.

Then later a horse galloped by. I colored and listened to the hooves clickety clop all the way till I couldn't hear them anymore.

The door squeaked open a bit. It was my aunt.

"You doin' o.k. in here?" she asked me.

"Yep. Just coloring," I said.

"Doodlebug still asleep?" she asked as she peeked at him nestled in a small portable playpen beside the big bed.

"Yep, still sleeping," I said. "Aunt Della, is my dad really coming to hurt my mom?"

"Nah, he's not going to do any such thing," she said confidently. "Everything's gonna be alright. You don't have to worry, o.k.? Just color for now and leave the worrying to the adults."

I smiled at her.

"Aunt Della, Mouse isn't going to hurt my dad, is he?" I asked.

"No, I don't even think your dad's going to come down here. Besides, if he was, I think he'd have been here by now," she said.

She went to close the door but opened it again. "You hungry?"

"Yeah, a little bit," I said.

"I'll bring you a biscuit with some homemade apple butter on it," she said as she winked. "Be right back."

I loved my aunt Della. I sometimes wished she were my mom because she seemed to worry for me and care about me more than my mom did.

A few minutes later she returned with a white plate edged in silver that held two biscuit halves spread with apple butter and a napkin.

"Thank you," I said.

"We'll get you some supper in you in a little bit, but this should hold you over," she said as she handed me the plate.

"O.k."

We both stopped cold, mid-action, to evaluate the sound of the car we heard coming.

I heard my mom scream, "That's him! He's here!"

I jumped up and ran to the bedroom door.

"Robin Lynn, come here! You don't need to go out there if they're going to just fuss and carry on now!" my aunt yelled after me.

I was quickly at the door leading out to the porch.

I looked out and Mouse was already taking off down the steps as my dad was walking up the driveway.

"Now, Mouse, this doesn't concern you," my dad said putting up his hand.

"Sure it does. You threaten to beat her ass, why don't you man up and beat my ass, if you can. Come on, ya fuckin' pussy," Mouse said.

"Mouse, I'm not here to deal with you. This is between me and Starlah and involves our family, not you."

"Well, this IS my family. I've known your wife a hell of a lot longer than you have and this family longer than you've been in it," he taunted my dad as he pushed his index finger into his chest.

My dad looked up the stairs to my mom.

"Starlah, you just gonna stand there and let him do this?" he asked.

"Harland, I'm not gettin' involved with this," she said.

"You're already involved!" he yelled. "You got this jack-off involved in it when you went runnin' your mouth to him," my dad said.

And with that Mouse pushed my dad in his chest.

A few punches were exchanged back and forth.

Mouse got my dad in a headlock and punched him rapidly over and over and over in the face. Mouse let go of him and he fell to the ground.

I ran out the door, passed my mom standing at the top of the steps, yelling, "If you're not going to do anything I will! Leave my dad alone! Leave him alone!"

Mouse was over my dad kicking him in the sides with his pointed cowboy boots.

"Stop! STOP IT!" I screamed.

"Robin Lynn, get up here this instant!" my mom yelled.

"No! I will NOT! Why are you doing this to my dad!" I screamed at Mouse. "Dad! Daddy! Please get up! Please!" I yelled at him.

My dad just covered his head with his hands and continued to be kicked all over his body.

Someone grabbed me and started to drag me from behind. And all I could do was watch as my dad was kicked until he was almost unconscious and had pink frothy foam coming from his mouth.

I screamed so loudly, I could taste blood in my throat. I felt like I was dying. I was crying and shouting, heaving and thrashing against whoever was holding me back and finally broke free.

"Leave my dad alone! Daddy… get up, please…" I begged as I knelt by his side.

"Robin Lynn, get up here now," my mom yelled down at me. "Your dad was askin' for it. He came here and this is what he got. I warned him not to come. But now maybe he'll leave us the hell alone once and for all," she said.

"That's MY DAD!" I screamed. "Why are you acting like this?!"

"Me? Acting like what? You heard him say he wanted to come here and beat my ass, but it figures, you cry for your dad," she said.

"No! NO! I don't want anyone to get beat up! Not you, not him! I'm tired of all this fighting," I cried out. "I'm so tired," I said as I cried, coughed and gagged. "Of all of this," I added. "I hate you. I hate YOU!" I yelled to her.

I no longer wanted Mouse to protect us. I didn't want him to love my mom. I didn't want him to care about us kids. I knew if my mom got with him next, nothing would be fine. He fought dirty.

I sat on my knees next to my father's side as he laid there, eyes rolling back in his head, gurgling on red foam coming out the side of his mouth.

"Daddy. I love you. Please. Wake up," I cried.

I looked up the steps to the house for someone to come help me, but everyone had walked back inside leaving me there by myself with my bleeding and half-conscious dad.

After the altercation with Mouse, my dad never came to talk sense into my mom again. And the cowboy-boot-wearing Mouse scurried from our lives like the rodent that he was.

And, well now, if my dad couldn't come see my mother to convince her to take him back, he'd send her gifts in the mail instead.

"Starlah, this was in the mail for you today. It's Harland's handwriting," my aunt said as she examined the box top.

"Oh brother," my mom said as she reached out for the box. "I sure hope it's not a dead animal in there, or a bomb," she added as she took the box.

My cousins laughed.

I didn't.

She placed the box on the kitchen table and carefully cut the glossy tape that held the box top together with a metal nail file and squinted her eyes like she did whenever she opened a can of biscuits.

I sat across the room, covering my ears, waiting for the explosion. She hesitantly pulled the paper back and strained to see what was inside.

She paused, looking confused, and then pulled the glossy beige statue of a boy with big black round eyes my dad bought for her for Valentine's Day. Its arms were stretched out and he held a banner that said, "I Love You This Much." But now the statue had a large butcher's knife sticking down through its head. He had melted red candle wax down over the top of the head to resemble blood dripping.

"This Much" now looked like "Please Help Me!"

I was the first to speak.

"Mommy. I'm scared," I said half crying.

Once my cousin Connie Ray got a look at it, she busted up laughing and my mom joined her.

When they finally stopped laughing she said, "Oh, don't be. Honey, your dad is just acting out. He's not getting his way and he's been used to getting what he wants his whole life and now he's pouting like a little child."

"He won't hurt you?" I asked.

"No, I highly doubt it. And after what happened between him and Mouse, I doubt he ever shows his face around here again," she assured me.

I didn't like what Mouse did to my dad. It was like a frightening movie that replayed in my mind that I couldn't shut off and it hurt me in my heart. But I didn't like what my dad was doing to my mom either.

"What a sweet talker," my cousin Connie Ray said and laughed.

"I know. Like this is a way to woo a woman back. What an asshole," my mom said.

And they laughed and laughed till their faces turned every shade of red.

Soon, my parents' divorce was final. My babysitter, Cathy, became my stepmother, and I would be living with my mom and Doodle in a trailer on the side of Rabbit Hill.

Part 4

Rabbit Hill

Wellsburg, West Virginia

Chapter 9

My cousin Ben and his friend Greg and I used to be so intrigued by an old car wreck we could see over the edge of the road on Rabbit Hill. It was so far down that it couldn't be excavated so it sat there to rot over the years. It was one of those station wagons with faux wood paneling on the sides, crunched and sitting on its side. We'd ride our bikes out to the area and peer over the edge, wondering if there were skeletons of the people that had died in that crash still in there. We'd get ourselves so worked up about it, we'd climb on our bikes and pedal as fast as we could away from there, not stopping till we got home, occasionally looking behind us as we pedaled to see if anything or anyone was chasing us.

We lived in a baby-shit-yellow gold trailer with white trim on Rabbit Hill. The trailer sat between my grandma Jancie's trailer and my aunt Adalene's trailer. It cost eleven thousand dollars and was part of my mom's divorce settlement; paid in full by my dad to forgo paying alimony and having to write that bitch a check every month, I overheard my dad say. It was odd that the man got the marital home and the wife and kids got thrown out, but that's what happened to us. My mom said my dad had a habit of falling into shit holes while coming out smelling like a rose.

So, my mom got the new trailer, the brown '76 Chevy Nova and two-hundred and fifty dollars a month in child support for me and my brother. It was a substantial amount of money back then, and I overheard the women of our family saying, to hell with that house, she got a hell of a deal.

I recall my mom sitting undecided between two trailers with the paperwork laid out in front of her on the salesmen's desk. She read back and forth between the two documents, tip of the pen resting on her bottom lip, probably her first decision made solely by herself. Finally the salesman assured her the trailer with the appliances in the hottest new color called Harvest Gold was the best choice. With that bit of prodding, she excitedly signed the papers, they shook hands, and just like that we had a new house.

I liked the trailer. I was intrigued that some of the walls came already wallpapered, there were already matching curtains in every room and the whole thing came furnished.

The bright daisies were gone and now my mother decorated everything in our new kitchen with gold, rust and brown mushroom decor. We had the mushroom toaster cover, canister set, magnets on the refrigerator and dishtowels that hung from the stove handle by their crocheted and buttoned tops. And a large gold soup ladle hung on the paneled wall in the kitchen that held a flower arrangement my mom made that had rust- colored mushrooms with brown dots on their tops scattered throughout.

That same color scheme was throughout the whole trailer. The living room was separated from the kitchen by a counter that never did have bar stools under it. The couch was a scratchy, stiff, gold, rust and brown-checkered pattern with buttons on the back of the cushions that poked into your back as you sat. In the summer months with no air-conditioning, no one wanted to sit on that scratchy thing that made you itch like you had bugs. On the wall that divided my bedroom from the living room were long mirrors that hung in strips between the panels of wood. The chemical smell of the high-gloss paneling, stiff new furniture, cheap carpet and linoleum made your eyes water and your nose sting. It was the same smell I remembered when I was little and played in homes being built around me on Highland Hills. And even though this was all new too, we were as poor as church mice. The life we were accustomed to living with my dad, as head of household, had completely and drastically changed after the divorce.

But we had a new home, new furniture and, she promised both of us, a new mom. It was a whole new beginning for her; a new beginning for all of us, she assured us with hugs.

She was tired of being controlled, beaten, terrorized, and now that the divorce was final, she could say the word: raped. Saving her seven-year-old from being admitted to the hospital for bad nerves was a plus too. We were all free now.

And she got rebellious.

No one was going to make her do anything she didn't want to again. Not ever again. So, in came the music. We played albums on the new stereo's turntable that she bought as her first new gift for herself and we sang our hearts out in what felt like total freedom. My mom would sing and dance around the living room wearing her cut-off jean shorts that showed off her lean, trim legs she swore were from wearing her Dr. Scholl's exercise sandals; a sleeveless, white, button-down cotton top tied in a knot at her navel; and a red bandana tied in a bow up around her short blonde pixie-cut hair. She looked like Rosie the Riveter, if Rosie had blond hair, wore Daisy Dukes and liked to dance.

I loved to see her happy and thought she was the most beautiful woman I had ever seen. That was my mom, I thought. And my goodness, when I watched her happy and free, I knew I would have turned myself inside out to show her how much I loved her.

She was twenty-seven years old.

Music filled our long metal tube of a home. We'd sing "Sunshine" by Jonathan Edwards and "I Can See Clearly Now the Rain is Gone" by Johnny Nash. We sang, danced and acted out the words of the songs with our hands in a theatrical way while facing one another. I didn't have to feel tingling around my mouth and a buzzing in my ears to gauge her mood; I knew by the music she played. Most songs were sunny and cheerful or "You're No Good" by Linda Ronstadt when she was feeling sassy.

She was proud of her new place and liked to show it off to her friends any chance she got. And I liked that, seeing her proud and happy of her life for a change.

Sometimes, we'd sit on the couch in our pajamas at night and she'd tell me the story about how I was named Robin.

"You see, your dad wanted to name you Edith after his mom," she said. "God love her, but Edith?" she wrinkled her nose. "I had to put my foot down on that one," she'd say. I'd giggle and listen intently, gazing up at her like I had never heard this story before.

"Three days passed and you still weren't named," she said.

"The nurses kept after me to name you because I was about to be discharged and they had to fill out the birth certificate," she added.

Knowing the story I'd chime in.

"You wanted to name me after the little girl you used to babysit, huh?" I said.

"Yep, that's right. And I just couldn't, for the life of me, think of her name," she said shaking her head.

She'd go on.

"It was December and there was snow on the ground. I sat in a chair in my hospital room looking out the window at a rooftop below. There, in the snow, was a robin, flapping its wings. Then, I thought to myself, how strange it was to see a robin in winter, and it dawned on me that that was the name I'd been searching for, her name was Robin!" she said amazed. "I said 'Robin' out loud and went out to tell the nurses your name. So… you see, you were destined to be a Robin."

"Thank goodness for Moms!" I said.

"Thank goodness is right!"

I didn't want the attention or the stories to stop, so I'd try to keep them going.

"Remember when you called me Roberta?" I said.

"Oh yes! Your father would get so mad at me!" she'd say. "I would wait until you were in your playpen busy with your back turned to me. I would call you by your name, Robin, Robin, Robin… and nothing. I'd call, Roberta, and you'd turn right around. It was the funniest thing ever, so I called you Roberta for years. I actually knew a girl name Roberta Henthorne growing up so I called you Roberta Henthorne," she said. "Your dad told me I had to stop calling you that and start calling you by your name, so that was the end of that," she said.

The paneled walls in my room were plastered with Shaun Cassidy, Leif Garrett and Andy Gibb posters, not a piece of paneling could be seen. Shaun Cassidy was my favorite. I'd write letters and send them to his fan club just hoping he'd read them. I had my KISS dolls lined up by my yellow ball radio with eight-track tape player, my small collection of Nancy Drew and Hardy Boys books, and *Teen Beat* magazines neatly stacked on the dresser.

My mom would come in from time to time and lay across my twin bed just to visit with me. She'd gaze over my walls and say, "Boy crazy just a little, huh?" and we'd laugh. She would ask what I was reading and what I was thinking. It was like we were not just mother and daughter, but friends too.

"Your room is always the nicest room in the whole house, clean and tidy, everything in its place," she'd say.

I never really minded my parent's divorce. I was sick of the fighting and locking myself in my room, pretending I didn't hear it all. Now, I could dance in the living room with my mom and be free.

My little brother was seven years younger than me, making me nine, and him two when my parents' divorce was final.

I acted like a big mommy to Doodle, but I was still a kid myself. And did stupid kid stuff. Like, how I told my little brother that the almond on top of Almond Joy candy bars were June bugs so he'd pick them off and give them to me. And I told him that the little chicken crackers he ate at the time that were shaped like drumsticks really did have bones in them and not to eat that part. We'd have ashtrays full of "the bones." And, I'd eat my mom's dietetic chocolate candies called Ayds, by the handfuls.

I entertained myself while washing dishes by reciting commercial lines I thought were funny after hearing my cousins doing it. There was the one for Shake 'n Bake. The little girl, with what we thought was an overly done Southern drawl, goes up to her grandma in the kitchen asking if she can help make her "special fried chicken." The grandma tells her she uses Shake 'n Bake and puts her to work shaking the bag to coat chicken. Later, at the table after the grandma admits it's not fried, but baked, the little girl says, "And I helped." I'd say, "space-cial fried chicken", "And I-iiiii helped" and crack myself up laughing. I was always my best audience and lived inside my head my mom told me.

And then there was Loretta Lynn, bless her heart, telling us that, "Crisco'd do us proud ever' time." We were called hillbillies but we didn't think we sounded like that at all and my cousins and I would laugh and laugh saying, "Crisco'd do us proud, ever' time."

One day when I was left in charge while my mom left I got on the phone with a friend and started talking like my mom always did.

"Stop bugging me, Doodle, I'm on the phone!" I said as I put my hand over the receiver's mouthpiece.

He ran the big metal Hot Wheels van over my foot while I talked. I was trying to manage him while I continued to talk on the phone and soon he was standing on the large van trying to skate on it and ran over my foot again.

I kicked out at the van and he went flying across the room and face first toward the pointy corner of the coffee table.

"I gotta go!" I yelled and hung up the phone.

Doodle got up and faced me, crying. His doughy white cheek was bleeding profusely.

"Oh my god, I'm sorry, Doodle, I'm so sorry!!" I yelled.

I grabbed him up, covered his face with a dishtowel and carried him over to my grandma's house.

"Oh my gosh, what happened?" my grandma asked.

"I pushed him and he fell on the table," I said. "Can you please call someone to take us to the emergency room? Mom's not home."

As I said that, I heard a car pulling in. It was my mom.

Without saying anything else, I ran to the car.

"Mom! Doodle's hurt! We need to go to the emergency room now."

"What happened?" she asked frantically.

"It's my fault, I pushed him and he fell on the table," I said as I strapped him in his car seat.

Once in the front seat I turned around and kept checking on him as she drove.

"I didn't mean to hurt him. He wouldn't stop pestering me while I was on the phone, he ran over my foot by accident and I kicked at the van he was standing on and he fell on the table," I recounted for her.

I walked into the hospital alongside my mom; stood feeling guilty about it all in front of the doctors and nurses who stitched him back up and picked him a blue lollipop for later as we left. I didn't take one for myself; I didn't feel I deserved it.

On the way home, he smiled at me while sucking on the lollipop. He had four black stitches that looked like upside-down ants with their legs sticking up in the air on his cheek. I never felt so bad before in my life.

"Awwww… look at him," my mom said, peering back at him from the rearview mirror as she drove. "He loves you, Robin Lynn, and you hurt his pretty little face."

"Mom, I feel bad enough, o.k.?" I said.

"That's going to leave a scar, you know," she said.

I turned around and faced forward and cried the rest of the way home.

At home, I could hear my mom on the phone in her room.

"Robin Lynn is getting aggressive. I hope she doesn't grow up to be hateful and mean like her father," she said.

I sat there and let those words tumble around in my head. Hateful and mean, hateful and mean. How in the world was I hateful and mean? It was an accident. I took full responsibility for it and apologized. I was normally taking care of him and he knew, I hoped he knew, I loved him.

My brother wore diapers till the age of four and no matter what anyone did, he would not go in the toilet. It drove everyone nuts and gave my dad just enough ammunition to sit and judge her parenting or lack thereof, he'd say. And just about everyone in our family at one time tried to teach him to use the toilet. Pee on Cheerios as a game? Nope. Sit down on the toilet? Nope. Face forward while sitting on the toilet? Nope. He wanted nothing to do with any of it. I have a photo of me trying to potty train him on visitation at my dad's house. He was about three and he's looking at the camera with a smirk like, Nope, I ain't doin' it.

And the kid ate anything he found on the floor. You'd have thought no one ever fed him. He was once taken to the emergency room for drinking my Avon perfume that came in a cupcake decanter. He unscrewed the cherry-on-top lid and drank my Sweet Honesty perfume. He sat there drunker than a skunk in the E.R., my mom said. When the doctor gave him medicine to throw it all up, she recounted that he threw up a button, some string, a piece of rubber band and something that looked like part of one of my hair clips. She laughed and laughed retelling that story but said she was scared to death at the time.

She said the doctor looked at her and asked, "What kind of diet do you have this kid on?" Needless to say, the Mr. Yuk stickers we had on anything and everything that was not edible did not deter him. Once, when my brother was in my aunt Della's shopping buggy, he told her to put back the lotion she chose and to buy another kind he liked better. When she asked why, he said, "It tasted good." When she told him he wasn't supposed to eat it, she said he just put his hand over his mouth and giggled.

One day while on visitation weekend with my dad and Cathy, I was riding bikes with a friend and fell. I became unsteady, going down the big hill too fast, and before I knew it, the back of the bike was flying up over my head and I was face down on the side of the road.

I tried to catch myself, landing on my wrist.

"Oh my God, are you alright?!" my friend yelled to me.

"No, I'm not," I said as I stood up starting to cry.

"Oh no, oh… God… let's get you home, your wrist is broken," she said as she helped me to my feet.

We left the bikes lying where they fell and walked the rest of the way to my house with me holding my wrist in the other hand.

"What the hell happened to you?" my dad said.

"I'm o.k., but I think Robin broke her wrist."

"Get in here and let me have a look at it then," he said.

We went to the bathroom and he clicked on the light for further inspection. I had two small abrasions that were bleeding and inside the opened areas were small speckles of blacktop cinders that looked like pepper.

"We gotta clean that out of there before it gets infected," he said.

He went over to the cabinet and got out the brown bottle of hydrogen peroxide he gargled with to whiten his teeth.

"Here," he instructed, "put your hand over the sink and let me pour this on it. It'll probably burn a little at first, but that white bubbling you see… it's cleaning out the germs from the road rash."

It did burn for just a bit and I squinted up my face until the burning went away. I stood there with my friend for that day and we watched the white bubbling foam get bigger and then finally disappear as my dad went to get a clean rag out of the laundry room.

"See… that didn't' hurt much, did it?" he asked when he returned. "When the bubbles are gone that means the area is clean," he added.

He wrapped the clean rag around my wrist and told me to hold it there.

As he squeezed my wrist, I screamed in pain. The swelling was getting worse and the bend in my wrist more pronounced.

"Cathy, come here!" he yelled.

She came in the bathroom to see what was going on.

"Do you think this is broken?" he asked as he moved my wrist up and down.

I screamed in pain.

"Oh, stop it. Stop it this minute!" he yelled at me.

"Dad, it's obviously broken, don't grab it and move it. Please!" I said.

"Oh, just calm down now. Come out here to the dining room table and have a seat for a minute, get yourself together," he said.

I sat there with my forearm resting on the table; hair all messed up, sweaty hot from being outside, tears streaking the dirt on my face.

"Why don't you eat some lunch while we figure out if we need to take you to the hospital," he said.

"I'm really not hungry, Dad."

"Well, you're gonna eat whether you want to or not. If you have to go to the emergency room, and you haven't eaten all day, well… that's just not gonna look good," he said.

He served me his usual tuna fish sandwich on white bread cut in half and potato chips on a paper plate. But he added onions to the tuna and I could smell them before I even took a bite. I hated onions. I even hated tuna, and he knew it.

"But Dad," I said, "this has onions in it. I don't like onions."

And in a split second, he was red and wide-eyed. "God damn it!! Why is it always a fight with you about everything?!" he screamed as he held the sides of his head. "You are going to eat every last bit of that god damn sandwich, do you hear me?" he tried to say calmer now.

I cried as I chewed a mouthful to appease him as tears rolled down my face.

"And if you throw it up, you'll eat that too!" he said as he walked away.

Cathy said nothing and my friend for the day quietly excused herself to go home.

I picked at the bread with the dirty fingers of my right hand. I'd take the tiniest bites I could, then eat a chip to cover up the flavor of onions.

I got the sandwich down and kept it down, chasing it with milk, which I also hated but nothing was worse to me than the taste of onions.

"Done?" he asked without looking at me.

"Mmmhmmm," I said.

"Good. Put your plate in the garbage and come here," he said.

He unwrapped the rag from my wrist. The opened area had started to dry to the bandage and was pulled off. The redness had gotten worse and now bruising was setting in. A large swollen area continued to grow and my wrist was deformed into a grotesque "U" shape.

Again, he grabbed my fingers and shook my wrist up and down like he was shaking my hand. I screamed and pulled back, crying.

Cathy stepped in and spoke before he could say a word.

"We need to get her to the hospital. Her wrist is clearly broken," she said, annoyed.

As we drove to the hospital, they talked between them like I wasn't in the back seat.

"Her mother is going to flip her lid to know she broke her wrist on my watch. She'll probably blame me like it was my fault," he said.

"It wasn't your fault, Harland, that's silly. It was an accident," she said. "Accidents happen. She'll understand, I'm sure."

"Fucking kids. More trouble than they're worth. Always into something, costing ya money," he said as he looked at me in the rearview mirror. I remember feeling guilty that I needed anything. I felt bad that I required any attention at all. I made myself as small as I could in the back seat all the way to the hospital, trying not to bring any more attention to myself than I already had.

"Well, the good news is, it's a clean break and should heal in about four weeks," the doctor said. "The bad news is, we have to admit her overnight so we can set it and cast it tomorrow."

"Why can't it be done without her having to be admitted?" my dad asked.

"Well, we could have, but she's already eaten. And we can't put a child under anesthesia who's already eaten."

My dad looked at me. "Should have listened to you when you said you weren't hungry, huh?" He rolled his eyes at himself.

I lay in the hospital bed with my left forearm in a white splint lined with a cottony white material. Over the top of the splint were white Velcro strips. I couldn't move very well or sleep on my side without having pain so I slept on my back that night.

Before dawn, the nurses came in and wheeled me down a dimly lit corridor, one on each side of the bed. All I remember after that, was waking up, turning my head to the left and seeing the nice doctor sitting at a little desk with a lamp on it reading paperwork.

"There you are," the doctor said when he saw I was awake and looking at him.

Then I threw up all over the bed.

The smell of tuna and onions permeated the air.

Soon, I would be sitting in the back bedroom with Cathy as she cried on the phone to her mother about how terrible everything was and whispering in case my dad was somehow listening to the conversation.

The marriage to Cathy didn't last long.

Just long enough to produce a child, my mom told me. A boy. I learned he existed when I was twenty years old, but I didn't dare mention him to my dad as warned by my mother. My mom said my dad signed away his rights when Cathy's new husband wanted to adopt him.

"Lucky kid," I said.

Chapter 10

As summer melded with fall, the newness of freedom and independence for my mom was winding down and the reality of being single and responsible for two young children was starting to set in.

"Dinner's ready!" I yelled.

Doodle ran in from his room in his white T-shirt, saggy diaper and messed up sandy blond hair. His big blue-gray eyes wide with excitement over Spaghetti O's and fried Spam.

"Again?" my mom said.

"Again," I said. "I can't cook what isn't here?"

"I know that," she said as she shot me a smart look.

She ate and excused herself to her bedroom and left me to clean up the kitchen.

Between the clanging and the rinsing of doing dishes, I could hear her crying and listening to music in her room.

I eased my way down the long tin hall and sat outside her bedroom door picking at the cheap carpet, worried for her, for us. She was crying softly listening to Elvis ask her if she was "Lonesome Tonight." When his singing became talking to her in that sultry, romantic voice, she cried even harder. I knew she was crying about my dad. I cried too sometimes, because I felt sorry for her and I worried she'd been broken beyond repair.

We tried to get through the best way we knew how. Sometimes the sadness would be soothed over by more dancing and singing, saying lines from commercials to make ourselves laugh, her telling me stories of when I was little, but deep down there was pain. And not just from recent events, but pain from things that happened before I was born.

The new trailer soon became a pigsty. Trash fell out of the garbage can in the kitchen and toppled to the floor, grass grew up to our hips and my mom was not motivated to do anything for herself or anyone else, but when Friday night rolled around she'd magically recover enough to go out on the town.

Once, on a Friday, I came home from school ready to bake brownies for the weekend and found that the oven was already warm to the touch. When I opened the oven door I found a large pan of leaves drying out.   When I asked my mom what it was, she immediately said she didn't know, that it wasn't hers, she was holding it for a friend. Laughter came flying out from her back bedroom. I thought it was marijuana but I wasn't sure at the time. Later, I found out it was.

As time went on, my mom got used to me stepping in and picking up her slack. I cooked, cleaned, took care of my brother, did my homework and extra-curricular activities. I was a high-functioning anxiety-ridden child that was being conditioned to take care of everyone around me and put myself and my needs on the back burner, or kill myself trying to fit it all in.

Around this time, I got a part in the play *Tom Sawyer* as Becky Thatcher, Tom Sawyer's girlfriend, and had to beg her to attend just one of the three performances we were giving of it at school. When I refused to stop bugging her about it, she finally gave in and came the very last night.

She didn't appreciate how I worked my butt off memorizing my lines while helping her or how I memorized more lines than any of the other girls at school that tried out. I recall one of the other girls at school trying out for the same part. She was upset, and said to the teacher, "But she was only supposed to memorize five lines."

"Yes," said the teacher, "five lines was the bare minimum. She went above the bare minimum, did it the best, and therefore Robin gets the part."

I was so proud of myself. And soon, overdoing and overachieving became my thing.

"So, how'd I do? Did you like it?" I asked excitedly on the way out of the school that night.

"You swayed back and forth the whole time," my mom said.

"I was nervous because I knew you were watching. I wanted to do extra good for you," I said.

"Yeah, well, you forgot some of your lines too," she said.

Gone were the days I could just walk over to my grandma's house next door to get away from her when I wanted to be a kid. I was too busy being in charge now. And my mom made it well known that nothing I did was good enough.

I missed being little and being with my grandma Jancie. She'd allow me to go through her jewelry box, look through her pocketbook and use her little Avon lipstick samples she had in her bathroom cabinet and purse. I would carefully apply the red lipstick, making sure to stay inside the lines, then blot with a tissue like she showed me to do.

After being there for a while, my mom would come after me.

"I should have known I'd find you over here. What the hell are you doing?"

"Just leave her alone, Starlah Jean, she's not hurting anybody," my grandma would say.

"She needs to get her ass back over to the house and get her chores done," she would say reaching for me.

"When she's done, I'll send her back over, she can spend some time with her grandma if she wants to," she'd say calmly as she held me tight in her lap.

My mother would grab my face, pinching my cheeks together tightly, and place a big smooch on my lips taking all my lipstick with it before she left. And she would laugh and laugh.

"Why do you have to torment her like that, Starlah Jean? She's minding her own business and you just want to see her upset," Grandma said.

"Ah, just send her ass back over when she's done here smearing in all this lipstick and perfume and shit," she'd say.

After she left, my grandma would remind me that I needed to mind my mother. She'd remind me of all the difficulties she'd been through and how I didn't in any way want to upset her anymore than she'd already been.

"Listen to me now. If Grandma's not around someday, I want you to remember to be a good girl… no, promise me, you'll be a good girl. I want to you to read this from time to time so you don't forget, o.k.?" she asked as she handed me a card.

I looked at the card and she wrote, "Be a Good Girl for Your Mommy!" And signed it, "Grandma loves you! XOXO Love, Grandma Jancie." And in my favorite red lipstick, she put two big red kisses on the inside of the card and one on the outside of the envelope.

"O.k., Grandma, I promise, I'll be good," I said, half paying attention as I turned my attention to examining the contents of her big grandma pocketbook.

Now, I was almost eleven and I kept the house clean, bathed my brother, cooked for us and was washing and folding laundry. I had graduated from heating up Spaghetti O's and frying Spam to being able to brown ground beef, drain it and make us Hamburger Helper. "Yes siree, Hamburger Helper was going to help me, make a great meal," I said as I stood at the stove. I made biscuits from the can and would toss lettuce in a bowl with dressing and call that a salad, later making a list of groceries I wanted from the store.

My mom had it made in the shade.

I felt alone and unwanted. I was either in someone's way, being told to get outside, go to my room or find something to do. The only time anyone wanted me around was if they wanted something.

Sometimes my mom would drop us off at my aunt Della's house if my dad didn't have me that weekend. My dad didn't take my brother overnight until he was much older so that put me at my dad's house, alone. If it was not visitation weekend with my dad and no one could watch us, I'd be home alone for the weekend in charge of my brother Doodle.

I'd sit and watch her and my cousins get ready to go out, trying not to be in the way. There would be a beehive of activity, usually with four women running around taking turns showering, picking out outfits, coordinating shoes and doing their hair and makeup in the four-way light-up makeup mirror. It had a green light marked "office" setting that no one ever used. No one I knew worked in an office so it was always set to the pink setting marked "evening." During the day my mom was fresh faced, something she got used to I suspect because my dad never liked her wearing makeup and would tell her to go wash that shit off her face she looked like a whore.

Now that she was single and going out on the weekends she wore bright blue sparkly eye shadow, dark lips and when her hair finally grew out from the pixie, she wore big, bouncy curls she got from hot rollers. Each of them got ready while singing and dancing in their bras and underwear with hot rollers or sponge curlers in their hair, cigarettes hanging from their mouths, disco music playing in the background.

My mom came out from her bedroom that night wearing a gold lame jacket, over a white T-shirt with the word "Bitch" in rhinestones on it, black strappy sandals that laced up around the ankle with gold metallic heels and black shiny skintight pants that looked like leather but were as soft as silk. Think Olivia Newton-John in *Grease*.

When she hugged and kissed us goodbye, she smelled of cigarette smoke, Skin Musk and the loose Coty face powder she wore.

I loved her so.

And I loved seeing her happy, even when I knew it wasn't me that made her that way.

It was early morning but still dark out and I knew my mom hadn't come home. I heard my little brother stirring in his bedroom that was next to mine, playing with his trucks and making truck noises.

"Doodlebug, Shhhh! go back to sleep, it's early," I said.

"No. I want my eggie."

"Doodle, Mom's not home yet, go back to sleep."

Soon I heard his toy chain saw revving up as he pretended to saw his way out of his room. My mom was scared to death to find him poisoned someday with as much stuff as he got into, so he was locked in his bedroom from the outside.

"Shhhh! Stop," I said as I poked my head in from the adjoining bathroom.

"No, I want my eggie," he said louder.

There was no quieting him. Sometimes when my cousin Bernice was there, she would get up and tend to him and his breakfast, and when she wasn't, I would. So, I took him out to the kitchen to feed him, but coaxed him to eat his Waffelo's cereal because I didn't know how to soft boil an egg, which was how he liked them.

Saturday morning came and went then night fell again. Sunday morning I was concerned yet hopeful, but still my mother wasn't home. Sunday night I knew I had school the next day, so I waded through the waist-high grass over to my grandma's house next door carrying Doodle on my hip.

"Just take your shower and get your clothes ready, do your homework as usual and your mom will be home shortly," she said.

"But, Grandma, she left Friday night. It's Sunday."

"I know, but she knows there's school tomorrow so she'll come home," she assured me. I walked back home. I was afraid there were snakes in the deep grass but we made it home safely and I locked the door behind us.

After Doodle was asleep, I took my shower, laid out my clothes, and got my books together for the next day. My homework was already done and I went to bed.

A car pulled in the gravel patch in front of the trailer, shut its engine off and cut its lights. There was a knock at the door. I got out of bed and went to the peephole. It was my cousin Connie Ray.

"Robin Lynn, it's me, Connie Ray," she said.

I opened the door.

"Robin, I came out to get you and take you to my house for the night. You can ride the bus from our house to school in the morning."

"How'd you know we were here by ourselves?" I asked.

"Your grandma called out and told my mom. Your aunt Della said I might as well come get you because she hasn't heard from your mother all weekend and it's anybody's guess as to when she'll be home."

"O.k., Doodle is sleeping but if you get him, I'll get his diaper bag and clothes."

She gathered my sleeping brother and I got our clothes and my schoolbooks and we left for my aunt Della's house.

I couldn't believe I had to ride a bus I never had ridden before and I couldn't believe my mom just left and didn't come back.

My mom was changing. I don't think my grandma approved, but I could never really tell for sure. Even when my mom knew I was in the room, she'd tell my cousins never to have kids because they were nothing but a fucking pain in your ass. Mark my words, she'd say, as she looked at me with disgust, "get pregnant and ruin your young life."

I knew from a young age that I was a big inconvenience and was told I had to earn my keep. I spent my young life paying for my existence and being told I should be thankful I was born.

You'd never know by the way she acted or spoke about kids, that she had had one child that had died already. She had him when she was sixteen years old when she and my dad were stationed in Germany while he was in the Army. The baby they named Bobby died three hours after birth.

My mom told me she fell down a flight of steps that were being cleaned when she was nine months pregnant. She had hit her belly up against the banister that caught her and later that evening she went into labor. My dad, not wanting to be bothered with any of it, and saying he needed his sleep for work the next morning, dropped her off at the bottom of the steps of the hospital and left her there alone. Three hospital workers had to come out and help her up the steps.

Once inside, and not able to understand German, she pushed when she wasn't supposed to. She said my brother flew out, hit the floor and died later as a result of the fall to the floor. When my dad came to the hospital to pick her up, she said my dad told her he was glad he died he didn't want him anyway.

She got to hold him and watched him die slowly over that three-hour period. The doctor telling her that he would have been in a vegetative state had he lived. She said he was fully developed with long eyelashes and had dimples in his fingers where joints would never form. He had a red mark and a large indentation in his forehead where he'd hit the floor.

They were flown back to the United States to have his funeral. Her baby wasn't flying bundled up in a cute layette set knitted for him by his grandma and sitting next to her, she recounted. He was flying underneath the plane, in a teeny tiny coffin and was now considered cargo. Cold, and dead, with all that noise, I remember her saying as she shuddered. She said he was laid out with his hands up over his head like he was sleeping, with a little stuffed lamb sitting by his side. She said he looked asleep in his gray blue coffin.

She told me how it all happened near Thanksgiving time and how my dad was just so inappropriately jovial and laughing at Thanksgiving dinner only a few days later, as if they hadn't just buried a baby boy in the November snow. It still bothered her all these years later. At the time, my mom was sixteen and my dad eighteen.

I used to sit and daydream about what it would mean for me to have a big brother and wished that Bobby were somehow here to watch out for me.

Many years later, I went searching for his gravesite after learning he never got a headstone. But, I could never find where he was. The funeral home where they had his funeral had lost records in a flood and they had nothing that dated back that far. And the onsite building at the cemetery that housed plot numbers and names was lost in a fire. The little metal plate that marked his plot had long since blown away in the wind.

Over time, things got even worse for us at the trailer. The electric and water were eventually shut off and we had no heat. It stayed off as a way to teach her a goddamn lesson, until my dad felt bad enough about it because of 'us kids' that he paid the bill and had it turned back on, he proudly reported to me one day.

My mom didn't work for very long and only had two jobs I can recall. A job at a the Big Wheel store downtown cutting fabric for customers, and a cleaning job she did for a few days and quit. She wasn't going to clean some fucking office buildings or people's homes for money, she said, she wasn't a goddamn maid, and fabric and sewing shit wasn't her thing either.

Before she said she was quitting the job at Big Wheel, I remember begging her to bring me home some green felt, green tights, a feather from the craft aisle, and some leather cording for a Halloween costume I wanted to make. When she said she wasn't making me a costume, I assured her I could do it myself.

"What are you going as, the Jolly Green Giant?" she asked.

"Nope. Peter Pan," I said.

We had a small cookie tin of thread and sewing needles but not much else, so I measured the best I could by holding and pinning the fabric to my body and hand sewed for weeks and weeks a Peter Pan outfit. I cut the short sleeves and bottom of the long green felt tunic into triangles to resemble a rough, leafy texture, braided the cording into a belt for my waist, made a triangular hat like the paper footballs all the kids made then, tucked the feather in it on one side, put on the green tights and a pair of leather moccasins, and on Halloween I walked out as Peter Pan.

"Well shit to bed," she said. "You look just like him with your Dorothy Hamill haircut. Hold on a sec, before you leave. I have the perfect thing to top off your costume."

She returned with her brown eyebrow pencil and drew tiny freckles across my cheeks and nose.

"There. Now, it's perfect," she said.

Chapter 11

My dad was a bachelor again which he said suited him fine and on my visitation weekends, he'd let me sleep in the den in a sleeping bag next to his desk on the floor.

He'd bought himself a Cobra 142GTL CB radio with a Golden Eagle 1976 Bicentennial Lollipop Astatic D104 mic that had a picture of a bald eagle carved in the back of it. It made a chirping sound over the airwaves when you keyed the mic.

His new hobby brought us closer together and reminded me of how he was with me when we raced bikes on our racetrack, or flew model airplanes together in the big green house.

Talking on the CB quickly became our new thing to do. And, when I couldn't come up with my handle, my dad named me "Super Kiddo."

"Breaker, breaker, can I get a break?" my dad said into the gold lollipop mic.

And we'd wait for a response.

After not getting a response he'd ask again…

"Breaker 1-9, breaker 1-9, tryin' to get a break. Anyone out there, over?"

The airwaves would crackle and come alive.

"Ah, this is The Night Crawler, can you read me?" someone answered.

"Roger that. This is Hambone," my dad said.

"Hey, Hambone, nice to have you on the airwaves with us tonight," he said.

"I should also tell you I have my daughter, Super Kiddo, here with me," he said.

"Well, welcome Super Kiddo! How you doin' tonight?"

"I'm good!" I'd say excitedly and then ask my dad what else to say.

My dad would whisper, "Ask him what's his 10-20? That's his location."

"Uh, what's your 10-20, Night Crawler?" I'd ask a little too loudly.

"I'm headed down 1-77, in South Carolina right now, goin' all the way down to Mouse Town. You ever been to Mouse Town, Super Kiddo?"

My dad whispered, "That means Disney World."

"No, never been to Mouse Town," I said as I giggled.

"Ah, come on, Hambone. When ya takin' yer daughter to Mouse Town?" he said teasingly.

"As soon as they give me a raise," he said laughing.

"Roger that," he said back.

"What do you do for work, Hambone?"

"I'm a steel worker," he said proudly.

Then someone else would chime in.

"Need the 10-36, over?" the voice said.

With my finger, I'd scan the index card of CB lingo my dad typed up and find 10-36, then the definition typed out beside it. It meant he wanted to know the correct time. I could answer that.

"It's now 5:25 p.m. where I'm at in West Virginia. Where are you? I mean... what's your 10-20, over?" I said.

"I'm not too far away from ya, Super Kiddo. I'm headin' to Pennsylvania via I-80 so we're in the same time zone. That sounds 'bout right. Time to pull over and get some supper. I'll be yakkin' at ya again. Thanks, Super Kiddo. Over 'n out," he said.

"Over 'n out," I said like I was a pro at this.

I loved talking on the CB with my dad.

I was told not to ever touch it or talk on it when he wasn't around and I had strict instructions to never be too specific with my whereabouts. My 10-20.

"You don't want none of those lonely weirdos out there, that haven't seen a girl in God knows how long, to come here tryin' to locate you," my dad said. "Promise me you won't ever try to talk on the CB without me here to help you, o.k?"

"I promise, I won't," I said.

We talked to all kinds of truckers from all over the United States. Sometimes well into the night. When it got too late, I'd lie on the floor in my sleeping bag and watch my dad, whose face was lit by the lamp on the desk, and listen to them talk. He'd be looking at a map that was strewn out across the metal desk tracking them as they told him their 10-20 or mile marker along the highways. The smoke from his cigarette in the ashtray danced up slowly in white string-like threads to the ceiling through the light from the lamp.

Sometimes the truckers would do what they called sandbaggin. That was listening in on conversations but not talking, and some called it "reading the mail." My dad did a lot of sandbaggin. Sometimes the truckers would key their mic as they drove and all you'd hear was the mesmerizing sound of their big wheels moving over the road.

It was all so exciting to me. And I knew that sound but I couldn't place it.

After some sandbaggin, he'd key the mic again.

"Breaker, breaker... 1-9 lookin' for a break."

A bit later he'd ask again.

"Breaker 1-9, come on. This is Hambone out here lookin' for a break. Anyone out there tonight?"

And slowly the airwaves would come to life.

"Hey, Hambone, this is Ratchet Jaw comin' atcha tonight, what's your 20?" he said, dropping the 10.

"Dad, he dropped the 10." I pointed out as he shooed at me with his hand to be quiet.

"I'm in the Northern Panhandle of West Virginia, over. What's your 20?" he'd ask back.

"Mmmmkay, Hambone from West Virginia. I'm comin' atcha from mile marker 301 on Interstate 17 in Arizona. How you doin' tonight?" he asked.

My dad quickly traced the whereabouts of the trucker on his map he had sprawled out in front of him, excited to be talking to people so far away.

"I'm good, Ratchet Jaw, just listenin' in tonight, hopin' to make contact with someone who wants to talk. I wish I was better at all this, but I'm a beginner, just learnin' my way 'round all the CB lingo and whatnot, over?"

"Well, sounds like yer doin' fine, Hambone, nice havin' ya on the airwaves tonight. It gets mighty lonely out here sometimes when you're drivin' at night. So, why don't you ask me anything and I'll try 'n help ya out as best I can," he said.

"What kind a rig you haulin' there, Ratchet Jaw?" my dad asked.

"I'm drivin' a Pete," he said back.

"A Pete?"

"Yep, that's short for Peterbilt," he clarified.

My dad would nod his head as if it all made sense now.

"Copy that. So, is it true what they say 'bout you old truckers, that old truckers never die, they just get a new Peter built?" he'd ask.

I didn't get it, but laughter erupted throughout the airwaves.

"Yep, that's about right, Hambone!" he said as they both laughed.

My dad would tell him about his brother-in-law who was also a trucker and ask him all kinds of questions well into the night.

"So, how'd ya get the handle Ratchet Jaw, over?" my dad asked.

"I worked as an auctioneer back in the day and I can talk a blue streak," he said as he demonstrated.

"Ah, I see. Makes sense," he said. "Do you really like drivin' that truck, over?"

"Sure do. It's nothin' but me, and the open road out here. It's clear as far as the eye can see at night. Only me, and an occasional car passing by the other way. I can think clear out here, Hambone, ya know what I mean?" he asked.

"Yeah. I can imagine how it would clear your head," he said. "You know any of the other people on here I been talkin' to? Like, how 'bout Rubberband Man? You know him, over?" my dad asked.

"Can't say that I do, but I'll be on a 10-10 when I park my truck and listen for 'em," he said.

"How 'bout Birddog, Skeeter, Thunderbolt or Sassy Kat. Know any of them, over?"

"I know all those guys and well… Sassy Kat ain't no guy, if you know what I mean, over?" he said.

"Sassy Kat, you out there tonight, over?" the trucker asked.

And about a half a minute later a sultry voice came over the radio.

"You askin' for little ole me, Rachet Jaw, over?"

"Woohooo! There's that Sassy Pussy Kat," the trucker laughed. It was clearly a man pretending to make his voice higher.

"O.k. Sassy, stop it. — Listenin' to that voice could get the mind goin' out here on the lonely open highway, am I right, over?" the guy said.

"Shit, no!" my dad said as he chuckled and keyed the mic.

I could envision all the truckers in my mind holding down the key of the mic they held in their hand, as they bumped around the highways in their trucks.

What fun this was, I thought. I loved sharing this with my dad. It was our special time together and no one else knew what we were talking about other than me and my dad and, well… all these truckers. It was like a secret world that had its own special language.

Kind of like when my mom and dad spoke pig Latin in front of me when I was little so I wouldn't know what they were talking about. They did that for years until I finally got my mom to teach me how to do it too. I never could understand it or speak it as fast as they could.

When I'd stayed at my dad's house I'd fall asleep in my sleeping bag on the floor hearing phrases like Kojak with a Kodak, Lot Lizard,

Mama Bear, Checkpoint Charlie, Affirmative, and Pickle Park. And even though I had not a clue as to what all that meant, I still loved every second of it, whether I was talking or just listening and watching my dad talk from across the room.

I sleepily gazed at my dad from my sleeping bag on the floor and watched him having fun talking on the CB in the dimly lit room and felt nothing but love for him, but I knew enough not to play on the CB without him there to supervise me. Or, as my parents would say in pig Latin, Iway, ewknay, enoughway, otay, ayplay, onway, ethay, CBay, ithoutway imhay erethay otay upervisesay emay.

And I never did touch that gold lollipop mic without my dad being around. I only stared at it from a distance admiring the golden beauty with a sort of awe I can only describe as love.

And I remembered, as I was about to fall asleep, that sound I knew I'd heard before — of the trucker's tires we heard while sandbaggin — it was the same sound the tires on the car made as we crossed the Steubenville Bridge.

"Mom, I need lunch money," I called to her.

She rolled over in her bed to look at me, hair all messed up and her eyes bloodshot. "Jesus Christ. Didn't I just give you money for lunch?"

"That was last week, Mom," I said as I handed her the purse.

She riffled through the bottom of her purse, then her wallet as if money would magically appear.

"You had money Friday, where'd it all go," I said as she looked.

"Oh shut up," she said. "I'm broke. Just charge your lunch for now."

"Mom! I can't just keep charging my lunch! It's already a reduced rate! It's 60 cents! Why don't you have 60 cents!" I asked.

"Stop lippin' off. I said, charge it and I'll get you some in the next day or two."

I rolled my eyes and left for the bus stop in a huff. I was so annoyed with her. She had money for beer and cigarettes and to go out every weekend, but no lunch money.

At school that day I got in the reduced-lunch line on the right side of the hall. The line down the left side was for the kids that paid full price.

It was degrading.

Kids stared and poked fun at you and I just stood there trying to act like I didn't notice or care.

I grabbed my plastic tray and chocolate milk when I got to the milk refrigerator and got up to the lunch lady.

"Where's your ticket? Didn't you pay for your lunch ticket this morning in homeroom?"

"No, I didn't," I said.

"And why not?" she asked as she crossed her arms.

"Because my mom didn't have any money," I said embarrassed.

"Again?" she said as she rolled her eyes and ushered me through, exasperated.

The lunch ladies shoveled food on our trays fast to keep the line moving.

A steaming-hot hot dog drenched in water was slapped into a bun, then mushy vegetables served from a slotted spoon were splashed into their indented portion of the tray, applesauce in its place and French fries that were wilted and dried from the hot lamp in another section of the tray.

I found a seat next to my friend Karen.

"You spendin' the night at my house this weekend?" she asked me.

"I doubt it. I probably have to watch my brother while my mom goes out again," I said. "Maybe you can come stay at my house since I'll be home by myself. We could bake cookies or make a pizza or something?"

"Yeah, that'd be fun, but my mom would want to talk to your mom and see if she's going to be home with us," she said.

"Oh, that won't work then," I said.

Chapter 12

I waited to see if my mom would go see what my little brother needed, but she didn't. I had school in the morning and was hoping I didn't have to go in there.

I opened his bedroom door and could see him sitting in his crib crying softly with his hair sticking up. He was holding his Stretch Armstrong and Baby Brother Tender Love baby doll next to him.

"Awww, what's a matter, Doodle?" I said as I touched his face to swipe back his hair.

He was drenched with sweat and hot to the touch.

"Oh my god, you're burnin' up, aren't you, little guy."

I went to my mom's bedroom door.

"Mom, Doodle's sick. He's burnin' up and crying," I said. I got no answer.

"Mom," I said, irritated. "Get up."

I went to the bathroom and got a thermometer out of the medicine cabinet above the sink and went back to his room. I turned the light on and turned the glass thermometer around in my fingers until I located the silver strand on the side of the glass. I didn't know where it was supposed to be, but I shook it anyway like I'd seen nurses do. The silver streak was now all the way down to the left.

I laid Doodle down explaining that I would take his temperature in his butt and let Mom know what number I got. I took his diaper down and put the thermometer in his butt. I held onto it while he just lay there and whimpered softly, too weak and hot to really fight it. My mom said us kids always cried and whimpered when we didn't feel good. After awhile I took the thermometer out and located the silver streak; it was all the way up high to the right. I placed the diaper up around Doodle's bottom and went to my mom's room again.

"Mom!" I said as I opened the door. "Doodle is sick and needs to go to the hospital. NOW!" I yelled. "Get up!"

She hurried to a sitting position on the side of the bed and cradled her head in her hands.

"What is going on?" she said.

"Doodle is sick, for the tenth time," I said. "He needs to go to the hospital, now!"

To further prove my point, I shoved the thermometer at her and said, "Here, this is his temperature, I took it in his butt. He's burning up and sick. Now get up!"

She hurried up, grabbed her pants and shirt, stumbling around tripping while trying to get her legs in her pants.

I grabbed Doodle out of his bed, put pajamas with feet on him, grabbed his diaper bag and headed to the door in some clothing I just threw on.

"Mom! Hurry up!"

"I am, I am. Honey, I'm just tired, ya know? Just didn't hear you, but everything's gonna be o.k.?" she said, trying to reassure me.

I had Doodle in the car seat and I was buckled in the front before she even made it to her side of the car.

"Mom. What is wrong with you? We need to hurry," I said.

She fumbled with getting the key in the ignition. She was talking and slurring her words and I realized she was still drunk.

"Mom. Are you drunk?"

"What, me?" She acted surprised. "No, no, honey. Just tired is all and I'm not feeling well either," she said.

"Not feeling well, as in drunk," I said.

It was like hitting a switch. Suddenly, she was wide-awake as ever.

"You watch it, missy. Don't you dare backtalk me," she warned with her index finger in my face.

"Whatever, do what you want, I don't care anymore," I said defiantly.

She turned the key, started the car and put it in drive as she didn't take her eyes off me. The car lurched forward and stopped again.

"Look. You're right. I'm still just a wee bit tipsy. Not drunk. I'm gonna have to drive slow and I need your help now to get there and again when we get to the hospital," she said.

"Yeah, fine. I can do that, let's just go. But go down Washington Pike, not down Rabbit Hill," I said.

"If I start to go off the road, just tell me and I'll stop and we'll start again, o.k," she said. "There's no one out at these hours, so we'll be fine."

We made it off Rabbit Hill, down Washington Pike and up Route 2 to the Steubenville Bridge where the silver-mouthed contraption sat waiting for us, ready to swallow us whole. I hated it. Was terrified of it. Had nightmares about it. I was falling off the side into the water, sometimes from the car, other times off the walkway as a pedestrian. I'd wake up sweaty, heart pounding out of my chest, grabbing for the edge of my bed. And now my mom was driving over it drunk.

"Mom. Just go slowly," I coached. "You're doin' fine. Over to the left a little bit, o.k. Now… just hold it straight," I said as I held onto my door and the dash.

We got off the bridge and headed up Market Street toward the hospital.

I let out a sigh of relief.

"Hey, thanks for helping," she said as if relieved to be off the bridge too.

"Yeah, no problem."

"You're alright, ya know," she said.

"Yeah," I said.

"Confident too," she said.

"Mom, pay attention, we're not there yet," I reminded her.

"Yes, yea, I am…" she said quickly as she turned her attention back to the road and sat up straighter.

"Hey," she said as she eyed the road, "because you're so good at being a big girl and all, I'm just gonna wait in the car and you can take your baby brother in, o.k.?"

"Sure. I'll need all those cards you carry in your purse, though. You know, the ones from dad for if we get sick?" I said.

"Oh sure, sure thing, good thinkin'," she said. "If anyone asks, just tell them I'm in the car and I'm sick too, that's why I didn't want to come in."

We got to the hospital's driveway where I got out. I grabbed Doodle's diaper bag then flipped the seat forward and got him out of his car seat.

She turned around and looked at me while I was unbuckling him. "Hey… thanks a lot. I really appreciate this," she said.

I went in and was met at the desk by a big nurse's head wearing a big white cap. It was like the one my grandma wore with her white uniform when we dropped her off at work.

She stood up from behind the desk when she saw me and said, "My, my, honey, where's your mother? He looks much too heavy for you."

"She's in the car, sick," I said as I grunted to hold him and put the diaper bag down. "I'm the only one not sick at the moment," I said as I giggled nervously. "Here's all the cards for him… my mother gave them to me to give to you."

"O.k.," she said hesitantly as she took them.

"My mom said I could sign for her anything she needs to sign," I added.

"Sure thing," she said, handing me a clipboard hesitantly.

Name, date of birth, address, phone number was about all I knew. I filled out what I could and handed it back and asked if the nurse could please fill in the rest from the cards and walked back to the waiting area.

A little while later, a door opened and out walked the same nurse.

She called my brother's full name.

"That's us," I said.

I lugged him up to my hip and his diaper bag over my other shoulder. She walked us to the exam room where she took my brother from me and placed him on the examining room table.

The doctor came in.

"Where's your mommy, honey?" he asked.

"Like I told her," I motioned my head toward the nurse, "she's out in the car sick too. I'm the only one not sick right now at our house."

He examined my brother, while the nurse took his temperature.

"102.4," she informed the doctor.

The doctor and nurse passed glances between them as she opened a cabinet above and poured liquid out of a bottle into a see-through cup. She gave it to my brother to drink as she rubbed his sweaty hair off his face and placed a cool cloth on his forehead.

"She didn't want to spread germs to anyone else so she's in the car laying down. You can go out there in the parking lot and check for yourself if you don't believe me," I added quickly.

He felt my brother's belly, listened to his heart and stomach.

"Any diarrhea?" he asked.

"No, none," I said. "Just crying, lots of whimpering, and hot, with a little cough," I added.

My brother sat making a whimpering sound I was too familiar with. It was a cross between crying and humming.

"My mom says us kids whimper like that when we're sick like this. She says she thinks we do it to soothe ourselves," I told them.

"Well, honey, looks like he's got a good old-fashion case of the flu that's going around," he said after listening to his lungs.

"There's nothing I can really do for him, it'll have to run its course," he said. "You know, it'll go away on its own," he clarified.

"Oh, o.k. So, what do I do at home? I mean, what can my mom do at home to help?" I asked.

"Just keep him comfortable, give him lots of fluids in his sippy cup, and make sure he gets plenty of rest. The nurse gave him something to reduce his fever," he said.

"What kind of fluids?" I asked.

"Tang is good, because it's got vitamins in it. But, water is good, orange juice is good too. Really anything he usually drinks," he said. "I'd stay away from milk though, it can cause more phlegm and coughing," he added.

"And Popsicles," he added. "To keep the fever down. And maybe you can help him eat some of those," he said as he smiled warmly at me.

"Here," he said. "Here's what I want you to get at the store on your way home. Tell your mom, o.k.?"

I took the paper and put it in my pocket.

"And because you were both so good, the nurse has a sucker for both of you. You can pick whatever color you want, how's that sound?" he asked.

"Good," I said.

I liked him. He was so kind and warm. And for some reason, before leaving, I felt the need to tell this warm, kind man in a white coat, that I wanted to be a nurse when I grew up. Like my grandmothers all were. I think it was because I wanted to feel a part of all that warm fuzziness I felt around caring, kind people.

"Well, honey, you're going to make a great nurse! Looks like you're off to a great start caring for your little brother so well like you do," he said.

"Thank you," I said, blushing.

On the way out, I picked a red Safe-T pop for me, and grabbed Doodle a blue one for when he felt better. I put his in his diaper bag, mine in my pocket.

"Thank you for everything. I'll tell my mom everything you said and give her your note," I said.

Heaving my brother back up on my hip and his diaper bag over my shoulder, I turned and walked out of the hospital. I was eleven years old.

When I walked back to the car I found my mother sound asleep. I tapped on the window a few times to wake her up to get her to unlock the car and let us in.

"Oh, how'd it go in there, everything all right?" she asked.

"Yep, just the flu. Not much they can do except let it run its course," I said as I got situated in the car. "And the doctor said he wanted us to get this stuff on the way home," I said as I handed her the note.

She opened it and read it. "Jesus Christ, people can't even be sick for free," she said.

"Mom, just get the stuff. I'll take care of him," I said. "You can go back to bed."

It was getting light out by the time we were done at the hospital. We stopped at the store that was just opening up on the way home and I bought the things on the list and got back in the car.

When we got home, I made my mom call me off school, which she usually refused to do but was policy if being absent. I was not going to have to explain why she hadn't called after having to take him in the hospital by myself.

I overheard her on the phone while I was laying my brother back down in his bed.

"Yes, she's sick. Yeah, we're all sick," I heard her say.

"Yes, probably tomorrow or maybe even the next day, who knows?" she said to the person on the phone. "We'll keep you updated," she said.

"What'd they say?" I asked.

"Nothing. They said nothing, Robin Lynn, now please, if you love me, you'll go take care of yourself and your brother and let me sleep," she said.

I shut her bedroom door, feeling pretty sorry for myself. How could I be responsible for all this by myself? How could this be my life? I replayed the night back to myself in my head and I wondered if I should tell my dad about this? I wondered if I should tell someone about what was happening to me, but I didn't know what telling might do to me, or to others.

I lay in my bed and thought that my dad only saw us every other weekend and he usually didn't even call to check on us in between visitation. Would he even care about me having to take my brother into the E.R. because mom was still drunk?

And I got an answer that just appeared in my head out of nowhere.

He would care.

Because, this wasn't about me, or my mom, this was about his son.

Chapter 13

I'd hear laughing and music late into the night and one morning woke up to find some strange man lying next to my mom in bed when I went in for lunch money.

"Mom. I need lunch money," I said.

"Again?"

"Yes, again. It's Monday."

"Go get me my… oh," she said as I pushed her purse down into her lap.

"Well, aren't you Little Miss Suzy Sunshine," she said as she squinted up at me.

"Mom, come on, I have to go or I'll miss the bus."

"Well, we don't want that now, do we, because if you do, I'm not drivin' you," she said.

She'd rummage around in her purse for change.

"And I still owe for last week's lunches you had no money for," I said.

The black-haired man with a mustache grabbed his wallet off the table next to the bed, opened it and pushed a five-dollar bill in my hand.

"Thanks. And Doodle needs to be fed," I said over my shoulder as I walked down the hall.

I didn't want to go to school but I didn't want to stay home. I never knew what Doodle endured when I was away and even though I cared, sometimes I was just too tired to worry about it. She had already forced him to be right-handed when he was clearly left-handed. She had removed every piece of food, utensil, crayon, or toy he ever reached for with his left hand, and put it his right. One day he finally succumbed to her and used only his right. Sometimes before grabbing for things in his high chair, he'd hesitate, confused, then he'd smoosh soft food into his mouth with his chubby right hand.

I climbed the steps of the bus and took the very first seat I came to and sat down.

"Look at her, she looks like she's high," someone said from the middle of the bus.

The kids on the bus started laughing.

"She must smoke weed like her mother does," someone from the back yelled.

"Stop it," the bus driver warned as he looked up in his wide mirror.

At the next stop we picked up a few more people, one being a gal that always looked tired and ragged too; her name was Suzanne.

She climbed the steps, looked down the isle of the bus and instantly flew into the seat next to me.

"Hi," I said.

"Hey."

After a few minutes of staring straight ahead, she spoke.

"Do you smoke weed?" she asked.

"Uh, no. Why?" I asked.

"Because your eyes always make you look high," she said.

"Nope. I'm just always tired."

"I'm tired too. My parents fight all night long," she said.

"Yeah, I deal with fighting too and a mother that thinks it's my job to care for my little brother while she does whatever the hell she wants."

"I'm glad I'm the youngest and don't have a little brother or sister."

"Yeah, you're lucky," I said.

When we got to school, I could barely keep my eyes open by second period. Second period was math class with Mrs. Travonie. I hated math. It was especially difficult when you were tired. I hated when she called on me to do a problem on the board too. I always got it wrong or took forever to arrive at the right answer.

And as luck would have it, this day we were learning to count by a certain number. On the board, in front of everyone.

"Robin, come on up to the front." She motioned for me with her hand.

I reluctantly got up and walked up to the board and picked up a piece of chalk.

"O.k., who would like to come up and count on the board by 5's to see who wins," she said excitedly.

Harold was selected. The brain of any group he was in and he always had the right answer. I knew I'd never win.

"On the count of three, I want each of you to count by 5's as fast as you can and write them on the board until I say stop."

Harold was on 25 before I could even think of what was happening. I could hear the kids in the back snickering, and one voice say, "Come on, Robin, you can do it!"

"It's soooo eeeeasy," someone said.

"I can't believe she can't count by 5's. That's the easiest there is!" someone else said.

Finally, it hit me as I watched Harold scribble by 5's across the board.

I hurriedly scribbled out the same: 5, 10, 15, 20, 25, 30, 35, 40, 45, 50, 55, and time was called.

"Ha ha! You lose!" someone yelled.

"Very good, Harold, very good," Mrs. Travonie said.

"Class… can anyone tell Robin how she can learn her numbers better?"

"Practice!" someone yelled.

"Do your homework!" someone said.

"Stop smokin' weed!" someone else yelled.

The whole class laughed at me as I was taking my seat.

"Stop. That's enough," said Mrs. Travonie as she clapped her hands.

The bell rang and everyone bolted for the door. I was the last one out of class.

"It's o.k., just practice at home," she said as she patted me on the back.

"I will. I'm just tired," I said.

"Honey, you need to go to bed when you're told at night so you can be well rested and have your thinking cap on when you come to class each day," she said.

I wasn't going to defend myself. I wasn't going to explain that no one told me to go to bed. I wasn't going to tell her that no one told me to do anything but to take care of my brother or go to my room.

I just smiled at her and said, "I know."

Outside the door, the girls who hated me were huddled together whispering and giggling as they stared at me. I felt like the dunce of the Universe.

I was smart, I thought. I was just so tired. Tonight, I would make sure I would sleep well and have my thinking cap on for tomorrow, just like Mrs. Travonie said.

My favorite class was next: gym class.

I had no choice but to wake up now.

Chapter 14

I learned my body would start having a menstrual cycle from Maddie Sayer's mom who, one night in the middle of a huge sleepover, taught all us girls what to expect and how to take care of ourselves when it finally came.

I remember vividly all of us girls listening intently while sitting in a semi-circle around her chair as she held up charts and pointed to things she was reading to us. I liked learning. She emphasized that although we couldn't swim or take baths while menstruating, that showers were absolutely necessary in order to stay clean and prevent odor. She also reminded us that once we got our cycles, that also meant we could become pregnant now.

We were in fifth grade when we got this impromptu seminar from Maddie's mom and she recommended that we all read *Are you There God, It's Me Margaret*, by Judy Blume that she also held up. Maddie, who wore her Girl Scout uniform to school on picture day complete with hat and sash, proudly announced that she had already read it and knew everything.

I didn't get to Fly Up from Brownies to become a Girl Scout when we left Highland Hills. Meetings were just too far away then. Now that Maddie's mom was a Girl Scout Leader and lived just down the street from us, I asked if I could please join again. The answer was no we didn't have the money.

I was the first one in line for the book when we went back to school.

Maddie's mom assured all us girls that night that even though it all sounded confusing and even scary, once we started menstruating it meant we weren't little girls anymore, we'd be young ladies she said wide-eyed like it was a glorious thing to be.

I didn't want to be a young lady, I just wanted to be a kid.

I remember it started in social studies class one day. The kid that sat behind me alerted me to the red bloodstain on my chair and the butt of my pants when I stood up. When the teacher saw, she tied my windbreaker around my waist and walked me out of class. She told me to go to the school nurse and let her know I needed a pad.

It turned out that the nurse wasn't there that day and her office was locked. The old grandma-like secretary called home and asked my mom to bring me feminine napkins. After becoming wide-eyed the secretary assured me after hanging up the phone that she'd be down as soon as she could and to just sit tight in the chair around the corner out of view. Within a half hour, here came my mom walking in and she was pissed.

"Here's my daughter's god damned pads," she said as she shoved two large white Kotex pads at the secretary. "Don't you people have pads here at this fucking school? Or one of those pad machine thingys in the bathrooms around here?"

She was gone before the woman could respond.

The grandma secretary hurried over to me and gave them to me.

"Go. Hurry," she said, guiding me to the door. "Before the bell rings and the halls are filled again with the other students."

I dreaded having to hear about this when I got home but to be honest, I was surprised she even came. I was so humiliated she brought pads to school unwrapped for everyone to see.

When I got home that night my mom gave me one of her purses and told me to start carrying my own damned pads. She wasn't going to have to get up and come down there again for such stupid shit.

Since my mom told everyone she divorced my dad because of his abuse, I thought she'd try to at least shield me from it whenever she could. So when she called him out to the trailer one night after school because she found out I liked a black kid, I was really bothered by it. She knew his rants went on for hours, but no matter how much time passed since their divorce, he still had his claws in her and she wasn't about to protect me from him now that I was a young lady with a monthly cycle.

I remember wanting to sleep once I got home from school that day. It was hot out and I was on my period, which was always heavy and debilitating. I'd usually miss gym class on those days because of the heavy flow and severe cramping by carefully hand printing an excuse and sloppily adding a signature at the bottom. Like yeah, I did write this excuse, but see... my mom signed it.

I laid down for a while on the brown ripped recliner that had foam protruding out the seat and tried to sleep but couldn't knowing he was on his way to our house.

I heard the tires hit the gravel patch in the front of the trailer.

"Robin. Get up. Your father's here," she said.

I turned around on the recliner, pulled the handle to release the foot and sat the back in the upright position. I turned to face them as they sat as a united front on the couch together. He started in on me the moment he got there.

"Your mom called to let me know a few things today," he said. "Seems you been hanging around one of the only three niggers we got in this town," he said.

I didn't say anything.

"Well? You been doin' that?" he irritatedly asked.

"They're not niggers, Dad. Stop saying that," I said. "Mom said you had a black friend in the Army named Smitty that you loved. You'd think these boys were nice too, if you got to know them," I added.

"Smitty? Smitty?!" he said, surprised. "Smitty happened to be one of the coolest motherfuckers I've ever known. And he didn't act like no nigger," he said. "So, don't even bring him into this. Two different things completely."

I sat quiet.

"Your mom here tells me you started raggin' it. I'll be god damned if I'm gonna have you knocked up with some little nigger baby. I know what those so-called nice boys want from young naive girls like you. I was a young boy once myself, remember?" he asked.

"Dad, they don't want anything. We're hanging out at school for God's sake," I said.

"Don't get smart with me, young lady. I don't give a rat's ass where you're hangin' out with them. I don't want you hangin' out with them anymore, you hear me? And if word gets back to me that you arc, and it will… you and I are gonna have some serious issues, you hear me?" he asked.

"Dad, we're in fifth grade. Nothing is happening or going to happen. We talk at recess at school, nothing else," I said.

He grabbed my book bag and removed my paper-bag-covered schoolbooks that I had decorated with colorful markers.

"What's this then?" he demanded.

"It's a heart with Robin and Isaac written inside the heart," I said.

"See. What do you mean nothing's going to happen? Shit like this is just the beginning," he said.

"Dad, all the girls put stuff like that on their books. One week we like one boy and the other week we like someone else. It's no big deal," I said.

"Don't you dare tell me it's no big deal!" he yelled. "I don't want those boys sniffin' around you like you're some dog in heat. And they are like dogs. They can smell a girl's period, ya know? I don't want you writin' this shit, hangin' out with this boy, or his friends… am I making myself clear?" he asked as he held up my covered book.

"Yes," I said.

"Yes, what?" he asked.

"You're making yourself crystal clear, I understand and I won't hang around him or his friends anymore, or write that shit on my books anymore," I said.

He cocked his head to the side as if he didn't quite hear me right like a dog does when learning a new trick they don't quite get.

"What did you just say to me?" he asked.

"Dad, I repeated everything you just said to me," I said.

"Did you use the word *shit* with me, young lady?" he asked.

"I was repeating what you said," I answered.

"You do as I say, not as I do. You hear me?" he said.

"Yes sir," I said.

He ripped the brown paper book covers from my books and then proceeded to rip them to shreds as he stood in my mother's living room screaming and ranting about these boys. It was all so overboard, but that's what he did. He went overboard with everything. Why she called him, I could only think meant that she hated me and enjoyed seeing me being yelled at and upset.

"Dad, why are you doing this? You are making way too much out of this and it's stupid," I said. "Nothing is happening. NOTHING!" I screamed.

He stood there looking at me.

He looked at my mom.

"Seems we have ourselves a real live wire here, don't we?" he asked her.

"Sure do. Seems someone's gettin' just a little too big for her britches and needs to be knocked down a few pegs, if you ask me," she said.

With that, he took his black leather belt off and slammed it into my legs. I screamed. I tried to move away but he grabbed me by my arm and shoved me face first down onto the recliner. He struck me a few more times before I was able to get up and run to my room and slam the door.

"Get out here now!" my mom yelled. "Your father is not done speakin' to you, girl."

I went out and sat on the recliner and folded my arms across my chest.

"Look at me," he said. "And unfold those arms of yours. No daughter of mine is going to act like that. Listen. I don't want to have to get called back out here again. If I do, it'll be much worse than you got this time, you hear?"

"Yes," I said.

"I know you don't think so," he said as he put his belt on, "but whippin' you hurts me much more than it does you."

"Don't you dare make me call him out here again, Robin Lynn. You hear me?" she said.

"I hear you," I said.

I went to school the next day with uncovered books and told Isaac that I was sorry but I couldn't like him anymore but didn't explain to him exactly why.

During class, the teacher reminded me that she'd told us to have our books covered and if I didn't have them covered by tomorrow, I'd get a detention.

"Make sure all those are covered by tomorrow," she said as she tapped her index finger down on the stack of them on my desk.

"I'll make sure," I said as I smiled up at her.

Chapter 15

My mom married the black-haired guy with a mustache six months after dating him. His hair was so black it had a blue sheen to it in the sun. He was Italian and had a big black caterpillar mustache that curled up slightly on the ends. His name was Ricky.

My dad called him a lazy fucking dago. I learned real fast that that was an insult for an Italian-American and not a nice word to call someone pretty quickly when I called him a dago to his face. Ricky said it was equivalent to when white people call black people the "n" word. But he was calm and nice about explaining it to me, and didn't hit me, which I thought was nice of him and I never used that word again.

Ricardo was his real name but he liked to be called Ricky. He came from a large Italian family in Steubenville. And I liked that we'd get together with his family every Sunday for a big Italian-style dinner. I especially liked it when one Christmas I got presents from everyone in his big family and they were people I never even met before.

The only time I remember really being excited about his existence in our lives though was when they were getting married and at Christmas. When they announced they were getting married, it meant I got to pick out my flower girl dress for the wedding. I picked a full-length lace and floral print dress with high-collared neck and had a bouquet of flowers to match.

I turned to admire my reflection in the mirror and spin.

"It doesn't twirl," I said.

"It's a full-length formal dress. They don't twirl," my mom said. "You couldn't care less about me getting married, all you're happy about is picking out a dress,"

"Pretty much," I said as I admired myself. "Why you'd want to marry him is beyond me. He doesn't work and doesn't even help you pay the bills," I said without looking at her.

"And how do you know that, young lady?" she asked.

I turned to her and put my hand on my hip.

"Mom, I hear you on the phone all the time, and it's not hard to figure out he doesn't work, when all he does is sit on the couch, drink beer and play his guitar all day when other dads are at work."

My aunt Della smirked and shot a glance at my mom.

"Well, she's right, Starlah. You don't have to do this if you have any reservations," she said.

"Reservations are for dinner," she said. "I know what the hell I'm doing."

My cousin Connie Ray, the artistic one of the family, joked that instead of buying a wedding card she'd make one instead. She'd make a card with a picture of a ticking time bomb on it with a caption that said "POW!"

Connie Ray was always a giggly, happy girl. Her laughter in a room full of people was undeniable. She had short reddish-brown ringlets for hair that sprung back into a curlicue after pulling them straight out from her head. She had a gap between her two front teeth, freckles, and her rounded cheeks would turn beet red in the heat. My aunt said she got cranky whenever she got too hot, and her temper would soar as the temperature rose. She also made a clicky, throaty noise in the back of her throat, and I remember thinking it was kind of like what I did sometimes when I was nervous.

She smoked cigarettes, walked barefoot a lot, cussed like a sailor and liked to drink beer. She laughed a lot, but let people know up front, she was not to be messed with and when she drank she ranted and raved with her finger in the air telling people the way it was. She had what my aunt said was a strong front but a soft back once you got to know her.

My mom told me that once when Connie Ray stayed over our house as a teenager in Marland Heights, she came home to find my dad in bed with her. At first, they both said nothing happened. Later, when my parents divorced, Connie Ray admitted to my mom that my dad had molested her. The only reason she didn't say anything then, was because he threatened to kill her if she said anything.

As far as I could tell my mom and Connie Ray got along fine and grudges were never held and no cross words were ever spoken. No one ever called the law, my mom said, because once my uncle learned of this, he convinced everyone it wasn't such a good idea to harbor any ill feelings or hold grudges, or get the whole world involved in the family's business. He instructed everyone that they'd handle this little incident within the family unit and let it roll off them like water off a duck's back.

When I was little I didn't understand what my mom and Connie Ray meant when they'd joke and laugh saying, if it was good enough for your kin, then it was good enough for them. My cousin Connie Ray said we lived in Dysfunction Junction as they all laughed.

It wasn't until I was in my twenties when I knew my uncle's reasoning for not calling the law. If they were called about what my dad did to his daughter Connie Ray, then they might find out what he had been trying to do to me.

So, everything was swept under the rug, all had been forgiven and life went on.

And still, no one knew about me.

My mom laughed at the idea of the homemade card but said, "You better not, Connie Ray, Ricky would be so mad, and it would hurt his feelings."

The wedding was nice. It was held at a little reception hall that looked like a tin storage garage but was decorated inside with paper wedding bell decorations that sat on every table and hung from the ceiling. Everyone danced and had fun that night and Ricky even danced a father/daughter dance with me.

My mom's dress was ivory lace and she wore a big floppy matching hat that had a Bohemian, hippie type vibe to it. Mouse came to the wedding and danced with my mom wearing, of course, his tight blue jeans that outlined his penis, cowboy boots and his black leather. People said they were like Ginger Rogers and Fred Astaire together on the dance floor. During their dance that night, he accidentally knocked the big hat off her head as he twirled her around and it landed on the floor. As he swooped her down, around him and up again, she had picked the hat up with her teeth and placed it on her head mid dance, not missing a step. The whole room laughed and clapped.

After the wedding, I helped carry the lace-covered box full of cards from all the guests to the black Cordoba with white interior that had replaced the Nova and we piled inside and went home.

Life went on with my mom and this new guy she called her husband.

He and I didn't talk much and I liked that just fine. He stayed out of my way and I stayed out of his. Turned out he was pretty depressive, almost despondent. Only a few months into the marriage and he had dark purplish, puffy circles under his already dark eyes, started to gain weight rapidly, and slept a lot.

Ping!

"What the?" I thought as I shot up in my bed. I sat there trying to figure out what the noise was.

It sounded like tin hitting tin.

Ping!

I was too afraid to pull the curtains back, but I could see a shadow cast on my bedroom wall that looked like an outline of Ricky. I finally got up enough nerve to peek my head out the side of the sheer to see him sitting on the hood of the Cordoba playing his guitar. He'd sing and drink and played the only two songs he knew how to play, "Please Don't Let Me Be Misunderstood" and "House of the Rising Sun" by The Animals.

And each time he'd finish a beer, he'd let out a big burp and pitch the crumpled can at the trailer. I could hear the pop and hiss of each new can.

And he'd begin singing again.

This singing and pinging went on till the wee hours of the morning. I had school in the morning and I knew there was no way I was getting back to sleep.

When I got up for school a few hours later, I walked out into the living room and had to step over empty potato chip bags, empty DiCarlo's pizza boxes and empty beer cans strewn all over the living room. I got my cereal and turned on the TV to watch cartoons before leaving.

"Turn that shit down!" my mom yelled from her bedroom. "I didn't get to sleep last night."

"You didn't get to sleep last night," I yelled back, "and I had to hear beer cans hitting the house all night long."

I walked outside to catch the bus. There were crushed beer cans lying all over the front yard, and I noticed what looked like mail on the ground, so I bent down to pick it up.

I turned it over to see Connie Ray's hand-drawn picture of a round black bomb with a lit orange-red fuse coming out the top. At the top of the picture in cartoon writing, it said, "POW!"

"POW! alright," I said out loud, "more like fucking KABOOM!"

She's so stupid, I thought, as I dropped the card back in the yard and left for school.

Six months later, they were divorced.

When I got to Mrs. Strickland's class that day, I realized that I had forgotten to do my part in a team assignment. To draw a picture of an onion cell after looking at it under the microscope the day before, of all fucking things.

Once in class, we all started goofing around and laughing and when I was confronted about where my part of the work was, I had to admit I didn't have it done.

We were all called out in the hallway, one by one. Me, and five boys. Our punishment was a paddling with a wooden paddle labeled "The Dept. of Education" that looked like a boat oar she pulled from the wall on her way out the door. We were all getting spanked for not working as a team. Three hard whacks.

And I went first because it was "ladies before gentlemen," the boys said.

"Bend over and touch your ankles," she demanded.

She counted out loud with each whack of the paddle.

One.

Two.

Three.

I had to think of something else while this was happening so my mind went to the commercial with the owl showing the boy that it takes precisely three licks to get to the chocolate tootsie roll center of a Tootsie Pop.

"A one, a two, crunch, a three. Three," says the owl.

But, I didn't laugh. I didn't even cry.

My ass hurt, but my heart hurt worse. I stood there with my stinging ass that burned like fire up against the cool metal lockers with my arms folded and had to watch the boys get their whacks too. I didn't know what hurt worse, getting spanked or watching other be spanked.

"O.k. Everyone, line up," she said. We all lined up quickly against the lockers, glad to be guarding our backsides from her.

"The next time I give an assignment and it's not done completely, as a team, you will all get another paddling. Does everyone understand?" she said, pointing the paddle at each of us.

"Yes ma'am," we all said in unison.

"Back to class," she said as she motioned to her door with the paddle in her hand.

"Thanks a lot, Robin," one of the boys said.

"Yeah, if it weren't for you…" another boy said.

"Sorry," was all I could say back.

On the bus ride home Suzanne pushed into the seat with me. "I heard you got paddled today by Mrs. Strickland."

"Yep. I did," I said still looking out the window.

"I'm sorry she did that to you. You didn't deserve it," she said.

"Thanks. I don't deserve a lot of things," I said.

I had never been in trouble at school much less spanked. Now, I was just a kid that was nothing but trouble, didn't do her homework, couldn't be trusted as a team member, and now everyone hated me at school. I tried to act as if it didn't matter, but it did. I was upset about the spanking and upset that I cared about getting spanked. I was hurt and mad. There was no safe place to be for me, I got spanked at home, molested at my aunt's and now, I was being spanked at school.

I decided that if I didn't want things like this to hurt so much, I had to stay on the line between caring too much and not caring enough. I didn't know the word for what I was doing at the time, but I later learned I was disassociating in order to cope. Just like everyone else in my family.

I sat and stared out the bus window.

Fucking onions, I thought. I hate fucking onions!

And my mind instantly tried to soothe me:

"A-one, a-two, a-three. Three licks to get to the center of a Tootsie pop," said the Owl.

Chapter 16

At eleven years old the glory of the morning at my aunt's house didn't remove the pain in my heart of my mom not returning for us yet again or what was happening to me in the middle of the night there.

"Oh please, Lord," I'd say in my head. "Please let my mom be safe and come for us. In Jesus' name I pray, Amen."

My mind would linger to the time my dad told me she was rumored to have been so drunk at a bar one night, that she smacked the bottom of her beer bottle across the table, holding it up with its jagged edges threatening to cut a woman she was fighting with. I'd try to change that image in my head by squinting my eyes and thinking of something else.

Instead, I'd try to think of times she'd be smiling. I'd think of her driving the brown Nova on the country winding roads, windows all the way down, her hair flying wildly around her face. It made her more beautiful to me than anyone else on Earth.

She'd sing as if she didn't have a care in the world, looking over at me, winking, and pushing her finger into my side to make me giggle.

"Here! Steer the car!" she'd yell.

"But —"

"Just do it!" she demanded.

And I would dutifully steer while she dug in her purse for her cigarettes.

"Don't you ever pick up this nasty habit." she'd yell over the radio and hold the cigarette out for me to look at it. She'd give me the look of "promise me you won't" and push smoke out the side of her mouth away from me after it was lit.

I'd smile and say, "Promise."

But, I didn't keep my promise.

I was joining the kids across the street from the trailer in sneaking their father's non-filtered Pall Malls. When we got used to taking those without getting caught, we started sneaking sips of clear liquid he kept in his bedroom closet in a Mason jar.

"Here, take a sip of this." Greg would say.

"What is it?" I asked.

"My dad's really pissed off vodka."

I turned out to be moonshine. I managed to swallow it only once, and it was like swallowing liquid fire.

We'd take the cigarettes out to the little house they had behind their big house and play pool and listen to music. We thought we were so cool walking slowly around the pool table eyeing out our next play, Pall Mall non-filtered cigarettes hanging out our lips, one eye squinted half closed from the smoke wafting up, occasionally removing it to spit a flake or two of tobacco from our tongues.

"Watch this," I'd say.

And I'd wet my lips, put the cigarette between them and ever so carefully open my mouth just enough to let the cigarette just dangle on my lower lip like magic. My dad did that all the time to make me laugh.

"Yeah, well, look at this," Becky would say as she blew smoke circles in the air. She created perfect round circles by forming her mouth into a circle and pumping her bottom jaw up and down. They stayed that way till she broke some of them apart with her finger saying, "Can't let that one die a virgin." We felt even cooler when she would get out her purple-feathered roach clip to hold what was left of the filter-less cigarette so we didn't burn our fingers. We'd pass it around as if we were smoking a joint.

I broke my promise to my mom about not smoking and for that I sometimes felt bad. But she never seemed to feel bad for breaking her promises to me so I just continued to smoke and try to drink with the neighbor kids.

"Roooobinnnn, breakfast!" yelled my aunt Della.

I'd jump out of bed, throw my pajamas off, put on my cut off jean shorts and Shaun Cassidy T-shirt, fluff my Dorothy Hamill haircut and run barefoot to the kitchen.

Homemade pancakes, eggs, and sizzling bacon hot off the griddle and the smell of coffee percolating. "Grab yourself a plate," she'd say. And I'd load up my plate with it all and drizzle my pancakes with syrup.

I'd looked up across the table to see my uncle Owen peering over the top of his paper at me. He wore a plain white T-shirt and would sometimes roll a pack of cigarettes up in one of the short sleeves. With a Pall Mall non-filtered cigarette hanging from his mouth, and his dark, greased-back hair, he looked like he was still stuck back in the '50s. When he was younger he looked like Elvis's twin. And he had a smirk that lingered in the corner of his mouth as he asked me, "So how'd you sleep last night?"

"Good," I said. "I slept good," I answered quickly and then ignored him.

I was eight when the inappropriate talk started. I remember wanting to learn how to play the guitar and was encouraged to go in the back bedroom where my uncle sat and played. He sat me in his lap and pretended to strum the strings and whispered in my ear.

"Hey, let me see your titties."

"Ew! Gross!" I said, as I left the room.

"Shhhh!" he said as he lifted his index finger to his mouth.

He made loud slurping sounds as he sipped his hot coffee and chewed with his mouth open. You'd see the food rolling around in his mouth as he ate. I loved him, yet I didn't. It confused me. He was my uncle, but he was doing things to me I knew he shouldn't be. When I was nine he started getting grabby with my body if no one was in the room. "Ah, come on now, no one will know if you let me finger your pussy," he'd say.

At ten, he walked over to me one night as I watched TV on the couch and shoved his hand up my nightgown. He got down on his knees to put his head under there and I kicked him in the chest so hard it knocked him into the coffee table. When my aunt yelled out from the back bedroom asking what in the hell was all the racket, he yelled back that he had walked into the coffee table and hit his knee.

Then one day at age eleven, I opted to stay at my aunt's alone while they ran into town for groceries, when shortly after they left, my uncle Owen appeared home from wherever he'd been.

I was in the bathroom when he barged in on me.

"What're you doing! Get outta here! I have to go to the bathroom!" I screamed.

"You can pee in front of me, don't be shy."

"Get out," I said as I grabbed a towel and put it over my lap.

He walked through the narrow bathroom while unzipping his zipper. He took his penis out of his jeans and shoved it in my face as I sat on the toilet.

"You see this? Some guy's gonna give you one of these one day and you're gonna take it like a woman," he said.

"It goes in there." He pointed to my lap as he tried to shove his finger through the towel.

"That's gonna get wet and warm and you'll want it like nothing you've ever wanted before," he said as he breathed heavily. "He'll put the head in just a little, then the whole thing."

"Quit it!" I yelled.

"Shhhh," he said. "At first it will hurt, you may even bleed… But you'll grow to love it and it won't hurt anymore… When you're bored of that, he'll lick your pussy and finger you… then you'll suck his cock and make him cum…" he said.

I was moving my head all around, moving in the opposite direction of his penis, pursing my lips tight.

"Stop it!" I screamed.

"You better not tell anybody I told you that. Your mom would kill you," he said.

"Me?!" I said. "I'm not doing anything! She'll kill you. Get out!" I screamed.

"You wanna touch it, see what it feels like?" he asked as he moved closer to me holding out his penis.

"No! Get it out of here!" I yelled, turning my face away.

"That's a dick, honey," he said as he pushed it to the side of my face.

I could smell it. It smelled like a dirty ashtray or maybe it was his hands.

"Yeah," he said as he stroked it. "Just rub it a little… like this," he said as he touched himself. "You wanna taste it?" he asked.

"No! Get out!" I cried.

"Just put your tongue out like this," he said as he demonstrated. "Just put the tip of your tongue right here and rub it around a little bit," he said as he rubbed his finger around in a circle on the head.

"No!" I said. "Gross!"

"That's cum, that clear stuff right there… that's what will get you pregnant," he said as he touched the clear liquid that came out the end.

"But, it's o.k., you can swallow it though and it won't hurt you," he assured as he tried to rub it around my face.

"Stop. Stop it!" I yelled.

"You hot, little girl?" he said as he laughed. "You'll get wet and hot and want your boyfriend to put his big, fat cock in your pussy. Let me feel," he said as he motioned to my lap. "You want me to show you how your boyfriend will eat your pussy? It's o.k. "You'll like it and no one will ever know. It'll be our secret."

"No. Get away from me. Gross!" I screamed.

"Ah, come on, darlin', don't be all shy about it now."

"Don't. Don't!" I said.

He grabbed me by my wrists to stop me from flailing.

"Come on now. Don't be like that."

I managed to stand up from the toilet, grabbed my underwear and pants together and pulled them as high as I could. When I tried to get past him in the narrow bathroom, he grabbed me from behind. He had yanked my pants down and was trying to turn me over to my back.

When he turned me over, he was trying to shove his face between my legs while pulling down my pants.

"Well, look at you… you're getting peach fuzz down there!" he said with amazement.

He stopped when he heard a car coming down the gravel road. He got up and went to look out the narrow window over the toilet. "The coast is clear, just a car," he said with his back to me, looking out the window.

By the time he turned around, I had my pants pulled up and was halfway through the living room headed out onto the porch.

"Aw, come on now!" he yelled out from around the corner of the bathroom at me.

"You don't know what you're missin'. No one's here, don't worry. It'll feel good," he said as he walked toward me. "You have to be a giver, not just a receiver, remember that," he said.

"I said no and I mean NO!" I screamed. "If you touch me again, I'll tell!" I yelled back at him.

I went outside to the porch and slammed the door behind me. I sat at the bottom of the steps to wait for my mom. My stomach hurt. I felt like I would be sick.

He peeked his head out the front door.

"Aw, don't be that way. You could get us both in a heap of trouble if you don't simmer down," he called down the steps after me.

I was confused as to how he referred to "us" getting into trouble. He was the one that barged in on me in the bathroom.

"What're you doing out here?" my mom asked as she carried in grocery bags.

"Uh, nothing, just sittin waitin' for you," I said.

"Well, go get your stuff, we're going back home," she said.

I went in and got my bag from the bedroom and came out and sat down on the floor to put my shoes on. I looked at him sitting in his recliner, not a care in the world. When he looked up and caught my disgusted look, he patted his index finger over the place where smirks lingered and winked.

I didn't want to come here anymore by myself. I didn't want to be alone in the house with just him. And during the drive home when I was sure I was going to be fearless and bold, and turn and tell my mom, I wasn't and I didn't. I kept my mouth shut and just stared out the window, glad to be going back to my own house. I would tell her when I could.

When my uncle Owen got his band together and played music on the porch my mom would join in singing the same two songs over and over again, "Bobby McGee" and "Mercedes Benz" by Janis Joplin. My uncle would sing "Act Naturally" by Buck Owens. He'd casually look in my direction as he sang into the microphone in his charismatic, on stage personality and wink at me. I learned that song meant that I should act like nothing happened and that it was probably best to clear my mind of reality. I had to let it go.

Some time after the bathroom incident, I was getting him his usual cup of joe. "Black, and make it quick," he'd say knowing I was famous for what everyone called dillydallying. By the time I returned with the hot coffee, he was fast asleep and snoring in his recliner, with a lit Pall Mall cigarette burned down into a white tube of ash that sat next to him in a tall ashtray, a newspaper lay opened across his chest. I walked ever so slowly holding the cup onto the white saucer and I was upon him when I called his name. He rose with a start and came up out the recliner knocking the cup from the saucer and onto his chest. He threw off the wet newspaper and screamed out in pain. He stood up from the recliner in a flash and ripped his T-shirt off over his head as fast as he could. My aunt came running and I ran for cold towels.

"Whewweeee! God damn that hurts!" he said as he whistled through his pursed lips. "Woooo!" he said as he panted and waved air at his chest.

"I'm sorry, Uncle Owen," I said. "Let me help you."

"No, no, you've done quite enough, thanks." he said.

I remember how he looked at me when that happened. He was scared and yet looked at me as if I somehow betrayed him. I know he thought I did it on purpose, but I didn't. When they returned from the hospital with sterile bandages and several tubes of ointments, his eyes were pleading me not to tell. I helped apply ointment and assured him instead.

"I'm sorry, it was an accident," I said.

"Shhhh!" he said. "Don't make a fuss."

I cried some that he was hurt and I was the cause.

When he saw I was visibly upset, he said, "Well, alright then. I'll just know not to ask you for my cups of joe anymore or ever ask you for a knife."

I didn't get it.

I have a picture of my uncle and me. He was sick and dying of cancer and in the last few months of his life. His face had a bloated, jaundiced appearance to it, and his Elvis-like smile that lingered was yellowed and worn from all the years of smoking and drinking. And there I was, hugging his neck from behind, smiling widely for the camera. In my heart and mind I told myself I was over it. I thought burning him that day with scalding hot coffee was an accident but now, knowing what I know about our subconscious, I'm not entirely sure.

But as he was being eaten alive by lung cancer, I was being eaten alive by secrets I started keeping when I was eight years old. I was thirty-five years old in that picture.

Turns out, forgiveness for others came easy to me, but forgiveness for myself was another matter altogether. I wouldn't speak a word about this to anyone for another fifteen years. No, I never betrayed him.

I betrayed myself.

He recovered and soon returned to playing music on the porch all hours of the night, keeping us awake. My aunt Della would get mad and say that she and these damn kids in here were trying to get some sleep and they ought to try to do the same. But they never did. They just played and drank and did what my aunt called "hooped and hollered all night long."

My uncle called it pickin' and a grinnin'.

"Ah, come on, Del... come out here and have a beer with us and settle down now," he'd say. She never did settle down and he never did quit drinking and playing. So, I guess you could say, she was always a pickin' and he was always a grinnin'.

If it wasn't him and his band keeping everyone awake in the house, he'd sit in his recliner smoking and watching black-and-white Westerns till the wee hours of the morning, the volume up full blast because he was half deaf from working in the mill around loud machinery. They were so dysfunctional that when he'd turn the channel, she'd yell clear from the back bedroom that she was listening to that and to turn it back, goddamn it.

I adored my aunt Della. She wasn't afraid of anything. My aunt didn't drive but that didn't deter her from high tailing it out the dirt road on foot to find my uncle. One night, she was so fed up with it all, and suspected he was with someone he shouldn't be, she walked barefoot up Parson's Run Road with a loaded pistol in her hand to find him. She found him all right; at the home of someone she called a friend. I heard after she started flailing the gun around, he came home in a flash and she and that woman never were friends after that.

My aunt Della was fierce. Always had her own way of being in this world and I always suspected she longed to be free to do her own thing. And for as long as she stayed, which was her whole life, she still had a way of walking to the beat of her own drum. She had elegance about her even if we were called hillbillies. She was a reader and knew a lot about the world she never got to explore. She wore her silver spoon rings and turquoise jewelry long after the fashion industry said it was out and people were into disco clothes and bell-bottoms. I remember her saying with a giggle when it all came back into fashion that she must have never gone out of fashion. No, she never did go out of style in my opinion, she was timeless in my eyes.

She wore long flowing skirts with jean jackets, stacked bracelets up one arm, wore chunky gemstone necklaces that balanced her chakra centers and mixed fabrics like leather and lace long before there were songs about it. She drank fancy Perrier water that mesmerized me with its bubbles as she took a handful of supplements to keep her young and healthy while everyone around her seemed to be hell-bent on pickling themselves as they drowned their sorrows and called it fun.

My aunt knew about other religions, other cultures and usually knew the answer to every question on every game show. You had to take care of yourself and your mind, she'd say. I remember once when she let me look through her purse, she had a piece of paper in there and when I opened it, it was a list of the counties of West Virginia. When I asked her what for she said to memorize as she waited at appointments and in lines. I thought she was the smartest woman I'd ever met. So once when she suggested I go back to her room and away from some drama with my mother and father, I memorized them myself. When I came out to the kitchen table, handed the list to my mom and proudly said them alphabetically as my aunt stood behind her reading the list, my aunt smirked with pride as I said them all in perfect order.

"How'd you do that?" my mom asked.

"She sat down, studied it, and applied herself, Starlah Jean, you ought to try it once in awhile," she said.

And for everything my aunt had been through, she had a way about owning any room she walked into. She didn't wear her pain like my mom did. She usually had a sunny, bouncy disposition and she didn't need you to like her. She liked herself enough not to give a shit whether or not you did. And she didn't need you to approve of her choices. She was unapologetically who she was and if you didn't like it, well, it just didn't bother her. And goddamn, did I admire and love her for that.

She wore her hair in a bob before it was named that and was pretty much barefoot at all times, her feet so calloused she could walk on gravel roads and not even wince. She'd let her house get filthy while she sat and read romance novels, and piles of books and magazines she was always in the process of reading surrounded her at all times and she never needed to follow a recipe when cooking because she had them all memorized. She hung clothes on a line, made homemade biscuits, and usually had no less than three dogs running around under foot at all times. And they could do whatever the hell they wanted; and you could just shut your mouth about them, they lived here, you didn't.

One night when my uncle was out carousing and my aunt Della was babysitting us, there was a pretty severe thunderstorm. Around 3 o'clock in the morning a loud banging started on her front door. The sound woke us both up.

I was up standing in the doorway as she passed the room I stayed in.

"You stay here," she said as she passed.

I came just out of the room and stopped to watch her walk down the hall toward the door.

She opened the door a crack and peered around the side of the door.

"Who is it?" she asked.

"Um, ma'am, I broke down, just a little ways down the road and was wondering if I could use your phone," a man's voice said over the loud rain hitting the tin roof.

She stood there and contemplated for a minute.

"Just a minute, I'll be right back," she said to the man as she closed the door and locked it.

She came back past me through the hall and into the bedroom where she opened a small drawer just inside her bedroom door. She quickly shut it and turned and headed back out to the door. She opened the door and the man was still standing there.

"O.k. You can come on in and make your call now," she said.

I snuck down the hall and got to the living room. I stepped to the left and halfway around the coffee table where I could see into the kitchen that was dimly lit, and there, dripping wet and scared to death, was a man stammering and fumbling to make a call on my aunt's rotary phone. As I walked around the table even further, there was my aunt standing across from him holding a gun with both hands aimed right at the man's face. When she saw me she nodded her head up to me and then looked back at the man.

"See," she said using her head to point in my direction, "I got kids here and I can't be takin' chances with them here, lettin' some stranger in to use the phone."

He didn't even turn to look at me, made his call and quickly scampered out the door into the rainy, thundery night.

Many years later, when we talked about it, we still didn't remember him talking to anyone on the other end of the phone and wondered whether or not he was legitimately broken down since no one saw for sure or if he was there to kill us and decided against it because of the gun.

My aunt Della was to me what Wonder Woman is to little girls. And I wanted to be just like her when I grew up. Bold. Fearless. Original. Powerful. Protector. My mom would tell me, as I grew older, I was more like my aunt Della than I was her.

After breakfast, I helped with the dishes. My aunt washed, I dried and put away. We'd while away the hours doing chores together, but nothing ever seemed to help the mess that was her house.

Outside, I helped my aunt hang clothes on the line while the dogs went running wildly around us as we walked. I'd walk slowly behind her carrying her basket of clothespins, afraid of snakes, calculating each of my steps to go inside her footprints left in the tall grass my uncle never mowed. She'd walked on without a second thought.

"You sure you don't want to go play, Robin Lynn? I can do this," she said.

"Nah... I want to help," I said. "Besides, there's no kids down here to play with."

"Well, you should really be out playing and being a kid, not doing chores, there's time enough for work when you're grown," she said.

But I was grown. I was more grown than she knew.

It wasn't my years that made me mature, it was my pain. And I got the feeling she was more grown than she was too. I'd watch her read some, then stare off in the distance, caught somewhere between this world and another. I knew we didn't fit here. We had big dreams. There were places to go and things we wanted to do. But right now we had chores to do, people and pets to take care of, and as she put it, "more pressin' things that needed tendin' to than our dreams."

And for all the recipes she had memorized she didn't have one for living life while living your dreams. And I knew by the smile she brought to my face whenever I was around her that I loved her too much to tell her the truth of what was happening to me.

Chapter 17

I was eleven when my grandma Jancie was diagnosed with colon cancer in 1978. My mom and Aunt Della took her back and forth to the Cleveland Clinic for all her appointments, and in the final stages of her disease, when she was admitted to hospice, they'd get a hotel room and stay there for days at a time.

Going to her funeral was my first. I can recall my cousin Ben, who was only two years older than me, preparing me ahead of time to touch her as she lay in her coffin. We'd put our hands together and he'd show me how to run my fingers down our two index fingers. "This is what she will feel like, hard but a little soft, like plastic and cool to the touch," he said.

I could see the thick funeral home makeup they had on her. It had a peachy tint to it and had caked in the crease of her nose. And now, two days into the viewing where everyone came to pay their respects, purple veins on her hands were starting to show through where people had worn the makeup off them from holding them while they cried.

Her hair was auburn red and red was her all-time favorite color, so the dress they buried her in was red too. It wasn't very funeral-like I heard some people saying, but that's what she wanted. Something red, with some glitz to it, she said. It was the dress she picked to wear for her last Christmas, the Christmas where she stood smiling for the camera as if she wasn't dying. She wanted to be buried in the shiny red dress that was gathered by a diamond brooch at the bustline should something happen to her, she said. She had her suspicions she was sick, she had all the symptoms, but right now she smiled big and wide.

Not six months later, she was dead.

My mom said she thought it was the colostomy bag that did my grandma in. It was the one thing she didn't want more than anything else. My mom told me when she awoke from surgery and saw the bag, she said, "Awww, Starlah Jean, ain't that awful?" as she looked down at it. They shook their heads that yes it was as they watched her grieve the loss of her bowels and her body image. They said my grandma Jancie had very specific rules about things and as a nurse she had a theory that air spread cancer cells once the body was opened to direct air in surgery.

They placed her tortoise-rimmed glasses on her face in the coffin. As I looked at her there with her hands folded, she didn't look dead, she looked like she might just be lying there checking her eyelids for holes.

And how weird, I thought, that my grandma's husband and her boyfriend were both at her funeral. And both cried like babies, even hugging one another. Even my dad was there and he called my grandma a whore.

I was told that my grandma Jancie got a boyfriend because she wanted to experience life. She wanted nice things, wanted to go to nice places and that's not something my grandpa could ever give her. She was sick of scratching shit with the chickens and had raised her eleven children and finally one day packed her suitcase and walked out the door. This was the rest of her life and she'd do what the hell she wanted with it despite what everyone else thought.

My grandpap Clay, my grandma Jancie's husband, was a passive, quiet man that never really had many feelings about much in his life. People said he didn't have opinions to share, no goals to obtain; he just existed from day to day and was all too content with how he was. His favorite saying was, if you don't have anything nice to say, don't say anything at all. So, I figured he must have never had anything nice to say because he barely if ever spoke and when he did, it was only a few words. My mom told me when she boarded the plane to fly to Germany at sixteen years old, she said, "I love you, Daddy." He said back to her, "Yeah."

Because of how he was, he just let my grandma Jancie live her life the way she wanted. He never did divorce her all those years, even when she went out and got herself a boyfriend.

Grandma Jancie was my favorite grandma and I would miss her. I had no one to hug me and tell me it would be all right. No more big red smooches on cards and no one to tell my mom to back off and to let me be a kid.

As I gazed at her in her casket, I thought about going through her pocketbook with her when I was little and her acting as if what I pulled out of it was somehow magic. When I said, "pay with dedicks gammall," she knew I was saying, "play with lipsticks grandma." I'd spray her perfumes as she sniffed her wrists, and I remember she gushed over the ugliest brooches I would buy her in Santa's workshop at school and proudly pin them to her apron.

"Good-bye, Grandma, I love you so much," I said to her lying there.

I can remember shortly after she died, my mom saying to me that it wouldn't have surprised her at all if all my god damned spraying of perfume over there was what caused her mother to get sick with cancer in the first place. I remember feeling hurt and horrified that I might be the cause that she got sick.

I cried some at her funeral, mostly when other people were crying. I never liked seeing people in pain. And in between showings, my cousin and I played outside in the funeral home parking lot.

"You know," Ben said as he pointed to the back door of the funeral parlor, "they say that's the room where they embalm dead bodies."

"Embalm? What's that mean?" I asked.

"They take their blood out and replace it with formaldehyde," he said.

"Ew, gross!" I said.

"They do that so we don't rot while people are at our wake," he said.

"I don't know about all that," I said. "She doesn't look awake to me."

When my grandma first died, my mom checked out even more. She cried constantly, drank because she was upset, and cried even more because she'd be drunk. I can remember my aunt Della telling my mom over and over that alcohol was a depressant and was only going to make things worse. It was her mother too that had passed away and she wasn't acting that way or coping like that. She needed to get ahold of herself, she said.

But, soon my mom had a new boyfriend that would come visit and stay for the weekends. During my grandma's illness, my mom met a guy named Wayne at the Cleveland Clinic where he worked as a security guard. He was a Cleveland Police officer doing some security on the side for extra money. When I met him, he wore mirrored sunglasses, had a much thinner mustache than Ricky, and walked with his chest puffed out at all times. He thought he was something, especially when he was in uniform. I hated him immediately upon meeting him. Once, when I wanted to try his sunglasses on, he looked at me as I was modeling them and said, "I can see myself in your eyes."

When I voiced my dislike of him she rationalized that maybe it was Grandma's way of changing our lives and that it was meant to be that she met him. Maybe, just maybe this guy would give her, give us, she quickly added, a new life.

I wrinkled my nose and thought, "Yeah, Grandma got sick with cancer and died so you could find another boyfriend. Weirdo."

Chapter 18

Everyone but me changed into gym clothes in a locker room located underneath the wooden gymnasium floor. My mom said she wasn't going to buy the school's shirt and shorts so I played in my regular clothes. And that day I just happened to be wearing the brand-new Jordache jeans I begged my mom to buy me.

That day we were playing softball for gym class.

The teacher chose two people to head up each team and call on the others they wanted on their team. The two people she picked were her favorites, Candice and Linda. Two of the biggest brown nosers of the school that thought they were better than everyone else.

Candice had flaming red-orange hair and thought she was God's gift to the world. She came to school every morning with perfectly coifed short hair always cut in the latest trend with a full face of makeup on, even in 5th grade. I didn't know too much about Linda other than she seemed to hang out with the more popular crowd and also acted like she was above you.

The less popular kids were chosen last. When Candice got to the last two people to be picked, me or Nan — an uncoordinated, pasty white girl who wore thick glasses and little girl barrettes on each side of her bangs — she'd draw out her decision like it was just so hard, then reluctantly pick me.

I was good in sports and they knew it. Choosing me near the end was what my dad called "their way of putting you in your place."

"Someday they'll get paid back for how they treated people," he added.

When I told my mom what he said, she said he was so dazzled by his own bullshit, he couldn't see the forest for the trees. Whatever the hell that meant. Sometimes adults say the weirdest shit, I thought.

It was bases loaded, a tied game and batters up for our team. Pitching to me was Linda. The first throw I didn't swing at. I heard encouragement being yelled from Candice and the rest of my team that sat on the aluminum bleachers behind me. And for just a little bit, it felt good to be included.

The second ball came straight and fast. I whacked it so hard it made a line drive down the middle of the field and Linda sidestepped it to miss her. I threw the bat behind me as I began to run and I yelled to the other players on bases to, "Go, go, go!"

As I ran, I motioned with my hands for my teammates to steal the next base as fast as they could while Linda's team fumbled to catch the ball.

Two outfielders slammed into each other while competing for the ball.

"I got it!" one yelled.

"No, I got it!" the other argued back.

The fumble cost them. Everyone made it home. And I had made it all the way around to third base by the time the ball got thrown back to Linda. She fumbled catching it while trying to keep her eye on the ball and me at the same time.

Struggling to get the bouncing ball up off the ground and into the too-big-for-her baseball mitt, I started to run for home base.

"No, go back!" I heard someone from my team yell from the bleachers.

"Linda! She's goin' for it! Hurry!" someone on her team yelled to her.

I ran with everything I had.

As I dove head first into home base, Linda had gotten a hold of the ball in just the tip of her leather catcher's mitt and she was also nose-diving into home with me. The last few seconds played out like a movie in slow motion that took forever.

My hands were stretched outward and my body curved backwards like I was swan diving into a pool, as she was sliding in from the right to touch the ball to the base. In her haste to tag the base, or me, she over shot the square white beanbag and the ball fell out of her mitt. My hands hit home plate and the rest of my body fell to the ground in front of it with a thud. The soft, dry dirt exploded up around my body.

Cheers and cries erupted from the stands; my team was pounding on the aluminum bleachers with their feet and hands as I lay in the dirt holding onto the base.

"Safe!" the gym teacher proclaimed. And with a few tweets of her whistle, she swiped her arms out to her side indicating the game was over, we had won.

I got up and stood on the base. I looked around to see my teammates going crazy about our win, high-fiving each other and jumping up and down.

The outfielders were slowly walking in from their positions with their heads down, slamming their mitts on the ground in defeat and kicking the dirt.

We had won! WE HAD WON!

And it was me that had won the game!

"Great game, Jessup! That's how it's done!" the gym teacher exclaimed in front of everyone as we headed back to the locker room.

Linda looked defeated, pale, but sweaty, with ruddy red cheeks. She kept eyeing me up and down, all the way back to the locker room. I thought she might say "good game" and shake my hand like they taught us was part of being a good sport. But she didn't.

And finally she spoke.

"You ripped your Jordache jeans," she said pointing to my brand new but filthy dirty jeans that now sported a hole in the knee.

When I looked down, I was mortified to see the designer jeans I had begged my mom for were now ruined. Designer jeans like Gloria Vanderbilt, Sasoon and Jordache were all the rage then and all the popular girls had them.

I didn't want to let on that I was upset about my jeans so I said nonchalantly, "Eh, they're just jeans."

"But they're filthy," she said.

"So I'll wash them," I said quickly.

The taunting and questions continued as a group of us walked to our next class.

"Yeah, so how're you gonna fix that hole?" she asked. "Your mom is gonna kill you when you get home."

I shrugged my shoulders. "I'll iron a patch on the knee."

"You hear that, everyone, she'll iron a patch on the knee after she washes them."

They all laughed, acting as if it was all so funny, they were falling into the lockers along the hallway. "She washes her own clothes cuz her mother's a drunk," someone said.

"Aw. No one takes care of her," someone else said as she pushed her mouth into an exaggerated frown.

"Poor wittle Wobin, has diwty, wipped pants," someone else mocked.

The mocking continued as some of us walked on to Mr. Jay's class.

Mr. Jay was our seventh grade history teacher.

"Stop it now. Right now," he said as we entered the classroom and closed the door. "That's enough. Time to turn your books to page fifty-six and get busy."

The class quieted down and was now filled with the sounds of books opening and pages being turned.

I wondered all through our quiet reading time how I was going to explain this to my mom. I didn't have to wonder how she'd react.

I never really wanted to go home, but on this particular day I was petrified. The taunting didn't stop all that day and pretty soon it was all over the school that Robin Jessup would ruin brand-new Jordache jeans to beat you at softball. I was both admired and looked at with disdain from those I'd beat that day.

I got off two bus stops away from my house and slowly walked toward the trailer. I was always embarrassed of the waist-high grass and weeds that clogged the entire front yard down to the unsteady wooden steps that led into the front door.

I didn't call out I was home. I stood on the square linoleum, listening.

I walked quietly through the trailer looking to see if anyone was there and I realized no one was home.

I ran to my room, tore off my jeans and put shorts and a T-shirt on. I stuffed my dirty, ripped jeans into my dresser drawer and covered them with other pants. I'd deal with fixing them some other time.

"So, how'd everybody like your new Jordache jeans I bought you?" my mom asked when she got home.

"They liked them," I said.

"That's it? They liked them?"

"Yeah. The other girls aren't going to welcome me into their popular circle of friends just because I have one pair of designer jeans," I said.

She nodded her head up not saying anything else. My mom knew everyone wore Jordache jeans because it was all I talked about and all I talked about wanting.

The night went on as usual. I did the dishes, took care of my brother, folded towels from the dryer and took my shower while my mother sat and talked on the phone.

I went to bed early that night, but all I could worry about were those damn ripped jeans lying there under the rest of my pants in that drawer. I worried I'd never again get another pair of designer jeans. And I worried. Just worried. All the time.

The next day, the gym teacher led us all down to a playground that was near the school. Mary and I were walking behind the rest of the class.

Mary was a cute tiny girl who was quiet, with short, dark black hair and round glasses. She kind of looked up to me and because I was taller than her, I felt it was my duty to protect her and look out for her. The other girls seemed to tease her as well so we stayed together a lot in class.

"Hey, you did really good yesterday in the softball game."

"Yeah? You think so?" I asked.

"Yeah, everybody's talkin' about it," she said.

"Thanks," I said as I giggled.

"And you showed those bitches," She motioned up to the rest of the group walking ahead.

I laughed. "I guess I did show those bitches." I said.

When we got to the playground, class consisted of whatever we wanted to do, as our gym teacher sat nearby on a bench talking to the boys' gym teacher.

Mary and I got on the merry-go-round while the rest of the class went to the tennis and basketball courts and a large jungle gym.

She got on and sat down, straddling one of the bars. I ran around the dirt ring outside the merry-go-round, running as fast as I could, one cool steel bar in each hand. Once I got the big wheel going as fast as I could, I'd jump on and lay down on the steel round contraption that had rough divots sticking up out of it to prevent slipping. The world would swirl above us and we'd laugh. It would finally slow to a stop.

"My turn," Mary said.

I stayed on. Once she got it to go as fast as she could, she'd leap on beside me and lay down.

"I wish you lived closer to me," she said.

"I wish I did too," I said.

I lived up the pike and she lived downtown so the only time we ever saw each other was at school.

"Look at these two. In a world all their own."

I raised my head to see one of the Key kids. Everyone called them dirtballs and no one liked them. They were forever in trouble with the principal, getting spanked in the hall or being expelled. There were three kids in all; two boys and a girl.

"Yeah, so what. Mind your business," I said. "No one's botherin' you."

"Yeah, mind your business, Tina," Mary said.

"I was talkin' to Mary, not you, Robin," she said.

"Well, she's my friend and if you're talkin' to her, you're talkin' to me," I said.

"Oh, you think you're gonna make somethin' of it?" she asked. "Look, everyone, Robin thinks she's Mary's protector now."

The few friends she had around her all started laughing.

I stood up then jumped down off the merry-go-round.

"Yeah, I do. What're you gonna make of it? Dirtball," I said as I poked her with my finger in her chest.

Her eyes got really big and she lunged toward me. I bent over and she flew over the top of me. I turned around to face her, but she was face down on the ground trying to push her way back up. I jumped on her back and sat down.

"You think you're cool always causin' trouble for everyone, don't you?" I said as I grabbed the back of her hair. "Well, everyone's sick of you and your whole fuckin' family here in this town; always actin' like a bunch of assholes."

"Get off me!" she yelled.

"No, I won't get off you till you apologize to Mary," I said gripping her hair even tighter.

"Ah! I'm sorry!" she said.

"Say it like you mean it."

"Mary, I'm sorry," she said.

"Good, now say sorry to me."

"Sorry!" she said.

"Like you mean it!" I pulled tighter.

"God! I'm sorry! I'm so sorry, Robin!"

I got up off her.

She rolled to her side and crab crawled backward away from me as fast as she could till she was far enough away to stand.

I was brushing the dust off my clothes when the gym teacher started toward me.

"You two," she said as she pointed to us. "With me. Now."

She marched us back first in line to the school when class was over. I turned around just enough to see Mary swiftly walking behind me with a look of terror on her face.

When we reached the front doors of the school, the gym teacher told the rest of the class, "Go to the locker rooms, I'll be there in a minute. I'm walking these two to the principal's office."

"Oooooh, the principal's office," someone from the back of the line said.

"Someone's gonna get it," someone else said.

We were seated next to each other in front of the secretary's desk and had to wait for Mr. Travonie, the principal, to get off the phone. When he did, the gym teacher went into his office and shut the door.

A few minutes later, the door opened and she motioned for Tina to go into his office and she went back to her next gym class, leaving me to wait my turn.

Tina got up and went in, closing the large wooden door with frosted glass window behind her.

I could hear every word.

"You. Why are you in my office again?" he said.

"Well, Robin got on top of me and pulled my hair."

"Yeah, but what did you do?" he asked.

"Uh, nothing. Nothing, Mr. Travonie."

"Don't give me that. You're in here every week and always innocent. I don't ever see Robin in here," he said.

When he dismissed her, she huffed and puffed her way by me with a pink slip that meant detention after school in her hand. I found out later that she was actually suspended from school for three days.

He fished out a file from a tall filing cabinet and went around the side of his desk and sat down. Without getting up, he motioned for me to come into his office and I shut the door behind me.

"Look. I don't ever see you in here. I'm surprised to see you in trouble, young lady. What's going on with you?" he asked.

"I know. I'm sorry. It's just that she's always picking on everyone and when she went after Mary at the playground… well, I felt I wanted to protect her," I said as I hung my head.

He was looking at some papers in my file, not saying anything for a bit. He looked over the top of his glasses after looking at the papers.

"And?" he said. "Go on."

"Well, sir," I said as I fumbled for what else to say. "I'm tired of getting picked on and I guess I just couldn't take it anymore."

"And who's picking on you here?" he asked.

"Um, no one until today," I said.

"But you said, you're tired of getting picked on."

"Yes. Some girls here are really mean to me. They tease me about my clothes, my parents and… I'm having a hard time at home too, sir," I said.

"Who here is teasing you about these things?" he asked.

"I don't want to get anyone in trouble by saying names," I said.

"Fair enough. If it gets worse though, you come tell me later, ok?" he said.

"Yes sir," I said.

"Now, about this hard time you're having at home? Tell me more about that."

"My parents are divorced now and I have to take care of my little brother, a lot. My mom is sad all the time and on weekends she's not home very much..." I started to cry. "I guess I just can't take anymore. I'm sorry," I said.

He read as I talked, looking up at me occasionally.

"I'm reading here that some of the teachers are writing in your progress reports that you have a hard time staying awake in class." He looked over his glasses at me.

"Yes, I don't get a lot of sleep. Sometimes my little brother needs something, or my mom wakes me up in the middle of the night with laughing and music."

"I see," he said, as he didn't take his eyes off me. After some deep breaths, removing his glasses and rubbing of his face, he said, "Well, you've never been in trouble before and the teachers say you're a bright young girl who's trying, has a pleasant personality, is helpful to her classmates... But I'm going to have to at least give you a detention one day after school for this."

"I understand. But, does it have to be after school?" I asked.

"I suppose we could have you serve it before class starts in the morning. Why do you ask?"

"Because my mom will be mad if she has to come pick me up," I said.

He scribbled some notes in my file, got up and filed the folder and said I could go.

I was about to shut the door.

"Just so you know, I'm on your side here. That girl is nothing but trouble," he said as he pointed up to the air. "You," he said, pointing back to me, "you have the potential to be someone, do something great someday." He smiled.

"Thank you. Sir," I said.

I left and felt like I had just been given a shot of energy. I felt happy and couldn't quite figure out why. I was supposed to feel bad because I just got a detention. Instead I was walking on a cloud.

When Mr. Jay saw me bouncing down the hall with my pink slip he started to hum the theme to the movie *Rocky*.

"Hey, slugger," he joked, "heard you were Rocky Balboa out on the playground today." He play punched the air back and forth. He was always joking with all the kids, making them laugh. He was everyone's favorite teacher.

I sat in my seat without saying anything and opened my book. It was silent reading time. When I looked up and made eye contact with Mr. Jay, he made a punching motion with his fist as he smiled at me as if to say, "Go get 'em."

When I got home to the trailer, I beelined straight for my room, but stopped short. There, lying out on my bed were my ripped jeans. I felt the color drain from my face.

My mom moved off the couch and came up behind me from the living room. "What the fuck is this?" she said as she pointed to my pants.

"Um, I was gonna tell you about that."

"Oh, you were, were you? Is that why they were buried under the rest of your pants in your drawer because you were going to tell me about them?" she asked.

"I knew you were gonna be upset so I was going to try to fix them, then tell you," I said.

"I used money from your child support to buy you an expensive pair of jeans and you do this to them?" she said.

"Mom, you don't understand," I said.

"Oh, I understand fine. I understand that you're an unappreciative brat that will never get another pair of designer anything as long as she lives!" she screamed.

She swung her hand across my face.

"You stay your ass in your room till I tell you it's time to come out."

"Mom! Why won't you let me tell you what happened?" I yelled.

"No! I don't want to hear it. You don't appreciate anything I ever do for you," she said as she slammed my door.

I did my homework while I was waiting to be called out from my room. I heard the whole ordeal spelled out on the phone call she was on as to what an ingrate I was, how horrible it all was to do so much for your children and they not care. How she was so tired of giving them everything and getting no appreciation. I heard her vow to never, "as long as I live, buy her another nice thing."

When I was done with my homework, I wrote in my diary.

Dear Diary,

She's always so dramatic!!! All I want to do is roll my eyes at her! ALWAYS some tall story about all she's sacrificed for her kids when she does NOTHING but yell, drink and sleep. NOTHING!!! And wouldn't you know it, the one day she decides to get up and do the laundry, she finds my ripped jeans!!! Do you believe that?! I know what this means, she'll use this for yet another reason to lay drunk and sleep the day away. And it will be ALL MY FAULT! I am nothing but the brat that causes her pain!!!

And, child support is for the child. To support it!!! NOT FOR YOU to SPEND on YOURSELF, YOU STUPID BITCH!!!!

I hate her!!!! I hate my life!!!

Fuck her!!! Fuck Tina!!! And fuck Jordache jeans!!!

Thanks for listening, Dear Diary. This is the only place I ever feel heard. See you later!

Love,

Robin

I loved writing with exclamation points and capital letters. I re-read my entry, screamed in my head at all the right places and slammed the book closed. I locked the tiny gold lock across the front of the book and put the key to it in my book bag. I hid my diary inside the track of the sliding door to my closet, right where the neighbor kids' dad kept his pissed-off moonshine.

One night, in late summer, I tossed and turned in the tiny hot room inside the big tin box. My pajamas stuck to my sweaty body and my hair stuck to my face. I kicked the covers down to the bottom of the bed and let the fan blow on me. I woke to the sound of my mom moving around in the living room and kitchen, and then heard my aunt Adalene's voice come in the front door.

Adalene was my aunt by marriage only. She was married to my mom's brother and she lived in the trailer next door. She was a germaphobe and cleaned constantly. Anytime her kids got hurt, out came the Mercurochrome, Bactine spray, peroxide and anything else she could think of, and she freaked out over the slightest cut. She washed their dishes in scalding hot bleach water and her hands were permanently scarred and red at all times from not wearing gloves. And for as clean as she was, I remember she was either always sick, or sick with worry. She made my cousin Ben wear a knit cap she called a toboggan, even in the summertime to keep his ears warm while riding a bike, thinking that would ward off a cold. She pronounced the word toilet with an "r" in it. So she said "torlet" and she referred to the console in the car as a "concert." And of course, she said she "worshed" the clothes. She had a nose that had a bump at the top making it resemble a hooknose, and with her frizzy, ratty black hair and heavy purple bags under her eyes, she reminded me of a Halloween witch.

I cracked my bedroom door and listened to their conversation.

"I just don't care anymore, about anything, fuck it," she said.

"Starlah Jean, you're upset because your mom recently died and drinking is just going to make you feel worse," Adalene said.

"Oh bullshit. I mean I am upset about Mom, but I don't drink that much. Just on weekends. Besides, I'm not hurting anybody," my mom said.

"I know, but alcohol makes everything worse, Starlah Jean," I heard my aunt say.

"Worse? I don't think things could get much worse than they are now."

"You've been through a lot the past few years," my aunt said.

My mom started to cry, raising her voice, her words slurred, stumbling about between the living room and kitchen occasionally to get something to drink and bring it back to the living room.

"Exactly, and if I wanna drink to cope, I will. I'm sick of hearing about how much I fucking drink," she cried. "I hear it from you, Della, even Robin Lynn."

My aunt sat on the couch with her hands folded between her knees just listening.

"Look," my mom went on. "I take care of my fucking kids. When and if I stop doing that, then someone can say something about how much I drink."

And with that I came barreling out of my room, and if it would have been possible, out of my skin.

I was livid.

"You don't take care of us! I take care of us! I'm the only kid I know that cooks, cleans, bathes her brother, takes out the garbage and takes care of her drunken mother, all while going to school, doing homework and sports!" I yelled in her face.

"Robin Lynn, don't you talk to your mother like that!" my aunt Adalene said, standing up from the couch.

My mom just continued to sit on the floor smoking her cigarette, flipping her ashes into a big yellow and orange butterfly dish that filled the middle of the coffee table.

"You don't know! I'm sick of it! She doesn't do anything around this house! So be quiet!" I yelled at my aunt.

"See," my mom said, crying and motioning up to me with her hand. "This is what I put up with every day."

"Liar!" I yelled.

"I do everything for these kids and this is how I'm paid back," she said.

"I don't have to pay you back! It's your job to care for us. You chose to have us! You don't care about me or Doodle, you never want to come to my school stuff, you don't ask me how my day was, you don't cook, everyone else potty trained Doodle but you, you don't even take care of us when we're sick, nothing... you're either sleeping or drunk!"

With that my mom stood up screaming.

She grabbed the large butterfly ashtray off the table and lifted it high above her head. She threw it straight down against the coffee table shattering it into a million pieces.

"You god damn little bitch! How dare you!" she yelled, trying to intimidate me.

"How dare YOU!" I yelled back. "I'm tired of you telling everyone how bad your life is, how much you do and how ungrateful your kids are when you're the one who's ungrateful. You don't deserve us! I told Dad how you are and he said he's going to take us off you if you don't change. He said all we are is a paycheck to you!" I screamed.

And with that she sat back down on the floor putting her head in her hands, crying.

Adalene bent down to console her, looking back at me as if I had pushed her down.

"Don't look at me like I did something to her. She does this to herself," I said to her coldly.

"Robin, your mom is hurting right now," she said.

"I've been hurting my whole life. Do you care about that? Does anyone? No, no one does," I said.

"See," my mom said as she pushed her arm out to me as if to show me to my aunt. "She's getting way too big for her britches. She hears what her dad fills her head with about me and I'm always the bad guy."

"No, Mom. I'm growing up and I see you for who you are and you can't handle that, that's all," I said.

She stopped crying and for a minute acted as if what I said sobered her up. When she finally looked at the pieces of bright orange and yellow glass, ash and butts strewn all over the living room floor, she started to cry again.

"Oh my God. I can't believe I did that," she said as she crawled over the floor picking up pieces of the ashtray.

She finally sat back on her knees cradling a large piece of the glass butterfly's wing in her hands. "This was my mom's and she gave it to me," she said as she cried even more.

My aunt started to try to clean it up for her.

"Adalene, don't. I'll get it," she said. "I made this mess, I'll clean it up," my mom said more crisply.

"Yeah, why don't you go home and mind your own family's business. If you want to come over here and tell me what to do, you can come over tomorrow and cook, clean, take out the trash, bathe Doodle, do laundry, all before you do my homework," I said.

She didn't say a word. She just excused herself and left, giving me a disgusted look all the way out the door.

It was in this instance that I realized that words, strung together in just the right way, with the right tone and inflection could make someone understand and that words, *my* words, could mean something. My mom would later tell me that I had a way of making people pay attention.

I stood outside my bedroom door and watched her clean up the mess she made. I felt sorry for her, but I wasn't going to help her clean up her messes anymore.

I was learning to defend myself and speak my truth, even if my voice shook. And I was willing to take the risk of back talking to get my point across. And besides, I was used to being hit by now and I figured that sometimes speaking up was worth a slap in the face.

The next morning, I got up and didn't bother her for lunch money nor did I wake her up saying that Doodle needed to be fed. I just left for school.

That day for recess we were given a choice to go outside and play or stay inside our health classroom and study, color, draw or talk. I opted to stay inside with a friend named Marci. We sat in the back and talked and sang.

The doublewide trailer she lived in sat nestled in some trees that cascaded off the mountainside. Her front yard was strewn with rusty, broken-down old trucks, rusted-out metal garbage cans that were used for burning trash, and litter was always flung everywhere. Marci was a chunkier girl with short blond hair and pasty white skin and her cheeks and neck turned rosy red everyday as the bus pulled up to let her off in front of her house. Kids would make pig noises and ask if this was her house or the city dump. I knew her embarrassment well and wondered what was going on in her life that was similar to my own.

"Sing me that song you sang the other day," she said.

"No, I'm no good," I said.

"Yes, you are. You have a beautiful voice. Please. I really love it when you sing that," she begged.

So, we sat together in the back of health class that day as I sang "Lady" by the Little River Band to her. And I guess to myself. She sat and watched me intently. When I got to all the right parts in the song, I made sure she knew I saw only her, and loved only her, and for a moment I forgot about my own problems. As I sang, it brought a wide smile to her face and tears to her eyes as she listened. We were self-soothers looking for wildflowers to pick in the midst of our hell.

"Thank you," she said when I got done, "you have no idea how much that means to me."

Chapter 19

It was December 1980 now and I was so excited! I was going to be a teenager!

Today was the day of my 13th birthday party! My friend Karen and I were able to convince her mom to let her ride the bus home with me and sleep over that night.

"I handed out all the invitations at school and so far almost everyone said they were coming, isn't that great?" I asked my mom at supper the night before.

"Yeah, great," she said.

The next morning I bounced out of bed.

"Mom, promise me you'll have the house ready for the party by the time we get home from school," I said.

"Yeah, sure, I promise," she said.

"And don't forget to take out the garbage too," I said over my shoulder as I was leaving.

"I won't," she said.

Karen boarded my bus after school that day and she gave the bus driver the note as we got on. Having another kid ride your bus was a big deal and everyone wanted to know why, so you had to have a note explaining why.

The bus driver read the note.

"So, how old are you going to be?" he asked.

"I'll be 13," I said.

"Ah, a teenager now, a big milestone… well, Happy Birthday," he said.

Our bus driver's name was William, an older man with white hair. He was the only bus driver that could round Deadman's Curve at the tail end of Rabbit Hill in one turn. Whenever we had a substitute bus driver, they'd have to back up several times to get the bus around that tight C curve, that turned almost completely back on itself.

Everyday, the whole bus would get quiet as we'd approach the curve and watch in anticipation to see if he could do it again. And he did it every single time. Even in the wintertime in the deep snow when driving the bus with chains on the tires, he managed it. We'd even clap for him on days like that. And in appreciation for our noticing, he'd hold his big hand up in the wide mirror above his head as if to say thank you and continue on, and the bus would go back to being loud again.

We got off the bus a few stops away from my house, and walked down to the slippery, uneven, wobbly wooden trailer steps. I opened the door and instantly wondered why I had believed her. The house was a mess, garbage was falling over in the floor, and the dirty dishes were still stacked in the sink. After examining the mess in the kitchen, I realized she hadn't even baked my cake.

I went back to her room down the narrow hall and opened her bedroom door. The odor of alcohol filled the room.

"MOM! What are you doing? It's 4:30, school is over, the house is a mess, Karen is here and you didn't even bake the cake!" I yelled.

She groggily rolled over to look at me.

"Home already? Oh…" She turned back over and went to sleep.

I slammed her bedroom door, determined to have a good party. I scanned the house again and started coming up with a plan and delegating.

"O.k. I'll do the dishes and empty the garbage while you take your shower first and get ready. Then, I'll take a shower and get ready and you make the cake. Deal?" I said.

"Deal."

By 6:30 p.m., the house was sparkling clean, not a dish in the sink, trash can emptied and we had a perfect chocolate cake with chocolate icing sitting in the middle of the kitchen table waiting to be eaten.

We laughed, took pictures, played games and rolled around on the living room floor wrestling with boys.

At one point during the party Karen said to me, "Do you realize anything about your party?"

I looked around not catching it.

"No?" I said.

"Everyone here, except me, is a boy."

"I invited the girls. They just didn't want to come," I said.

That night, after everyone except Karen was gone, I opened my mom's door to check on her. She rolled over to face me as she heard the door open.

"Did you have your party?" she asked.

"Yes, Mom, I had my party."

"Did it turn out nice?" she asked.

"Yes, it was fine," I said.

"Oh good, glad to hear it. Goodnight," she said.

"Night."

"Oh, and before you go to bed, my sweet girl, can you do me a big favor?" she asked.

"What," I said coldly.

"Can you get me some soup and bring me a glass of ice water? Dry pipes," she said as she grabbed at her throat.

"Sure," I said.

We went back to the kitchen; I opened a can of chicken noodle soup, poured it into the pan and heated it through, got her a glass full of ice water, put it on a tray and took it back to her room.

Karen opened the door and I put the tray down on her bedside table.

"Huh? What's this?" she asked as she rolled over again.

"The soup and the water you asked for," I said.

"Oh, oh... yeah. Thanks, honey," she said as she tried to sit up in bed. "What's this?" she said as she held up the glass squinting to see what was inside. "What's that floating in there?"

"Those are ice cubes, Mom."

A few days later my mom bought me a birthday cake from Kroger's, not because she felt bad, but because according to what I'd overheard her saying on the phone, that I'd never let her hear the end of this if she didn't.

I still have a picture of me smiling for the camera while posing with my cake in the white box sitting on the table in the mushroom kitchen. My smile isn't as wide as it usually was and my head is slightly turned downward from the camera, I'm almost embarrassed and in the photo I don't know why. I didn't realize why it felt awkward at the time, but now I know. If you have to make this kind of ruckus to be seen and valued as a person within your own family, it's hardly worth it when they finally act like they do. I never had another birthday party as a kid. My next birthday party wasn't for another 27 years. It was a huge blowout complete with an Elvis impersonator who serenaded me, asking me "If I Was Lonesome Tonight."

It was thrown as a surprise by my husband.

I was 40 years old.

Chapter 20

July in a trailer with no air-conditioning is miserable. July in a trailer with no air- conditioning with chicken pox, at age thirteen, is an excruciating hell I won't soon forget.

I woke up one morning and realized as I laid in bed that I had blisters all over my arms.

I got up to examine my face closely and started picking and popping the water-filled blisters. I got undressed and they were everywhere.

I was tired and felt fevered, but with no air-conditioning, who could tell.

When I showed them to my mom she said, "Yep, looks like chicken pox. Probably got 'em from those kids you babysit out the road from your dad's."

Later the blisters had started turning red and itching. Horribly itching as if bugs were crawling all over me. And I couldn't stop digging, or crying, or whimpering as my mom called it.

"Stop being such a baby," she'd say. "You'd think she was dying or something, it's the fucking chicken pox," I overheard her telling someone on the phone. "Yeah, I know. But she's having a goddamn conniption fit in there," she'd say.

I knew I shouldn't scratch but I couldn't help it. With the heat of July and all the crying, I was hotter and sweatier which only made it worse.

"I want my dad," I cried as I cradled my legs up to my chest, rocking back and forth. "I need someone to help me," I cried out to the ceiling.

My bedroom door opened and it was my mom.

"Jesus Christ, Robin Lynn, will you quiet down, the neighbors can hear you in here making all this god damned racket," she said and pulled the door behind her.

"I just need to get the fuck out of here, this kid is driving me insane with all this crying and shit," I heard her say to someone on the phone.

Between crying and being in and out of sleep, the next thing I heard was my cousin Bernice at the door.

"Starlah, I'm here, it's Bernice," she said.

"Oh, good, glad you're here. Do you hear her in there crying? You'd think I was in there killing her."

I heard my mom drive off.

A few minutes later, my bedroom door slowly opened and it was Bernice.

"Come on, I'm running you a cool bath, let's get you in the tub. I made you a paste of baking soda we can rub on your spots so they stop itching and it'll help them dry up so they heal faster."

Already developing breasts and having light pubic hair, I got undressed in front of her without even caring.

There was barely an inch on my body that didn't have a blister on it and the one that I was particularly worried about was the one right on the end of my nose. The one I had popped first.

"That's the way they spread and scar, you stupid ass," my mom had said to me.

"How was I supposed to know that?" I said.

I didn't want to have a scar on my nose but I could already see there was a circular indent just at the tip of my nose that wasn't going away.

"Don't worry about it, Robin Lynn. It may end up healing and you won't even know it's there," Bernice said as she saw me examining it in the mirror.

She carefully applied the paste to areas I couldn't reach. And carefully dug through my hair to put paste on the ones buried within my scalp. She got clean pajamas from on top of the dryer and helped me get dressed and walked me back to my room where she had already changed my sweaty sheets to clean, fresh crisp ones.

She brought a fan from my aunt's and placed it in my room, aiming it at me. Then, placed a pan of ice water in front of it.

"Here, this will help cool the air and help your fever. And I want you to take these," she said, as she pushed her closed hand toward mine. "Chew them up and then lay down for a bit and I'll go make you something to eat, o.k.?"

"Yeah, thank you," I said as she pushed the already sweaty hair off my forehead.

I drifted off to sleep listening to the sound of the fan, but awoke later to the sound of people talking outside my window.

"See, she quiets down for you," I heard my mother say.

"Yeah, but, Starlah, she's sick, she's feeling miserable. All I did was run a cool bath and put paste on her blisters to help the itch," Bernice told my mom.

"She's old enough to take care of herself, she's thirteen years old for Christ sakes," my mom said. "I'm not a fucking nurse, I didn't sign up for this shit."

I could smell cigarette smoke waft into my room from outside through the opened window where she sat and smoked cigarettes on the front steps of the trailer. Bernice was in the kitchen making me a tray of food.

"Here ya go. A grilled cheese and chicken noodle soup. I know it's hot out, and soup is the last thing you'd want to eat, but it's all there is, and if you eat or drink something hot in the heat, it will help cool you down," she said. "That's why your aunt Della can drink hot coffee in the summertime. Says it cools her down," she added.

I ate what I could, leaving some of the sandwich and soup uneaten on the tray.

A week went by and the blisters started to dry up and scab over. My fever was gone and all that was left was the intense itch. I sat in my room and picked and picked at my scabs until they were opened and bleeding again between falling asleep and waking for what turned out to be another full week.

When I was finally feeling better and there was barely anything to pick open anymore, I showered and put on clean clothes. I cleaned my room, changed my sheets and washed my clothes and sheets. My mom was in the living room smoking, talking on the phone.

"Feeling better now?" she asked when I came out.

"Yeah, better now," I said.

"Good, maybe you can help me around this house now and with your brother so I can get the hell out of here for awhile."

"Sure." I said. "What do you want me to do first?"

"You can start by making your brother something to eat, then when you're done, you can take out that garbage."

I went to the kitchen and opened a can of Spaghetti O's and a can of Spam and began to heat it on the stove. The empty can didn't fit in the garbage, which was overflowing with trash that spewed onto the floor.

My mom was in her room with the stereo playing, singing to "I Love the Nightlife" by Alicia Bridges, getting ready to go out, doing her hair and makeup in the pink light of evening four-way mirror.

It was only a matter of a few weeks and my little brother Doodle got my chicken pox. He was as miserable as I had been with little to no relief for him in sight either. When some of the chicken pox on the bottoms of his feet turned black and he could no longer walk, he was finally admitted to the hospital.

I remember visiting him once in the hospital. There my mom sat doting on him at the bedside.

"How come he gets to go to the hospital with chicken pox and I didn't?" I asked her.

"Because he's much sicker than you were. Just look at this sweet face," she said as she smooshed his cheeks together in a kissing motion with her hands.

"Oh," said the nurse at the bedside, "that's probably not true at all. They were probably both equally miserable, and didn't you know... chicken pox are more dangerous the older we get," she said.

"Well, that may be so, but she has to learn that not everything's about her," she said to the nurse.

"Awww... poor baby," she said to my brother as she wiped his forehead.

Chapter 21

After a late-night game of hide-and-seek and Marco Polo in the pool at my dad's, Karen and I took our sleeping bags to the den. Our hair was still damp and smelled like chlorine; our feet still dirty from running around outside all day.

The den used to be an attached garage, but was turned into a rec room by the previous owners after slapping down some cheap padding and carpet over the cement floor, and building a two-car garage down over the hill. That room was always much colder than the rest of the house because of the two glass sliding doors and three windows. It had two heavy wooden sliding doors that housed our washer and dryer. The door going into the den was closed off from the rest of the house by a breezeway off the kitchen and a wooden slider door with a tarnished gold handle. I can still hear the sound of that door opening and closing. It made a hissing sound as the wood door scraped against the wood frame.

We liked to sleep out there in our sleeping bags in the summer. Out there by ourselves, we were cut off from the rest of the house where my dad was and could talk without intrusion or him eavesdropping which he was famous for doing. One summer night as we sat in my bedroom he snuck outside and sat beneath my window listening to every word we said. He eventually jumped up and we both screamed sending him into a laughing frenzy.

When the house was finally dark that night and I thought the coast was clear, I got up and lit the cigarette I had hidden earlier in the day from what was left in what my dad said was his last pack.

"Karen, make sure if you hear anything to let me know."

"I will, go ahead."

I went outside, around the side of the house just outside the glass sliding door we left cracked open, and smoked. Karen stayed in the house sitting on the floor near the crack in the door so we could whisper to one another.

The red tip lit up the night's sky with each long drag of the cigarette. The country night so quiet, the sound of the crackling tobacco as I sucked the filter sounded much louder than it actually was.

"Anything?" I whispered around the side of the cracked sliding door.

"Nope. Coast is clear."

I kept smoking, fast, getting a bit light headed and fanning the white smoke with my hand as it wafted up against the night sky.

On the last drag of the cigarette, when the white paper met the brown filter, I flicked the butt off the end of my middle finger and thumb and watched the red light sail high in the air and land in the grass about ten feet away. It would burn out soon with the dew of the grass. I went back inside where we closed the door as quietly as we could.

We were drifting off to sleep when I heard it. The hissing sound, it was wood against wood, then, a snapping, cracking sound. It would stop periodically and start again. I knew instantly what it was but it had snuck too close by this time to whisper to Karen to play it cool. It was my dad's foot and ankle that snapped and cracked as he walked.

I lay there stiff as a board, pretending to be asleep, trying to pace my breathing to that of someone who had already long been sleeping. I knew not to say a word and hoped Karen wouldn't either.

The clicking stopped abruptly and it was silent for what seemed like an eternity. Then the clicking and snapping sounds started again. It walked all around the room stopping to look out each of the glass sliding doors.

It came close. Right up to our heads.

It walked in circles around our heads as we lay on the floor in our sleeping bags. He was so close to my head I could feel and hear the carpet and padding press down under his foot.

And I could hear his breathing.

I was sending Karen telepathic messages with my mind. "Don't move a muscle!" I screamed in my mind. "Act like you're sleeping!"

My throat constricted and my heart buzzed in my ears as I wondered if he had seen the red light from the cigarette.

I prayed to the God I wasn't sure heard me or even liked me. "Please, Lord, don't let him do anything to me and please, let the grass be wet enough and the red light of that cigarette be out," I prayed.

The breathing continued.

It got louder.

The clicking had stopped as he stood over us just breathing. Slow and steady deep in through his nose at first and then faster through his opened mouth.

I wanted to crack my eyelids open just a bit to see what he was doing but I was too afraid at what I might see, so I lay there pretending to be asleep and thankfully so did Karen.

The breathing quickened from his mouth and finally slowed and disappeared. The clicking noise eventually walked over to the sliding wooden door. Wood against wood to open. And wood against wood to close.

I can still hear it in my head.

I was still sending Karen telepathic messages…

"Don't move yet! He could still be standing there trying to trick us into thinking he left! He does shit like that, don't trust him!" I screamed in my mind.

Thankfully, she didn't move. We lay that way for what seemed like hours until I thought to act as if I was rolling over toward the door in my sleep to try to catch a glimpse of whether he was standing there.

He wasn't.

But I still couldn't take my chances to whisper over to Karen. He could still be standing on the other side of the door waiting and listening for us to talk, so I said nothing.

Soon, daylight streaked through the room in panels of light on the floor. We woke up, looking at each other, realizing that even in the midst of being terrified we had fallen asleep.

As we rolled up our sleeping bags and got ready to go outside, I said, "Don't say a word. We'll talk later."

She nodded in agreement and we went to my room at the other end of the house and got dressed for the day.

After breakfast, we went outside and walked down the street as far as we could, stopped and perched ourselves up on a fence.

It was quiet for a few minutes and then Karen broke the silence.

"No offense, but I don't think I want to spend the night anymore. Maybe you can stay at my house instead from now on," she said.

I nodded, looking down at my swinging feet.

"I don't blame you. I was hoping you wouldn't talk last night. I wasn't sure he was out of the room," I said as I looked over at her with a furrowed brow from the light of the day. "I know this sounds nuts but I was sending you telepathic messages to act like you were asleep," I added.

"I worried about that cigarette you flicked in the yard. Wondered if it was still smoking or lit," she said.

"Me too! Oh my God, I know! I was hoping it went out. He didn't say anything about it this morning so I think it was out," I said.

"Don't you have to pick up the butt?" she asked.

"Nah, he'll just think it's one of his. I stole it from his pack. He's trying to quit so I'm going to have to get cigarettes from somewhere else now."

We both stared out over the road into the trees before us in silence, feeling the warmth of the sun warming up our backs.

She was the first one to speak.

"Somehow I think that cigarette is the least of your problems, Robin. I worry for you. Your dad is what my mom calls a deranged pervert."

"I know. My own mother calls him that. She told me he liked young girls and she and my cousins joke about him finding his next girlfriend in an elementary school playground. My mom told me it wouldn't surprise her at all if he ever tried to force himself on me," I said.

"Your mother said that to you?" Karen asked.

"Yeah, she doesn't care what she says to me or around me or how it makes me feel. It scares me, but what can I do?" I said.

"Don't visit him anymore!" she said.

"Yeah. I'm not allowed to make those choices," I said. Even though up to that point, the thought never crossed my mind.

I couldn't bring myself to think he would do anything to me. He was my dad. But my uncle was my uncle and that didn't stop him.

It was all so confusing and terrifying.

Chapter 22

It wasn't long after we both recovered from chicken pox that my mom decided we were moving to Lakewood, Ohio, so she could be with her boyfriend Wayne.

I had no idea, but my dad did. He let me visit the whole weekend with him and didn't say a word to me until Sunday evening before my mom came to pick me up.

"Dad, can I just stay here? Please! I don't want to go with Mom. I don't want to live in Cleveland, I'll hate it there!" I said.

"I know, but you can't stay here. With me working shifts, you can't be here all hours of the day and night by yourself," he said.

"I won't be in the way, I promise. I won't ask for anything and I won't be a bother. You won't even know I'm here. I'll do all the chores and earn my keep like you always say, o.k.?"

"No, now you gotta go with your mom. Girls belong with their mothers, you know that," he said.

"But, Dad, please. All she does is move and date losers. I just want to stay at one school until I graduate and I hate her boyfriend Wayne," I said.

And even though he chuckled, he said, "Robin, please don't make this any harder than it already is. I know it doesn't sound fair, but your mother and I already discussed this."

"Dad! You're supposed to talk to me! To ME!" I said, crying and pleading.

"Now, stop it. I made you a bite to eat before you leave. Just get your stuff from your room, put everything in these trash bags and come eat. They'll be here around 5:30," he said as he turned and walked out of my room.

"I don't want to go, Dad! Please don't make me go! You love me! I know you do!" I yelled after him.

But he didn't return and didn't answer whether he loved me or not. It was final. I was going with her whether I wanted to or not. And this time, instead of taking just my clothes, I had to pack my whole room because God only knew how long it would be before I'd be back.

My heart sank, and I felt my stomach churn like I was going to be sick. I sat up against the dresser and looked around my room in disbelief that this was happening.

What did I do to be kicked out of my home? Why did my dad hate me so much? I thought of how useful I'd been. I mowed the grass, burned the trash, did the dishes and I cooked, baked and helped with my brother.

I pulled the overly stuffed garbage bags down the hallway, sat them up against the back of the couch in the living room and sat down at the dining room table.

I bent over the plate on the table, holding my head with my hands at the sides of my temples. "I'm not hungry, but thanks," I said.

"Suit yourself. But you have a three-hour drive ahead of you, so if you don't, you'll be hungry later."

I didn't eat.

Instead, I put my sandwich and chips in plastic bags and put the bags in a brown paper lunch bag. I looked out the window above the kitchen sink as I was rinsing my cup to see my mom and Wayne pulling up in the driveway in Wayne's brown Jeep. I ran to the bathroom and got sick. Outside the bathroom I could hear them come in the house.

"Harland, this is Wayne. Wayne, Harland," my mom said.

"Nice to meet ya," he said. "She's not happy about it, but she'll get over it," my dad added with a chuckle.

"Where is she? Is she ready?" my mom asked.

"She's in the bathroom, she should be out in a minute. She didn't want her dinner, so she packed it in a lunch bag for later," my dad said.

"Good, cuz we're not stopping," my mom said.

I don't know why I thought I could talk some sense into them, but I tried when I came out of the bathroom. Quietly at first, then more loudly, pleading for someone to please listen.

"Hi, Mom. Hi, Wayne," I said.

"Well, get your stuff and let's go." Wayne motioned to the garbage bag with his head.

"I don't want to go. Please. I want to stay here. But, even if Dad doesn't want me," I quickly added, "then how about I stay with Aunt Della?" I bargained. "I could just finish school here?"

"Nope. We're not havin' any of this now," my mom said as she motioned with her hand across her neck. "We don't have time for it, Robin Lynn, we need to go," she said.

"But, Mom, you never listen to me. It's all about you and what you want. All I want to do is stay in one place and graduate from the school I go to now." I said.

"Get your stuff and get in the car. Now," she said louder.

"No. I won't. I'm sick of you and I'm sick of how you never care about me," I said defiantly.

Wayne flew around the side of the counter, his eyes wide with anger. He grabbed me by my arm yanking me over to the door. I sat down on the floor defiantly and refused to move. Wayne kept pulling and tugging at me to stand, but I wouldn't.

"That's it! I'm not going!" I announced. "And you're not gonna make me! You're not my dad and you can't touch me!" I said as he was trying to get hold of my flailing arms and legs.

I looked over at my dad who was just standing there watching my mom's boyfriend do this to me in his house.

"Dad! Why are you letting him do this to me!" I yelled at him.

"You gotta go. I'm sorry, but you have to, don't make it harder on yourself now, just do as he says," he said with tears in his eyes.

My mom picked up my bags and Wayne dragged me to the car by one arm and one leg down the hill to the driveway.

I was pushed in the back seat of his brown Jeep behind the driver's seat. Wayne got in the driver's seat and slammed his door.

My mom threw the garbage bags in the back seat with me from the other side and slammed the door and got in the front passenger seat and slammed hers.

She turned around, out of breath, and said, "You really know how to make a spectacle of yourself for Christ's sake."

"Mom, I don't want to live with you in Cleveland! Please! Why can't you listen to me?" I cried. "I just want to stay here with my friends!"

Wayne turned around in his seat to face me and brought down the back of his closed right fist across the middle of my face.

I screamed as blood shot out of my nose and mouth.

"You know, Robin Lynn, you just have to go and make things worse, don't you?" she said as she handed me a tissue.

I coughed up a dark red blood clot in the tissue and bright red blood spewed from my nose.

As we pulled away, I turned to see my dad standing in the glass sliding door and he quickly disappear behind the curtains.

At the end of Manner Ridge when we could go left, and down Washington Pike to go to Cleveland or right to my aunt Della's house on Parson's Run Road, we turned right.

"We're gonna have to stay there tonight till she calms the hell down," my mom said to Wayne.

I was sweaty and exhausted from fighting and blood smeared my face.

As we drove down the dirt road to my aunt's house, my mom kept looking in the back seat at me and handing me tissues to spit the large amounts of red blood that continued to spew from my nose and mouth. I coughed and gagged and cried.

"Robin Lynn, when someone asks about your nose, you can tell them you brought that shit on yourself, you hear me?" she said.

I shook my head no as I continued to spit up blood and glare right back at Wayne who was staring at me from the rearview mirror. I didn't care if he killed me. I wasn't agreeing to that.

I couldn't help but notice my nose was swelling rapidly and it looked crooked to me now.

"I'm never gonna hear the fucking end of this one," my mom said to Wayne.

I stormed up the stairs to my aunt's house and went in first.

"What the hell happened to your nose, Robin Lynn?" my aunt Della asked immediately.

ROBIN DONNELLY

"Wayne backhanded me in the face for not wanting to go to Cleveland, but my mom wants me to tell you I brought that shit on myself," I said.

I defiantly walked to the start of the long hallway leading to my aunt Della's bedroom, stopped and turned around to glare at them where I stood. I knew he'd not touch me at her house.

"Is that true, Starlah Jean?" my aunt asked.

"Yes, it's true, but she"... My mom trailed off as if not knowing where to start. "Della, you weren't there... the way she talks to me, to both of us," she added quickly as she was pointing to Wayne.

"I don't care what the hell she did or said, you shouldn't be allowin' no man to hit your kids, Starlah Jean," she said.

"Go back to my bedroom and I'll bring you some ice in a minute," my aunt said to me.

I gave Wayne one last glaring look as he stood sheepishly at the front door of my aunt's house. I snubbed my bloody nose up at him as I turned in a huff and went to her room.

I laid down with the ice pack on my face and cried myself to sleep. And I think it was the first time in my life that I sobbed, feeling all my feelings about it all. I saw it all so vividly, this dysfunction that I lived. How my mom treated me differently than my brother, allowed people to hit me and sided with them, and then told others I brought it on myself. How my dad allowed my mom's boyfriend to waltz into his house and manhandle his daughter and then carry her off down over the hill to the car as I screamed out for him to do something.

The molestation from my uncle had stopped two years before, right after the hot coffee incident, but I was still reeling from it and trying to deal with it without telling someone. I was hurt to the core of my being and cried myself to sleep.

Later that evening, I awoke to the sounds of talking in the kitchen. I snuck out of the bed with the baggie that now contained hot liquid and crept up to the door that was cracked. I snuck down the hall I was used to sneaking down and stopped right before the hall entered the living room.

"You can't be allowin' no man to beat your kid like that," I heard my uncle Owen say to my mom.

"And you," he said to Wayne, "should fuckin' know better. You're a fucking cop for Christ's sake! You're gonna get locked up someday for doin' that kind of shit," he warned.

It felt weird that he'd defend me, and it confused me. He was convincing himself he was the good guy and nothing bad had happened here. He was announcing here in front of this police officer and everyone listening that he was the protector in this house and I was safe. But I knew I wasn't. Hearing him talk like that, I got the sense he was talking to himself. All he was doing was reminding himself that he better not touch me again or he himself might just get locked up.

Part 5

Lakewood, Ohio

Chapter 23

The first day of school at Horace Mann was one of the scariest times for me. Moving to Lakewood, Ohio, to a girl from Wellsburg, West Virginia, seemed bigger than life and I'd never felt more alone than I did there.

"Mom, they need you to come to the school with me, I can't just enroll myself," I said.

"Sure you can, you're a big girl. I'm tired," she said from her bedroom.

"Mom, they need my records from my last school and you need to sign papers and stuff," I said.

"Just tell them the address of your last school and they can send for the stuff they need. Bring home any paperwork I need to sign. Go," she said.

I didn't think about it much after that. I found if I thought too much about things, anxiety got the best of me and pretty soon I wouldn't be able to do whatever it was I was about to do. Off the cuff was much better. No time to think. It was how I learned to face difficulty and do scary things. Hard front, soft back, my aunt would say.

I walked down sidewalks that lined the busy city streets and passed groups of kids walking together that morning. This was all new to me. I'd never walked to school before. Never been to a big city.

Upon entering the large red brick school, I looked for the office down both sides of the hall. It was down to the right with a small, metal arrow sign above the door that said "office." I walked right in, head held high. "Like a Jessup would have," my dad would say.

"Hi, I'm new here and I need to enroll myself in this school," I said confidently to the lady sitting behind the desk.

"Um... well, honey, is your mother with you?" she asked, looking behind me.

"No, she couldn't come today, she's been sick with the flu," I said.

"Aw, well... this is very unusual. Let me get you in to talk to the assistant principal. What is your name, sweetie?"

"Robin," I said.

She disappeared behind the partition for a minute and returned with him peeking around the side of the half wall, motioning to me with his finger to come with him.

"So, Robin, you're new here?" he said.

"Yes I am."

"Where'd you move from?" he asked as he walked to and sat down at his desk.

"Rabbit Hill," I said. "In West Virginia," I added quickly.

"Well, Robin from Rabbit Hill, do you have any paperwork from your last school, perhaps some transcripts?" he asked.

"No, I don't. Like I told your secretary here, my mom's been sick with the flu and told me to have you send for them and then send any paperwork home for her to sign."

"I see," he said as he rubbed his chin with his index finger and thumb.

He tilted his head, looked out the window and pursed his lips to the side like he was thinking.

"Well, I can't say I've ever encountered this before."

"Encountered what?"

"A kid enrolling themselves in a school without a parent present," he said.

"Oh," I said as I squirmed in my seat.

"I'm going to go get a new student packet and I'll be back in a minute," he said raising his index finger.

I sat there and looked out the big window that his desk sat near. It looked out onto the front parking lot of the school and some homes that lined that street.

I heard whispers around the half wall about the girl who was trying to enroll herself in school without a parent.

He peeked his head around the wall.

"Honey, you wouldn't happen to have a phone number to your last school, would you?"

"No, I don't, sorry," I said.

"Can you tell me the name of the last school you attended, then?"

"Wellsburg Middle School in Wellsburg, West Virginia," I said.

"Ah! Now we're gettin' somewhere," he said as he smiled at me and disappeared around the wall again.

The bell rang and the halls swelled with the echoes of kids talking and laughing, metal lockers opening and closing. And, like clockwork, it all suddenly ended and became quiet again after the second bell sounded.

He came back and sat at his desk with the large packet of papers.

"Well, there are quite a few papers here to fill out, but let's just see what we can fill out here and what can be taken home," he said.

I heard the secretary on the phone calling information for the number to Wellsburg Middle School. My heart sank knowing this was real now. In a few minutes, I would no longer be going back to my old school with my old friends. It was scary, but I also hoped this was the end of the Candice's of the world and kids that were cruel to those who didn't have what they did.

The man was writing some things down as I heard the secretary speaking.

"Yes, hello. I'm calling from Horace Mann Middle School in Lakewood, Ohio. We're here with a Robin Jessup who is trying to enroll herself in our school today and she doesn't have any transcripts or school records or a parent with her. I was wondering if you could help me out?"

"Mmmhmmm. I see," she said.

"You didn't know…" she trailed off.

"Oh, that's too bad. It all makes sense now," she said.

"Well, yes, can you please send what you have to our address here and we'll take it from there. And thanks again," she said before hanging up.

"Ok, here ya go, kiddo. Just fill in your part here," he said, pointing to the top of the form. "Just full name, address, phone number, birth date and social security number." he said. "I'll be back."

I filled in the top of the paper as he excused himself. I could hear them talking around the corner again.

"They didn't know she was moving?" I heard him say in a low voice.

"Yeah, apparently the mother is a real winner," she said. "The person I spoke to said she is barely passing any of her classes, almost falls asleep in class and they think there may be..." She trailed off into a whisper.

I acted like I was still writing as he came back around the corner.

He sat down with a bounce in his big leather chair and smiled at me across the desk.

"All done, honey?" he asked.

"Yes," I said as I pushed the paper back across the top of the shiny wood.

"O.k., these are for your mother to fill out. And this half green sheet right here is a form for reduced lunches... you know... if you need those," he said, holding up the paper for me to see.

"O.k," I said, hoping I didn't still need to stand in that line.

I pushed all the papers in my book bag and waited for more instruction.

He pulled out a big book and started shuffling through the pages. Forward then back.

After some careful deliberation, he said, "Looks like... I'll put you in Ms. Parrish's class. I think you'll like her," he said without looking up from the book.

He pushed a small piece of paper marked "hall pass" with her name and room number on it to me.

"O.k. You go out the door, hang a left and when you come to the first hall, turn right. She's that first door on your right," he said.

"Thank you," I said.

"She'll assign you someone to pal around with for the first few days and they can help you find a locker and everything else, sound good?" he said as he got up and patted me on my shoulder.

"Sounds good," I said as I mustered a smile.

I walked out of the office and stopped. I turned around before heading left just in time to see him standing next to the secretary, talking. She was standing there with her hand over her mouth, looking disgusted, and shaking her head as they continued to discuss this situation.

I took off down the hall toward my class.

I tried to be hopeful that the new school, in a new state, would indeed be a new beginning. I hoped my mom would be more of a mom here, maybe I'd make new friends… and once she got her rest, things would be good.

But right now, I needed to stop off at the bathroom on the way to Ms. Parrish's class to be sick.

I got myself together and knocked on the rectangular glass window that had a metal crisscross screen between the two panes of glass in the wooden door. The teacher and I made eye contact and she waved me in while she kept talking.

I walked down the left side of the room and up to where she was sitting on her desk and handed her the note.

She stopped talking to read the note and then pointed me to an empty seat near the back of the room. She went right on with her speech about what she expected of her class and continued to go down the list of rules on the blackboard.

Finding your seat in a new school was like walking the gauntlet; you're eyed all the way by everyone in the class. And it may as well be in slow motion because it seemed to take forever to reach the back of the room. I sat down and looked straight ahead at the board trying to ignore the eyes.

They were on rule number seven by the time I got there, which was: "Parents must sign your homework every night."

I knew right then, I had to get better at forging my mother's signature.

Rule #8 was: "no lying."

At the end of class I was waved up to the front.

"Karen, this is Robin. She's a new student here from West Virginia. Can you please escort her around today?" she asked.

"Sure," she said.

"Another Karen," I thought. But this Karen was a chunky girl with long, dark black hair that went down her back and black plastic glasses that slid down her skinny nose. We were the same height.

She was nothing like my friend Karen back in West Virginia, who was tall and thin and beautiful and nice and who was going to be a dancer one day and who... I already missed like crazy. And who didn't even know where I was.

"Show her where her locker is, the lunchroom, introduce her to some of your friends, you know what to do... make her feel welcome," she said.

"Hi, Robin."

"Hi, Karen," I said awkwardly.

"Can I see your schedule?" she asked.

I fished the papers out of my folder, found a class schedule and handed it to her.

"Looks like we have lunch together but not much else. Did you pick these classes yourself?"

"Pick them? No."

"Did you get to pick your classes where you used to go to school?"

I shook my head no.

"Well, here we get to pick the classes we want to take."

I was amazed at this new way of attending school. Walking to school, picking your own classes, it all seemed so grown up.

"You're in all different classes than me. See?" She pointed to the schedule.

"Third period, Remedial Math with Mr. Mannuso," she said.

"I hate math," I said.

"That might be why you're in a remedial class." She giggled.

I giggled too, not knowing what the word remedial meant.

Later, in English class when we were told the rules of the class, one of them was: "The Teacher will Not Tell you the Definition of a Word, You will Look it Up in the Dictionary." The kids all balked at that and rolled their eyes saying how in the world could you look something up, if you didn't know how to spell it.

So, during silent reading that day, I mustered up enough courage to get up and walk to the front of the class to get one of the red dictionaries that sat lined up on a metal cart in the front of the room.

The teacher looked pleased as he smiled at my eagerness.

I scrolled to the R's to find the word remedial. It meant, "intended as a remedy or to cure." Cure me of what, I thought.

I ran my finger further down the definition of the word remedial. "Provided or intended for students who are experiencing learning difficulties," it said.

Learning difficulties? I thought.

I was humiliated.

I got through my first day of a new school and walked home with this new Karen. She lived only a few streets away from where I was staying and although she was nice, we were just too different to be good friends. We not only had different classes, but different maturity levels. She thinking it was her that was more grown because she was in more advanced classes. And me being smart enough to know better than that.

When I got home I gave my mom the papers to fill out and stressed to her that I needed them for tomorrow.

She was up out of bed when I got home from school, which was different than usual and was cleaning the duplex we were staying in.

After she finished cleaning she asked, "So what do you want for dinner?"

I was surprised by the question.

"Uh… I don't know, what do we have?" I asked

"Well, I could make macaroni and cheese with hot dogs or I could make Spaghetti E.oi. with a salad," she said.

"Spaghetti E.oi, and salad," I said.

Spaghetti E.oi was like fancy buttered noodles. It was cooked spaghetti noodles with an oil-based, egg and garlic sauce. Once the pasta is cooked and drained, you pour two raw eggs on top of the cooked noodles and pour the hot oil over. The heat of the burner cooks the eggs into a white scrambled egg as you pull and part through it with two forks. Its official name was, pasta aglio e. olio, but we pronounced it "I-Oy" because that's how Ricky's Italian mother said it. It's simple, but delicious.

We sat at the table like a family night after night. I liked the new mom I saw. This might just be what she needed to get herself out of the funk she was in. It had been two years since my grandma Jancie passed away and my mom certainly seemed happy enough and was acting much different than she had in the past. Whatever the reason, I wasn't going to question it. And even though I hated Wayne, I was going to just sit here and soak in all the newfound happiness.

I went to bed after doing my homework with a full belly and a shower and didn't have to help take care of my brother. I lay in bed thinking that maybe the past was over and this new chapter was going to be good. I imagined new friends, maybe a boyfriend here someday and graduating from this school. I was excited for the future. I was smiling and fell asleep that way.

Shortly after starting there, I remember a fall dance I wanted to go to and all the other kids were talking about it. It was held in a large, wooden-floored gymnasium type room on the second floor in an area I had never been in before. And it was in this area that I'd have my first fight at my new school. It was with a girl they called Big Berta, short for Roberta. She was overweight and always looked mad and hot with her fat red cheeks. She had a smaller group of girls that followed her around like baby ducklings follow their mother. She bossed them around and they did whatever she told them to do. She and I hadn't formally met, I only knew her from her reputation of being mean and watched her stomp around from a distance with her fists clenched.

Some time during the dance, a circle formed around a popular boy named Nick doing some new dance moves called break dancing. As he fell to the floor in what looked like a fit, twisting and turning around and spinning on the floor, we gathered to clap and cheer him on. Sitting in a chair directly behind me, was Big Berta.

Someone tapped me on my shoulder.

"Excuse me, but Berta over there, wants you to move out of her way so she can see Nick dance," said one of her followers.

I turned to see her moving her head about trying to get a better look. When we caught eyes, she motioned with her hand for me to move to the right. To be kind, I moved. When I turned to see if that was good enough, she motioned for me to move back to the left. This went on for several more times and I could never get it right according to Berta. Finally fed up, and without hesitation, I walked right up to her, bent down in her fat face and told her that if she'd get her fat ass up off the chair, others wouldn't have to move so she could see and I walked back to the circle.

It wasn't long after that and she had three of her girls huddled around her telling them what I said. They were all listening to her story as they stared over at me. I turned to ignore them and continue clapping for Nick.

At one point during the dance, Big Berta made her way to the semicircle and pushed me in my back. As I turned to face her, her friends were cheering her on to beat my ass. My mom used to tell me, the bigger they are, the harder they fall. So, I hauled off and shoved this girl with both my hands against her chest with all my might. And with that, Big Berta didn't budge an inch. She just stood there, unfazed, literally unmoved. We stood there, toe-to-toe

and eye-to-eye and after what seemed like forever, she stomped off
with her fat red cheeks and clenched fists.

Shortly after this, we moved back to West Virginia and back to the
trailer that sat empty waiting for us to return to it.

Later, when I told my mom what had happened at the dance, and
how Big Berta just walked away, she said that she was sizing me up,
and just wanted to see what I was made of. When she realized I would
fight her, she backed down. Just a bully. Always better in packs than
they are alone, she said.

What my mom didn't tell me, is that the littler you are, and the
more abuse you take in your life, the less likely you are to take shit
from anyone no matter how big they are or how they fall. Or how
they don't.

Part 6

Rabbit Hill/Manner Ridge Road

Wellsburg, West Virginia

Chapter 24

When I got back home, I excitedly told my dad about Big Berta. "That's my squirrely girl, you're definitely a Jessup," he said proudly.

Our trailer had sat there for months unattended. The grass and weeds grew up so tall they kissed the bottoms of windows. The air inside the trailer was stale, and dead mice dotted the long, hot hallway. When I examined the dead mice, their little tongues were hanging out of their mouths, dead from the heat, my mom said. They must have chewed up through the flooring and made their way in, she added.

I cleaned my room first. Then I helped clean up the rest of the place. I hoped my mom wouldn't start crying and laying in bed all day like she did before. For now she was energetic and happy to be back here and away from Wayne.

I'd take it. I was happy too.

In between cleaning and getting settled, I'd hear my mom talking on the phone to my aunt like old times. Visitation that stopped while away, was now back in force and things were back to my normal. This time, my mom sounded different.

"No man is going to beat my children like that," she said, standing with her hand on hip talking on the phone.

"Yeah, it was awful to see her like that. He can do whatever he wants to do, but he's not going to talk his way back in my life after that."

"This time's going to be different though," she said. "I'm a lot stronger than I was then and I can handle it."

From what I could piece together from the one-sided conversation, I'd apparently taken a beating from her boyfriend so horrendous I didn't even remember it.

Soon, we had the trailer cleaned top to bottom, she got her brother to sickle down the tall grass before cutting it with the mower and life in the trailer started to take shape, and there was music filling the house again. It was filled with music from the Eagles, Boston, Fleetwood Mac, and Foreigner. I could talk with my mom and feel like I was heard. And, I wasn't spending my life in my room.

I loved having a strong mother who defended me. I loved hearing her be tough, defiant and independent and I loved that she was taking care of herself and us. I prayed at night Wayne would just stay away for good and never call or come around again, maybe even die.

When my dad started to date Tammy, he wooed her with gifts of jewelry, clothes, art, beautiful porcelain statues of fancy birds and cockatiels, and a new puppy; a black and brown Yorkshire terrier. I don't recall its name but the poor thing couldn't lay eyes on my dad without peeing where it stood.

Tammy was beautiful. She was short but voluptuous, with long flowing golden brown hair down her back. She waitressed downtown Follansbee at the Anchor Room and wore the short nautical outfit that fell just below her butt crease. It was navy blue with two rows of gold buttons up the front and she wore a small red and white satin handkerchief tied in a bow on her neck.

I'd watch her get ready for work, which took her hours. She'd carefully apply her makeup at the vanity in the bathroom, dry her hair by flipping it around mostly to air-dry, then finishing it off with the blow dryer. When she was completely done with her hair and makeup, she'd come out from my dad's bedroom in her uniform wearing tan pantyhose and her tiny, size six black patent leather open-toed high heels. She always smelled of Opium perfume.

My dad would walk her down the big hill to the driveway to her car so she wouldn't fall, her holding on tightly to his arm, them giggling all the way.

She had two boys, Ronnie and Roger. Ronnie was my age, same grade and was taller than me with dark black hair and was overweight. Roger was a few years younger than us and was short, thin and blond. I liked them both.

Things were nice, we all got along great and my dad seemed happy. He was proud of her and liked showing her off to people. The neighborhood boys could barely contain themselves when they saw her in her sexy uniform and did anything and everything they could do to visit while she was there.

She was always laughing and didn't need to act sexy or seductive, she already was, just by being. She was glamorous and cute at the same time. It didn't take me long to see that it was only sometimes that she thought she was pretty and worth something more. I'd catch it when watching her get ready for work. She'd admire her body and face, sometimes her lean legs in the mirror, but would quickly act as if she wasn't anything but plain and wasn't too bright when she caught you looking.

Once, she innocently came out of the bathroom with just a white towel on her head and one around her body. She walked out toward the den we were all sitting in to ask my dad a question and stopped short on the step, where one of the neighbor boys sat. After he answered, she turned and walked away not thinking much more about it. I could tell by her reaction she had no idea what she'd just done.

Later, my dad beat her in the middle of the living room in front of all three of us kids for allowing that boy to stare straight up her towel. He accused her of sending seductive messages to underage boys and being too seductive. He called her a whore and warned her that if it ever happened again, there would be trouble that she and her pretty little face would not soon forget.

At first, my dad would hold the new puppy he bought for her. Cuddle with it, take it outside, try to teach it tricks.

As the months passed and she continued to work, leaving her boys and her puppy there because I was there, it seemed all hell broke loose.

"Look at this," he said, as he grabbed the dog by the scruff of the neck and held it up high.

"Dad! What're you doing?" I screamed as the dog yelled.

"Anyone for a game of tennis?" he said as he heaved the dog across the room with one hand. It hit up against the wall on the other side of the living room.

"DAD!" I screamed. "Oh my God!"

I went over to pick up the dog and it laid there yelping.

"Don't you dare touch that fucking dog!" he screamed at me.

I backed away.

Its leg was obviously broken and I was crying and screaming for him to stop.

He picked it up, walked back across the room to where he was the first time and threw it one more time, this time even harder. It landed with another yelping scream.

"DAD! NOOO! WHAT ARE YOU DOING!" I screamed.

"I'm not taking this little fucker pissing in my house one more second!" he yelled.

He went over and picked it up by the scruff of its neck and headed out the back sliding door with it. He was headed to the only tree stump in the yard and lying next to it was a hatchet.

I followed yelling, "What are yooooou DO-ing!? Why are you doing this?!" I screamed.

"I'll show you what I'm gonna do!" he said as he picked up the hatchet.

"NOOOOOOO! STOP!" I screamed until I tasted blood in my throat. I watched his right hand raise up and start to cut the air as he forcibly held the squirming and screaming dog's body across the stump with his left.

Without another thought, I ran out and pushed him away from the dog and grabbed it from his grip.

I ran and ran holding onto the dog until I finally stopped a few houses down at a neighbor's house and knocked on the door. "Please, hurry! Let me in!" I yelled.

"Hurry! My dad's gone mad and almost killed this dog," I said to the lady who answered the door. "Its leg is broken and I need help. Can I please use your phone?"

The lady dialed the phone and handed it to me as she wrapped the yelping dog in a towel.

"Tammy, you gotta get home, now!"

"Why?" she asked.

"Dad's gone nuts and almost killed the dog for peeing on the floor!" I yelled into the receiver of the phone.

"What? He just called here. He told me to expect a call like this from you."

"What?" I was so confused.

"Yeah, he said the dog fell off the couch and he thinks it broke its leg."

"Tammy, you gotta believe me! He did this to your dog, it did NOT fall, he threw it! You gotta get it to a hospital now!"

"O.k. now, calm down, I'll be there in a few minutes," she said.

I can't remember much after this. I had never been so terrified in all my life as I was that day. I'm not sure if I blacked out or what, but I still can't remember this without sobbing and feeling as if someone is tearing my heart out. It feels exactly as it did that day.

I'm not sure how, but my dad ended up with the puppy again, taking it to the vet's office. It needed pins surgically placed in its leg in a few different places and needed to wear a tiny little cast. As a way to show Tammy he wasn't the monster I said he was, he got it a playpen and kept it in there when she worked, removing pee pads and putting in clean ones as it soiled the pen.

My dad never spoke of the incident again or even mentioned it to me when we were alone.

It was like it never happened at all.

Eventually, my dad had to pick on someone.

"Watch this," my dad said to me. "Ronnie, Roger, get your asses up!" He covered his mouth with his hand to stifle his laugh like a little kid.

"Dad, it's Saturday, don't —" I said.

"You're gonna stand there and shut your fuckin' mouth!" he said with his finger pointed to the ceiling. "You're just like your fucking mother, always ruining someone's fun... I'm just havin' some good, clean fun," he said as he motioned to backhand me in my face. "Besides, these fuckin' bastards get on my nerves and deserve to be tormented," he said as if he was giving me a legitimate reason for what he was about to do.

The boys came out of the room rubbing their eyes.

"Look at you, Ronnie boy, what a fat ass! Look at all that blubber on you. Whew! You could afford to lose a few pounds, whale," he said. "I'd make whale sounds at you, but what does a whale sound like?" he said laughing.

"You're mean," I said to him.

"Yeah, well... what're you gonna do about it anyway?" he said. "Always so highfalutin, you are. Better than anybody else in the family, always on your high horse," he said as he wrinkled his nose to me as if smelling something bad. "One day someone's gonna come along and knock you off that horse of yours," he warned.

"I'm not highfalutin, I mean, I don't try to be, it's just mean to treat people that way."

He hurried them to the table with bowls filled with cereal and milk.

"Hurry up, the bus will be here in a few minutes," he said.

He looked at me across the room and eyed me that I better not say one word to them or else.

They wolfed down the cereal, grabbed their backpacks and walked down the dirt driveway to stand and wait for the bus at the mailboxes at the end of the drive.

My dad stood there watching from the bay window, knee-slappin', gut-wrenching laughing, with tears coming out his eyes, that he had convinced them there was school today and they were going to be late. He let them stand there long enough for me to empty out the milk from the bowls and wash, dry and put them away.

I watched out the window, seeing them both stand there and my heart felt sad for them. Their mom was at work and they were left alone with my dad to do this sort of shit to them.

"Dad," I said.

He looked at me and said, "Yeah, I'll go get them and tell them it was a god damned joke. You gotta ruin all the fuckin' fun around here all the time, don't ya?" he said as he waved his hand in the air in defeat.

I watched all three of them walk back to the house.

As they walked in the house and Ronnie and I caught eyes, I mouthed the word, "Sorry" to him.

"Now go put your book bags in your room and then get out here when you're done."

"What're you gonna do now?" I asked.

"That fat-ass Ronnie needs to get in shape," he said. "I think it'll do him good to run laps around the house for awhile, you know... get in shape like me," he said as he puffed out his chest and patted his flat stomach.

"Dad. Why're you doing this?" I asked.

"Shut your god damned mouth! I'll do whatever the hell I damn well please in my own house," he said.

"Ronnie," he said as he put his hand on his shoulder, "I'm going to do you a favor. You may hate me for it now, but when you're older, you'll thank me. But I want you to go out there and run 30 laps around the house. Run like your life depends on it, Ronnie! You need to lose some of that blubber on you, boy." He smacked at his stomach.

Ronnie went outside with his face red, humiliated, and Roger and I followed. We both started running around the house with him. Ronnie was winded, red-faced and soaked with sweat within half a lap around the house, panting and gasping for breath, unable to talk. Roger and I ran right alongside him, coaching him every step of the way.

My dad sat on the front step of the house and every time we came around that side of the house, he'd yell another insult at him.

"Come on, Ronnie boy, you can run that fat ass of yours right on around the house. Keep going." As we neared the front step where he sat to make one lap, he yelled, "Only 29 more laps to go!" and he would laugh hysterically.

"Ronnie, don't listen to him, he's nuts," I said.

"Yeah," said Roger.

"Just pretend you're in a movie and you're doing this because you want to," I said.

As we rounded the house again, my dad made pig noises at him.

"Come on, my fat little buddy, only 28 more laps, you can do it!" he yelled. "Maybe this will make you stop stuffing your fuckin' face with food all the time, you fuckin' fat lard ass."

We'd round the house again.

"I'm gonna wake you up every morning at 5 a.m. like they do in the Army and get your fat ass out here to run laps around the house until you start to lose that baby fat, you hear me, Ronnie boy?" he yelled after him.

Ronnie couldn't respond. He slowed to a fast walk.

"Don't you dare stop, Ronnie, or I'll tack on another 30 laps," he yelled to him.

"Don't stop, Ronnie," I said.

"Yeah, don't," Roger warned.

"One more lap you fat pig, one more!" my dad yelled.

As we rounded the house for the last time, my dad yelled, "30!"

My dad came up to him as if he was greeting an old friend.

"How'd that feel, Ronnie? You feel nice and warmed up now? Why don't we go on a jog down the ridge now or are you too tired, you fat slob?"

There was no answer from Ronnie as my dad put his arm around his neck like they were buds.

"Ah... go on now and take a shower, and don't forget to use soap when you clean that fat ass of yours. Anyways, I'm just kiddin' around with you, don't be such a sore loser," he said as he pushed him away.

Ronnie came out later still red-faced from the run but clean with wet hair and smelling of soap.

"You o.k., Ronnie?"

"Yeah, I'm alright."

"I'm sorry he treats you guys like that."

"It's not your fault," he said.

"Ronnie, I would tell your mom what my dad does to you and your brother when she's not around," I said.

"Yeah, I think I'm going to."

"If you don't, I will," Roger said.

"Whatever you do, don't tell her I said to tell her, my dad would kill me," I said.

"I won't," Ronnie said.

During one of their volatile fights, my dad grabbed two expensive porcelain statues he bought for her and smashed them both together right in the middle of the living room. Shards of glass flew far and wide. He stood there with both his hands cut and bleeding, screaming, "That right there… THAT is what I'm going to do to your fucking head the next time I catch you flirting with anybody, you got that!" She sat there on the couch and recoiled from his rant saying nothing. She shielded her head as he got down in her face and screamed within inches of her ear.

He made her get on her hands and knees and pick up all the broken pieces of glass as she cried.

He left for work that night and told her that she had better be there when he got home or else he'd hunt her and her fucking kids down and kill them all.

We all got in the same bed that night. No one slept.

"Do you believe me now?" I asked.

"I do. He used to just be moody, and jealous — but the dog — and now these threats," she said, "has gotten out of hand. I won't live like this or have my kids subjected to his abuse."

"I'm not trying to cause problems for you two but he's got a screw loose." I motioned a clockwise motion around my temple with my index finger.

"You ain't kiddin'," she said.

"What're you gonna do?" I asked.

"I'm gonna have to get an apartment of my own and move out one day when he's not home," she said, "and then we're outta here."

"Mom," Ronnie said, "let's just go now. I hate him and I hate it here."

"Yeah, me too," said Roger.

"I hate both my parents," I said. "I wish I could just run away from both of them and live on my own. Maybe I could live with you guys?" I asked.

The Steubenville Bridge came to me in my sleep often during this time of terror. I'd sometimes go ages without so much as a nudge from her. Then sometimes I'd dream of her for weeks on end.

Sometimes I was approaching the bridge on foot in the middle of the night. In my dream I was determined to leave and find a place of my own to live on the other side of the bridge. When I got up to the pedestrian walkway on the side, I'd walk on it only to get halfway across and come to an area of missing walkway and have to jump. The jolt from the sensation of falling would wake me up and I'd be drenched in sweat.

Sometimes, I'd dream that I got to the other side of the bridge and was out looking for an apartment to rent and was trying to explain to people that yes I was a kid, but I couldn't live with my dad or my mom anymore and could they just please let me stay there till I found a job. I woke up once yelling, "Please!" drenched in sweat.

Soon after the night of being huddled together in bed, Tammy and her boys moved out and got their own place, but she still dated my father, which I never understood. She'd come over for dinner from time to time whenever I was around for visitations and my dad would be on his best behavior. He'd be overly nice to the boys, putting on his best show to woo her back, and we'd all eat at the dinner table like a nice normal family. Other times, they'd still fight, she'd storm out and it would be over yet again.

When it was over, my dad would sit for hours in front of her new place, watching where she went, who came, who went, where and what time. He called it "casing the joint." He recorded it all in a little notebook he kept in his car. I'd overhear him bragging how he'd recite to her when she answered the phone, all she did that day, and with whom. He'd laugh hysterically as he talked about imagining her just standing there listening on the other end of the phone. Too afraid to speak, looking like a deer in headlights wondering who was tipping him off to her whereabouts. He bragged to someone on the phone how he pranked her in the middle of the night and would whisper, "I'm gonna kill you."

On weekends with my dad, I started going over to her new apartment instead to be with her and her boys. Then one day, it was as if she didn't like me at all, she just turned on me and no longer wanted me around. But she came over to my dad's house one last time.

"What did I do? What did I do?" I screamed.

"Who do you think you are flippin' people off?"

The thick black military belt struck my back with laser precision. I screamed in pain.

"I didn't flip anyone off!"

"Pull your fucking pants down, you hear me... pull your god damned pants down!"

"Nooooooo! I screamed. Just spank me on my pants! Who did I flip off? Tell me! Who?"

As I turned, I could see Tammy standing in the hallway, watching.

"Tammy! Help me!" I called out to her.

She stood there with her hand over her mouth crying but didn't move.

He struggled with my pants and managed to pull them down to my ankles from behind. But that wasn't good enough. My underwear had to come down too and I was humiliated. He made me hold on to the bedpost as he whipped my bare ass. I winced and braced myself as the belt cut the air behind it and struck my lower back and legs. I held onto the footboard of the bed screaming as she watched from the hallway. When he was done, I was told to get my shit and get to my room.

Finally, the whippin' was over and I was sweaty and sticky from crying, but I was safe in my room. I trembled, cried, cussed and wondered what the hell I did to deserve that. The skin down my back and legs burned like fire.

Later the door to my bedroom opened; it was him.

"You," he said as he pointed to me from across the room, "are not to step ONE foot on the floor." He walked slowly around my bed at first, then around the side faster and all at once came right up to my face where I was crouching on the floor.

In a low voice he said, "If I so much as hear a floorboard creek, I will be in to deal with you and I'll tell you right now... if THAT happens... the coroner will think a pack of wild dogs got ahold of you, you got that? You get your fucking pajamas on and get to bed, you hear me?" he said crouching down in my face.

"Yes," I said, "I hear you."

"Yes, you hear me, what?" he said.

"I don't know what you mean, Dad," I said trembling.

"I don't know what you mean," he mocked in a girly voice. "You don't know what I mean?" he said. "SHE doesn't know what I mean!" he said as he bent backward looking at my bedroom ceiling.

He went back to the low whisper voice. "When you address me. You will call me sir. Do you hear me?" he said with his face shoved into mine.

"Yes sir," I said.

"Yes sir, what?" he asked.

"Yes, I hear you, sir?"

"It's not a fucking question!" he screamed as he pushed me backwards. Say it!"

"Yes, I hear you, sir!" I said loudly.

"Now say it like you mean it!" he yelled.

"YES, SIR! I hear you, SIR!" I yelled as loud as I could.

A few hours later, I had to pee. I called out the crack of the bedroom door to ask if I could go to the bathroom.

"Go piss then get your fucking ass back in your room and in your bed," he said.

I went to the bathroom. I lifted my pajamas to see the long red welts raised on my back, butt and legs. At some time during my whippin' the buckle had slammed into my spine and had left a raised lump that was turning purple.

I didn't eat supper and didn't get to shower before bed.

"Look at you... you look like something the cat dragged in," someone said as the whole bus broke into laughter.

"Nice hair!" someone yelled from the back of the bus.

"Yeah, and it looks like you were crying," someone said, and then made crying sounds.

"She rides the bus here to her Dad's and then rides the bus out to her mommy's house on Rabbit Hill, why don't you make up your mind where you want to live," someone said.

"Yeah, pick one. Either your drunk, lazy mother or your perverted, psychotic dad that stands naked in front of the window when the bus goes by," someone said from the back of the bus.

I didn't want to go back to my Dad's house that day, I dreaded walking up to the house. I had no idea what to expect after yesterday, so I beelined straight to my room.

I stopped dead in my tracks at the doorway of my bedroom. There on my bed were three brand-new outfits. Three tops, three pairs of pants. I felt him come up behind me in the doorway.

"Oh! You scared me!" I said. "Dad? Whatever I did, I'm sorry, I didn't mean it."

He motioned with his head toward the new clothes lying on the bed.

"I thought you might like those," he said.

"Oh?" I said. "What're they for?"

"Tammy admitted to me this morning, that she lied to me. She said you flipped her off to see if I would take her side over yours.

Seems you were telling the truth after all," he said and he turned and walked away.

I sat on the bed next to the new clothing.

I thought Tammy loved me like her kid but she lied to see if I'd get into trouble. I got beat with a belt as she watched for something I didn't do. I just couldn't take it all in. And, now the older kids were telling me my dad was walking around naked in the window as the bus went by?

My mind couldn't absorb all this.

My dad and Tammy broke up for good after that, but not before he broke out every one of the windows from the little black Pacer she drove with our Great Dane's heavy metal dog chain. I only heard about it from some neighbor kids after talking about the pretty green glass I found in thousands of pieces laying all over the gravel in our driveway.

I eventually had to stop being friends with Tammy's boys and even had to stop babysitting her niece and nephew that lived down the street from my dad. He had her entire family living in fear that he'd kill them all. And he liked it that way. He didn't care who he hurt or how his behavior impacted anyone.

While he was casing her house, pranking her all hours of the night and using threats to continue controlling Tammy and her family from afar, he had started screwing a girl from the neighborhood who was only a few years older than me.

Chapter 25

When my brother was old enough for visitation weekends with my dad, my grandma Edith, my dad's mom, would come to his house to babysit us. My dad didn't want me being responsible for him while he worked and thankfully she agreed to come out and stay for the weekend, because now that I was older, I didn't like going to her house.

My grandma Edith's house was overly warm at all times, and had smells. She wore a heavy Estee Lauder perfume that was the color of maple syrup in the bottle. My grandpap smelled of grease and chewing tobacco and only sponge bathed at the sink in the bathroom. My grandma had a Chihuahua named Pepper and she kept her box of dog biscuits in a stairwell leading up to the attic. The door leading up to the attic was open at all times and was right off the tiny, stuffy kitchen. A small window at the end of the steps allowed the sun to beat in on the box of dog treats, and made the kitchen and stairwell going up to the attic smell of a cardboard, dog biscuit, mothball smell. The further up the steps you climbed the more pungent the smell of must, mildew and mothballs got. The attic was my dad's room when he was a little boy. I remember wanting to see where my dad spent time as a little boy but was never able to fully see what was his bedroom. The darkness of the attic and stacked-up boxes that had long since accumulated, and something I could only describe as the feeling of danger, told me to go back, so I did.

My grandma Edith constantly crocheted, and as she counted stitches under her breath, her lips moved as she silently counted. If you got close to her, you could smell her old-lady breath. When she'd sit me on the floor in front of her, to teach me how to crochet, it was her breath that deterred my learning.

Every night, as a treat to herself, she ate a bowl of vanilla bean ice cream and let her dog Pepper lick the bowl. The dog was so fat it waddled. It slept next to her as she crocheted for its entire life and died from being obese.

When you hugged my grandma, you had to bend over as if hugging a child because she was only four foot nine inches tall. My dad inherited her short height and was only 5'8". It gave him what my aunt Della said was the Napoleon Complex.

At night, the Estee Lauder smell that usually coated my grandma Edith's skin and clothes during the day was replaced with the smell of Ben-gay that burned your eyes when you inhaled around her. She'd bring all her toiletries in a blue train case and slept with a hairnet on.

My grandma's husband, also Harland, was referred to as "Old Man Jessup" around town. He had a white Santa Claus beard that lay just above his large, rounded stomach. Years of chewing tobacco and spitting had left orangey, brown marks around the corners of his mouth. He wore the same gray work pants, brown work boots and white T-shirt stained with tobacco spit down the front all the time I knew him. Supposedly he was a self-made millionaire but loved free things. He'd brag to anyone that would listen about the free ball cap he'd get at the bank, or some free letter opener he scored at a store that day. His car was a 1967 something or other, in the eighties, and when he'd drive out to visit my dad at his house, my dad said it embarrassed the shit out of him.

My grandpap was missing his ring and middle finger on his left hand down to the second knuckle. And because he held a spit cup all the time, it was usually the second thing you noticed about him. The beard being the first, the missing fingers second, his smell, then his beady eyes. My dad had his eyes.

He was never a warm, fun-loving, or a cuddly type of a grandpa and that was fine by me. Once when I was in my twenties, I walked up to him after not seeing him for years. His eyes flew open wide as he came toward me, his arms opening for a hug. When he realized it was me he quickly closed his arms, lowered his eyes and turned and walked away from me in the other direction. He walked in and lovingly greeted my sister-in-law instead, calling her his sweet darling girl just loud enough for me to hear. When I told my dad, he said he'd take care of it and confront him about it, but later explained it away saying that he must be getting dementia.

When my grandma came to the house to babysit, my dad tried to be on his best behavior in front of her. But even when she knew he was doing things he shouldn't be, and was blatantly screwing around with a girl from the neighborhood, Grandma Edith sat there and crocheted and acted like she didn't hear them in the bedroom laughing and carrying on.

I was pissed.

"Grandma, don't you hear Dad in there with her, you know she's underage, right?" I'd say.

"What... I don't hear anything?" she'd say after pretending to strain to listen.

"Grandma. Listen," I'd say, irritated with her.

She'd pretend to listen again.

"Oh that, they're just in there talking. They'll be out in a little bit," she said.

"I'm going to go see what they're doing," I said.

"No, don't bother them, you just sit here and I'll teach you how to crochet," she said.

I loved my grandma, but she had to know her son was up to no good. I mean, I was just a kid and I knew what was going on, there's no way she didn't know.

"Sometimes in life, honey, you just have to learn to pick and choose your battles," she said. Pick and choose your battles. I didn't know how you got to be a person who chose not to see things going on around them and not say anything, or know things are not right and not get up and go do something about them? I knew then and there, I'd never be one of them.

When I told my mom about how she sat there not doing anything, she told me that my grandma Edith had been an abused wife and mother her whole life. She said my grandfather abused her, physically and mentally, and that he allowed his kids to do it too.

She'd been stifled so many times in life and told to shut her mouth, she learned to sit and make herself small, never saying a word. My mom said she crocheted like she did as a way to escape her living hell of a life.

It made me sad to think that my grandmother, who was an independent registered nurse and head nurse of an operating room at the time she met my grandpap, was now reduced to sitting, mindlessly crocheting and counting under her stinky old lady breath to avoid battles she didn't want to face.

I would never be like this, I thought.

Not ever.

Chapter 26

"Hey, do you like this song?" Cindy said as she raised the volume on the large towering stereo behind the glass cabinet.

Cindy was an older girl that lived down the street from my dad's. I didn't realize it then, but Cindy was a good friend to the neighbor girl my dad was screwing around with.

"Oh yeah! Who doesn't?" I said.

It was Rod Stewart's "Do You Think I'm Sexy."

With her eyes squinted in excitement she turned up the volume. Her face scrunched up as she sang to the song and we danced together around her living room.

After the song was over, I asked, "When's your mom comin' back?"

"Not till later, why?"

"Because I wanna have a smoke," I said.

"Sure, let's just go back in my room, we'll blow the smoke out the window."

We thought we were cool. We'd smoke and do our hair in her vanity mirror. It reminded me of when I saw my mom getting ready to go out.

"What're you two doin' in here?" her brother Bubba asked as he barged in.

"Get outta here!" Cindy said as she threw a bed pillow at the door. "He likes you, that's why he's doin' that," she said.

"He's cute," I said.

"Ew. Gross." Cindy said. "Hey, are you going to be at your dad's next weekend?"

"Yeah, why?"

"I thought we could have a pool party at your house." she said.

"Yeah, sure, sounds good to me. Who do you want to invite?" I asked as I curled my hair, not looking at her.

"I was thinking my sister, Becca, you, me and your dad."

I wrinkled my nose.

"And my dad?" I asked.

"Yeah, he's cool. He's like one of us," she said. "You're lucky to have a dad who's that cool who lets you smoke and drink if you want."

"Well, I don't smoke in front of him, but he lets me have beer once in awhile, it's my friends he lets do that stuff."

"Well, still," she said, "my parents suck."

"I think my parents suck," I said back.

"Why?"

"My mom's what my dad calls a nutcase and he's what everyone else calls a perv. They're both too concerned with their own shit to see they have kids."

"Oh, that's too bad," she said.

"He acts cool and hip in front of my friends, but that's just because he's trying to get in my friends' pants. That's what my mom told me," I said.

"Not mine," she said.

"Maybe not yours, but he's definitely screwing around with Carla," I said nonchalantly as I curled my hair in the vanity mirror. "I caught Carla coming out of his bedroom one night when she told her parents she was babysitting me and my brother and she stayed over. My dad snuck home early when I was in bed and didn't think I heard. I caught her in the bathroom with her hair all messed up and lipstick rubbed all over her face."

"What?" she said wide eyed. "So, she's being your friend because she wants to screw around with your dad," she said.

"Yep. I think he has a thing for Leanne down the street and that Holloway girl too, I've noticed. He thinks he's being sneaky but he's so obvious. All those girls are older than me and not even my friend, but he keeps telling me to make friends with them and invite them to sleep over or see if they can babysit overnight."

"Wow. So you think your dad is trying to get you to be friends with the older girls in the neighborhood so he can lure them to bed?" she asked.

"Yep," I said.

"I don't know about the other girls, but Carla is a fucking whore," she said.

"Yeah, well, my dad's the predator and she's a minor," I said. "She's underage and if he ever gets caught he'll be up the river," I said, repeating what my mom said about him. "It pisses me off that she uses me as her friend to sneak around with my dad, and they both act like I'm stupid and don't know what they're doing."

"I think all parents act like their kids are stupid babies. Like we can't put two and two together," she said.

I could put two and two together. I knew what a whore was, and what a predator was, but I didn't know what up the river meant. And, he had a pool so; I knew for sure he could swim.

A few days later, when I walked outside, I found Cindy and Carla sitting on Carla's back porch together. They both looked over at me and then Carla got up and started to walk across the road toward me. When she got up to me she slapped me right across my face.

"I'm not a fucking whore," she said. "You're a little cunt."

My dad watched the whole thing from the sliding glass window. He laughed and said the slap in my face served me right. He was a grown adult and what he did, and who he did it with, was none of my fucking business.

Chapter 27

Eventually, my dad lost interest in following Tammy and camping outside her apartment at night, and he even got tired of screwing around with the neighbor girl. Instead, he found religion to occupy his time and mind, and just like that, all his sins were forgiven and he was a new man.

He was a born-again Christian.

You could not have a conversation with him that he couldn't turn into some lecture about religion. Anything pretty was a gift from God, anything he deemed dark and evil was from Satan. And, oh, how he loved to preach. Now, even things like Halloween that he used to love so much, were off limits and unholy. He no longer put his light on October 31st and refused to acknowledge trick-or-treat calling it devil's night. When I told my mom about it, she said if he would be an expert on anything at all, it would make sense that it would be about the subject he talked about most. Satan.

Before religion, if my dad ran out of Halloween candy, he'd become almost distraught over it thinking he was disappointing the kids. He'd rummage around looking for anything he could give away. Once, after running out of candy, he started giving away those little boxes of cereal that come twelve to a pack. After running out of those he gave away dollar bills from his billfold.

I can still see him in his last-minute homemade costume. A white sheet ripped and pulled down over his head, worn draped from the shoulders down to the floor, and just the leg cut off of a pair of women's panty hose pulled tightly over his head.

When he came out of the bathroom, I asked, "What the heck are you supposed to be? That's not even scary." But he wasn't quite done, he said. He was coming to the kitchen to smear peanut butter all over his face and smash it into a paper plate of Rice Krispies. Doesn't sound like much, but the heat he generated from jumping in and out of all the Fall leaves and bushes made the peanut butter run making him look deformed and burned half alive. He walked by dragging his right foot behind him and arms held out in front of him like Frankenstein, moaning and groaning at the kids.

The peanut butter would become warm and drip slowly down and hang there suspended and sway in long strands as he walked before breaking off completely to the ground, or slide down the front of the bloody sheet.

I can still hear the kids screaming and laughing, leaves rustling, see them running away and then tentatively walking ever so slowly back to the door for their treat, calculating their every step.

What fun he was sometimes.

After religion, anyone who loved it or participated in it was a heathen and was going to hell for their Satanic worship, he said that the night was all about. I learned to equate religion with no fun, no smiling and the seriousness that I just hated. I wondered how anyone recruited people to a religion like that.

He liked to drone on for hours about how God and Satan actually talked daily. He was fascinated with that, and explained to me how Satan used to be an angel but got kicked out of heaven for wanting to take over. He'd tell me that Satan would ask God who he could test that day, and if you were in good with God, you may just get a free pass making Satan move on to someone else.

He would talk about how wonderful it would all be someday to be with the Lord and went into explicit detail about how the streets in heaven were literally lined in gold. He would get a glazed look in his eye describing it like he'd actually been there before and was just recounting it all for me. The sinner.

He read the Bible constantly, preaching that I "better get right with Jesus before it was too late," "respect my elders," and to "honor thy father and mother."

He decorated the house with Jesus pictures everywhere, a Jesus bust with a crown of thorns complete with dripping blood and a Bible was placed in every room. The big thick, family heirloom Bible with gold-edged paper sat on the coffee table. It showed detailed pictures of tormented souls trying to claw their way out of the pits of hell.

I looked through those books for hours on end. Seeing the agony on the faces of the heathens worried me. I couldn't believe it. We have such hell in life only to die and have this kind of agony too? It just didn't seem fair. Some days I felt like the heathens in those pictures just clawing my way through my life and wondering if I'd ever make it out of the pits of this hell. And I didn't find anywhere in any of those Bibles anything about "respecting thy children" because I looked and looked. It didn't say anything about molesting young neighbor girls, calling your daughter a whore, calling people niggers, beating and raping wives and nieces being acceptable behavior, but I was the one that had to get right with the Lord?

"Honor my father and mother, but… what if they act like my parents do?" I asked the bust of Jesus that sat on my dad's curio cabinet.

He didn't answer.

My dad reported that not only was he saved, but he was very highly favored by God.

"So, you can just treat people anyway you want and all you have to do is say a prayer, ask for forgiveness and poof, like some sort of heavenly wizardry, your slate is wiped clean?" I asked.

I lay in my bed at night and wondered how anyone that evil, mean and nasty to people and animals could be favored. It was just beyond me. I just couldn't wrap my mind around any of this. There should be limits to forgiveness, even with God. You shouldn't get to do whatever the hell you want to others then, magically when you pray about it, you're forgiven? If you pass a certain threshold of badness, there should be no more favor, no more passes from prayer just because you ask for it, because you're never going to change. God doesn't change people. People change themselves.

But my dad had a way of convincing people of things. And he convinced me that he was the highly favored one, I was the heathen, and that made me hate God even more.

I inspected the Jesus bust that sat there staring off into space. Blood dripped off the thorns that pierced his forehead and his mouth hung slightly open showing agony and pain. I wondered why in the hell anyone would want to look at something this hideous let alone display in their home. When I looked deep into Jesus' eyes I saw nothing but pain for what he was going through at that moment and highly doubted that he knew about me or even cared about my life.

But, my dad said that he had plans for everyone's life and knew us in our mother's womb before we were even born.

"What about my baby brother Bobby? Did you know him?" I asked Jesus.

Distant and in pain, mouth partly opened, Jesus remained quiet.

As far as I could tell, everything was agony. Evil was agony, but so was Good. Death was agony, but so was Life. There was no way around the pain of agony.

I'd study his bloody face and wondered what plans he had for my life? If he loved me so much and had such great plans for me, why would he give me a dad that would tell me the best part of me ran down the crack of my mother's ass? Why did he tell me I should have been an abortion? Why did this Jesus guy not talk about listening to and respecting children and women in his big rule book on life? If he didn't love me enough to give me an earthly father, how in the world could I believe in a heavenly father, I asked.

If he thought so little of me, of kids in general— then, fuck him, I thought.

So, I turned my nose up to him and his pain like he did mine, and I continued believing in myself instead.

The church life became my dad's life, and he soon became a deacon in the church and it was all he talked about. When I told my mom about it, she laughed and said that, apparently they'd let anyone hold that position then, and said that they'd shit themselves to know they'd let Satan, reincarnated, into their tiny little church.

He did independent Bible study classes at home even on days he went to church and studied into the wee hours of the night.

Long gone was the CB and gold lollipop mic that we used to talk with truckers all over the United States. The small wobbly metal desk of the seventies was replaced with a more scholarly looking wooden rolltop desk now, and the cigarette that would burn down to an ash in the green glass ashtray was replaced with a sucker lying on a coaster when not in his mouth. The new desk was toppled high with Bibles, reference guides, piles of notebooks filled with his frantic writings, pens and highlighters. He was manic about it and he wrote constantly. He was trying to be accepted, he was working to be loved.

And there I stood next to him doing the same.

He would go almost the entire weekend ignoring me on visitation.

"Dad, what're you doing?" I asked.

"Gettin' right with my Lord and Savior," he said. "He's always watching you, you know."

"So, he's like Santa Claus was when I was little?" I asked. "He knows when you've been naughty or nice?"

"Uh. No. Like, this guy is Omnipotent, he's the Alpha and the Omega. It means everything begins and ends with him," he said as he saw the confusion on my face. "He knows exactly what's in our hearts," he said.

Paying attention to his kid wasn't in his heart, paying attention to some guy in the sky that didn't answer was.

When I told my mom about my weekend she said, "Yeah, yeah... gettin' right with the Lord. And learnin' just enough to finagle his way into someone else's pants and her family's hearts all while hiding behind some God." When I asked how she knew all that, she said, "Nothin's private in this podunk town, there are eyes everywhere. I already heard he's on the prowl again."

Lana lived just down the street from my dad and was still young enough to live at home with her parents. She was only five years older than me.

Lana jogged past our house for exercise everyday and that's how my dad first spotted her. When he found out she went to church he about broke his neck to go there too. If he spotted Lana running down the road as he sat in the den, he would quickly run out to the living room and out the front door and sit on the front step as if he had no idea she was coming.

"Oh, hey… how're you?" he'd yell out to her.

I was there the day she mustered up the courage to jog up the hill to talk to him versus her usual wave and smile as she continued on. They stood in the front of the house making small talk, they were both smiling and giggling and sometimes Lana looked down at her feet and swayed back and forth.

I watched out the front bay window from behind the thick rubber-backed curtain.

"Good God in heaven, are you gonna spare this girl the agony of this and be her Savior, Lord, or are you just gonna let this happen?" I asked in a whisper to the window.

Jesus didn't answer me.

And didn't save her.

Chapter 28

I liked Lana instantly. She was a bit taller than my dad, thin, and athletic. She exercised, liked lying in the sun, and swimming like my dad and I did, and we'd both get brown as berries in the summertime. We'd use my dad's homemade suntan oil that was his own concoction of Baby Oil and iodine. You'd have color one way or another with his formula, he said.

She was the first girl I'd ever met who worked in an office. She could actually use the green light, called office on a four-way light-up makeup mirror, but she didn't because she didn't need to wear much makeup. She was a natural beauty, my dad said. The longer they dated and the more he got to know Lana and her family, the more he bragged. He was proud of her, telling anyone who would listen that his new girl was not just a secretary, but the secretary to the president by god, of a major college nearby and what a prestigious job that was. He called her his "Most Precious" after the perfume she wore.

I remember her laughing nervously around him. My dad had a bigger-than-life personality that took up the entire room and only got louder and more obnoxious the more he thought you were entertained by it. She'd turn red in the face from embarrassment and look away.

I'd think about things I saw my dad do, as he stood there trying to woo her with his many jokes where someone else was always the butt and he the hero. He lavished her with admiration and phony baloney praise and later he bought her gifts too. I remember an emerald ring once; her birthday was in May and that was her birthstone. He took me with him to buy it. He was enraged that he couldn't find a clear green stone. When the lady at the counter said that a genuine emerald stone had imperfections in it, he said she obviously didn't know the recipient of said ring and no girl like Lana was going to wear a stone with imperfections in it. He got what he wanted though. A clear, green stone he thought was much prettier even though it was synthetic.

He was either with her, or was busy planning for her visits to the house. Everything had to be in its place and nice for her so she could be comfortable after her long day at work. He was one way with her and another way completely when she wasn't around. My mom called it his Jekyll and Hyde.

He read the Bible, dated Lana and worked like mad to be loved by Jesus and accepted into Lana's family. But there, just underneath the light he was trying to find and beam for all to see, was his darkness. Darkness that he just couldn't outrun or hide for very long.

One night around dusk, after Lana went back home, my dad let our Great Dane, Dana, outside when she spotted an old, one-eyed toad we had that hung around my dad's house for years. We called him Old Mr. One Eye and my dad and I would catch flies for him to eat in the summer as we reminisced about that fat old bullfrog I caught when I was little. When Dana spotted Mr. One Eye on the porch that night, instinct set in and she set out after it and clutched it inside her mouth. She instantly dropped it and started foaming at the mouth, and it hopped off unharmed, but it pissed my dad off so much he hauled off and slugged her right in the snout.

Usually my dad would say how much of a lady Dana was when she sat with her two front legs crossed out in front of her. He bathed her in our tub, or outside with the garden hose in the summertime, and spritzed her with her very own bottle of Jean Nate after-bath spray he labeled with her name on it. He bought her a bottle of her own nail polish and painted her nails black to match the black dappled spots on her coat. But now, in a rage, she was a piece of shit that he should just kill by putting a bullet in her fucking skull.

Chapter 29

The longer my dad worked to learn everything in the Bible and the harder he tried to be accepted by Lana and her family, the more erratic and bizarre his behavior. So, one night, when my dad should have been at home gettin' right with the Lord, he was off tailing me, and my friend Karen, to the new arcade downtown because he was obsessed I might be doing something I shouldn't be. He didn't want me going there with all the fornicating going on between me and the boys in there and upon dropping me off at my friend's sister's house downtown, gave me strict instructions that I was to go nowhere else.

When I told Karen this, she was disappointed and devised a plan saying that we should call my dad and tell him we were in for the night and not to call back because her sister's husband was already sleeping and had to work in the morning.

"No, that's a dead give away that we're up to something," I told her.

"You think?" she said.

When I told my mom of Karen's plan later, she laughed and said, when you don't live with Satan himself, you don't have to learn to think around corners.

"Look," I said. "I know him. He'll get in the car and drive down here to see if he can catch me lying to him. He'd drive to the ends of the earth to see if I was doing something I shouldn't be," I said.

Not able to come up with any other scheme, I eventually called and said just that.

Once at the arcade, we were off playing videos games. She played the Pac-Man video game that sat just inside the door to the left, and I played Centipede, which was toward the back of the storefront to the far right. My dad couldn't see me back here even if he drove by, I thought.

I could get my name to the top of the high-score list almost every time. Slamming and rolling the ball with my right hand and holding down the shooting button with my left, I played and played.

Karen was over at the jukebox with Gerald and Isaac, the only two black boys in our school. Isaac was the boy I had to tell I didn't like anymore because my dad was enraged he was black.

Not wanting to spend the extra twenty dollars my dad gave me on more games, I joined Karen near the jukebox to help her pick the next round of songs. She picked "Celebration" by Kool & the Gang she had danced to in our school talent show the year before and I selected "I Love Rock n Roll" by Joan Jett. We put our money in, pushed in the letter and number combination and waited for the music to start.

I looked outside to see if the coast was clear just in time to see my dad's silver Nova snaking ever so slowly down the street through the rain. He had his head turned and was trying to gawk inside the storefront that was the new arcade as he drove slowly down Main Street. The windows were steamed and I hoped he hadn't seen me, but that was not to be.

We both got in the back seat.

We didn't say a word. My dad announced that, no, he would not be dropping my friend off at her sister's house that was on the way, and if her parents wanted her they could come pick her up themselves goddamn it.

When we got to my dad's house, we stopped in the kitchen as if we weren't welcome there as he paced back and forth, between the dining room and kitchen, wiping his hands through his hair; he was manic. He acted as if he just learned some terrible news that he had to save me from.

"Dad, here's your twenty dollars back, I'm sorry I lied to you about being at the arcade," I said as I laid the twenty-dollar bill on the counter.

"I don't want that money," he said as he dismissed me with his hand. "You probably got that from sucking those niggers' dicks in the alley."

"Dad, nothing happened," I said. "It was all innocent, we were just picking songs at the jukebox at the arcade. That's it. I did nothing else with those boys," I said.

He rolled his eyes at me.

"Dad, I'm fourteen and I'm still a virgin. I've never been with a boy. Why can't you believe me when I say that?" I said.

"Doesn't matter. You're just a fucking whore, like your god damned mother. And your grandmother and her mother before her! You'll never amount to a god damn thing,"

"Dad, we just —" I tried to say.

"A fucking nigger lover is what you are! Get the fuck away from me, you and your whore friend over there."

I looked at Karen and she just stood there wide-eyed with tears streaming down her face. She excused herself to go get her belongings and call her mom for a ride.

"If you were my daughter," he said as she walked past him to go to my room, "I'd beat your ass. In fact, when your mom answers, give me the phone, I'll talk to her and tell her I'll beat your ass for her," he said to her as she stopped to listen and not provoke him more by continuing by.

"Go on," he said, "get the fucking phone and call your mother, then get your shit and get outta my house. I don't allow no nigger-lovin' whores in my house," he said as he motioned for her to get down the hallway.

He grabbed the phone from Karen who was crying to her mom on the phone and butted in. "Hey, just so you know, I'll beat her ass for you if you want me to, these god damned girls with these fuckin' niggers down at the arcade at the jukebox, I'll tell ya!"

There was silence on his end and we could hear Karen's mom on the other as he held the phone out and away from his ear. "I know what these boys are like! I know what they want!" he yelled back into the phone.

Later, at school, Karen told me what her mother said to my father on the phone that day.

"She's my daughter and you'll do no such thing. You're making too much of this, Harland. They were only talking to these boys, nothing else... They all go to the same school, for God's sake. They aren't up to no good like you think. They are good girls. My husband is on the way as we speak. You aren't to lay one hand on my daughter," she said.

"Just come get your fucking kid. You do with yours what you want and I'll do with mine what I want but I'll be god damned if mine is gonna flat out lie to me about her whereabouts and who she's blowing in the alleyway. I'll beat her so bad she won't be able to walk for a month!" he yelled into the phone. "Your whore daughter will be outside waiting in the driveway for you," he said as he slammed down the phone.

As she left, she turned to look at me. She gave me an, 'I'm worried for you' look over the roof of the car as she got in the car to leave.

"You! You can get your stupid, nigger-lovin' ass in your room, missy, you hear me?" he said.

I nodded.

"I expect an answer when I'm asking you a question, you hear me?"

"Yes, I hear you," I said.

"Yes, SIR, I hear you," I added quickly.

I felt safe in my room. I spent tons of time in my room by myself, both at my dad's house and at my mom's place, and I liked that just fine.

Then the door opened.

"Here, read these!" he screamed as he threw a pile of Bibles at me from the doorway of my bedroom. "They're called Bibles. If you weren't such a slut, you'd know what they were," he said. "You're going to hell and I'll be god damned if I'll ever claim you as my fucking kid! Not here on this Earth, and certainly not on Judgment Day!" he screamed.

I crouched behind my bed, crying. He was enraged, glassy eyed and red in the face with every vein in his neck and face bulging with rage.

"I know how boys think at your age. You've developed boobs now." When I looked confused, he said, "Boobs, tits, knockers. Get it? That's all those boys are interested in at their age." He came closer to me to twist my nipple through my shirt.

"Ow! Don't do that!" I said as I recoiled and turned my face to the wall.

He left me in my room and I could hear him out in the living room ranting, laughing his ass off, making fun of me. "She's getting boooobs!" he would yell. "I have a god damn nigger lover with tits for a daughter." He was screaming and mocking. I could hear him out in the living room raging at no one. And it went on for what seemed like hours.

"Flee fornication!" he yelled. "Every sin that a man doeth is without the body; but he that committeth fornication sinneth against his own body," he raged.

I didn't want to know this person, this beast that beat women and children and abused animals. He was a crazed lunatic that quoted the Bible while he abused others for conjured-up stories that were never true. I didn't want to have this be my dad but it was. I didn't want to associate with it, be related to it, or be around it. I made it rage for some reason, I brought out the worst in him and I couldn't understand why.

I found a passage that night in one of the Bibles: "As long as I am in the world, I am the light of the world."- John 9:5. That told me I was good. But I knew deep down I couldn't be if my own father treated me this way. I had to be rotten to the core. I had to be an evil piece of shit that should never have been born. So I begged for forgiveness as I lay there.

"God, please. I'm sorry. I'm sorry!" I said as I whispered and cried to the wall. *"I'm sorry for everything I said — for lying about the arcade, for cussing, for stealing cigarettes, writing bad things in my journal about my parents, and whatever else I upset you about! Please. Just make it stop!" — "I'm sorry. I didn't mean to yell at you. I'm asking nicely, I'm not mad, just upset, please? Can you? Thank you. By the way, this is Robin Jessup, if you didn't already know that. Please send help. Amen."*

I cried myself to sleep with my head on top of a heap of Bibles that night.

I woke in the morning in the same clothes I had on the day before. I went to the bathroom and saw that I had dried blood smeared on my face from my forearms where the corners of the Bibles tore and poked triangular-shaped divots into my skin and a large goose egg on my head. When I separated my hair to get a closer look, I found it had the same dried bloody triangular center to it.

He walked by the bathroom and saw me in the mirror checking my head.

"Serves you right. I bet you don't lie to me anymore, will ya?" he said.

"No. I won't," I said. "SIR," I quickly added.

"You just remember this, young lady: Good will always win out over evil," he said. "Always has, always will, you got that?"

"Yes, sir," I said.

Chapter 30

"Robin, can you get that, I'm in the bathroom with your brother," my mom yelled.

"Hello?"

"Is your mom there?" he said.

I knew instantly who it was. And I didn't speak. I didn't want to say she was here. But I didn't want to get in trouble if I lied and said she wasn't.

"Hello?" he said.

"Um... yeah. Hold on a minute."

I threw the phone down on the couch and ran down the hall to the bathroom.

"Mom, it's Wayne."

"What?" she said as she turned around.

"It's Wayne. You want me to tell him you don't want to talk to him?"

"Yeah."

I was happy and ran back down the hallway of the trailer and told him she didn't want to talk to him. "And don't call back," I added as I slammed down the receiver.

"What'd he say?" she asked.

"Nothing. I didn't give him a chance to say anything. I just hung up."

"That's my girl!" she said.

I went to bed happier than I ever did that night and woke up fresh and rested. I wore my best clothes that day, did my hair and wore a little makeup, which consisted of blush and a spritz of Love's Baby Soft perfume, and off I went ready to take on the day.

When I got home that day, I knew she'd talked to him. She was distant and in her own little world. Distracted.

"Mom. Tell me you didn't talk to him," I demanded.

She just stared at me.

"Mom. Please. Tell me you're not going to get back with him."

"Robin, I don't know what I'm going to do. I just heard what he had to say. I didn't promise anything. No decisions are going to be made right now," she said

"Mom. What could he possibly say to make you want to take him back when he's not only beat your daughter, but has beat you and cheated on you?" I asked.

"I said I don't know what I'm doing..." She trailed off and turned around, looking at the wall at the side of her bed.

I turned around in a huff and went straight to my room. I was pissed.

This couldn't be happening. Again.

I hated her. I hated him. I hated my father. I hated my life.

But, the first chance I got I pleaded my case with my dad to please tell her not to take me away from my friends here and not to move me again. And he was all too happy to oblige me, preaching to her how kids needed structure, strict discipline and roots. "Spare the rod, spoil the child," he said.

So we stayed put for a while and my mom did a little "sowing of her oats" as she called it. At first, she'd just go out with my cousin, she'd stay out a few hours and come home. Later, it would be a whole group of them and soon Friday turned into being gone until Monday again.

When I was left in charge, I knew not to answer the door, what to say on the phone if someone called and how to handle things most kids my age didn't. I may have needed remedial math class but I had street smarts. And I knew that 1+1+1 in our house didn't equal three. The answer was two.

I was a distance runner in track, but was also pretty fast. I was used to running long distances with my dad now as he worked hard to get in shape and quit smoking for Lana. Instead of smoking cigarettes and drinking alcohol, he now inhaled the Bible and drank Geritol. When I wanted to quit running, he'd tell me "No, don't be a quitter, it's not in your makeup. You're a damned Jessup and Jessups don't quit."

So I learned to be quick just to be able to stop.

Linda, the softball player who was still upset that I'd won the last softball game by stealing home, was absent the day we were timed for our 8/80 run. As a result of her absenteeism, the gym teacher said she had to let Linda know who had been the fastest up to this point, and what their time was. It was me, I was the fastest, and my time was two minutes and eighteen seconds. That's two times around the football field.

And I thought telling Linda my time was an unfair advantage.

Our gym teacher favored her. The day Linda ran her race she coached her around the track, cupping her mouth with her hands, yelling to her where she was in her time, pushing her harder and harder to beat my timed score as I stood on the other side of the bleachers watching. She beat me by two seconds. Her official time: two minutes, sixteen seconds.

I kicked the dirt. "Son of a bitch!" I yelled to the air.

I so wanted to beat her. I wanted to tell my parents that I beat her and how well I did. I wanted them to be proud.

Later in the summer during one of our track meets that year at Follansbee Middle School, when the kids were getting back on the bus to go back to our school, the assistant coach was handing out that day's track ribbons. She was busy trying to manage a clipboard, record stats, and hand out a pile of ribbons at the same time to a loud bus full of screaming, excited kids.

I sat in my seat discouraged I hadn't placed that day.

Then John, an older kid by only a few years, said, "Here. Maybe this will get your mom to notice you once and for all," as he slipped a blue ribbon that had fallen to the floor at me.

John wore his brown hair a little longer than the rest of the boys at school. My mom called him a rebellious hippie-type. I knew my dad wouldn't like him but luckily he lived nearer my mom's place and only visited me there. When he came by to visit me at the trailer on a few occasions, my mom commented on how he lit up like a Christmas tree when he looked at me. I think he was the first boy to ever really see me.

Once when he came with a fist full of flowers he picked along the roadside on his walk to the trailer, she said you would have thought he was looking at an angel when I answered the door. She didn't like that.

"Put it in your bag. Hurry," he said.

And without thinking about it any longer, I did just that.

I grew excited on the bus ride home thinking of how my mom would be so proud of me. I couldn't wait to get home and tell her I placed first and show her the blue ribbon.

"Mom! I'm home!"

"I'm back here!" she yelled from her bedroom down the hall.

She walked down the hall to meet me at the door to my room.

"Here," she said.

"What's this?" I said as I reached out to grab it.

"It's a garbage bag. Pack your room and your clothes, we're movin'," she said.

"What? Just like that? Why!" I asked.

"Just do it!" she said.

"Mom, I don't want to move, please!" I said.

"Well, I don't know what to tell you," she said as she walked down the hall to her room.

"Mom! Where are we going? Does Dad know?" I asked.

"No, he doesn't know. I'll tell him when we get there."

"I'm calling my dad!" I said.

"You'll do no such thing!" she yelled as she turned back and walked toward me pointing her finger my way. "You'll pack your shit and I'll not hear another word about it."

I sat on the linoleum floor in my bedroom and sobbed. My face scrunched up in pain, my heart broken, I could barely breathe and it felt like I was going to throw up.

My mother passed back and forth in front of my bedroom door carrying loads of her clothing to the car, not even looking in my room.

"Lay there and cry, I don't care. We'll leave and you won't have your stuff with you," she said as she came back in past my room.

I ran out of the room and up to her in the hall, grabbing at her to stop.

"Mom. Please. I don't want to go. Please. Just let me stay here. I'll be o.k. by myself. Dad can check on me. Please."

"Robin Lynn. Stop it. You're not old enough, you can't be here by yourself. You're going and that's final. Get your stuff or I'll beat your ass all the way to the car. Do it now."

"Why can't I stay here by myself now?" I asked.

"Because I said so, that's why," she said.

"I can stay here by myself for days at a time taking care of myself and Doodle when you want to go out, though, huh?" I said.

She bent down, brow furrowed, with her finger within inches of my face.

"You little bitch. You'll shut your smart mouth if you know what's good for you and do what the hell I tell you to do," she said.

I turned away from her in a snap, lips tightly together as I stomped back to my room. I tore clothes from my closet, the hangers swinging wildly back and forth. I yanked the drawers open so hard they fell out. I crammed everything I owned into a garbage bag. On top of the clothing, I threw in my books and my belongings from my bathroom and on top of that my book bag from school.

When I stopped long enough to take in what was happening, I slid to the floor and sat there next to the bag. I looked at my book bag lying there on top and realized I'd no longer see my friends. There was no time to tell anyone or call anybody. I didn't even get to say goodbye. I had no records to take with me to a new school. And no one would know what happened to me until I could get in touch, not even my dad.

When I turned to look back into my room for the last time, there in the window, tucked behind the white sheer curtain was the stick to a large pink paper rose that stuck out over the top of the curtain. I loved that thing. My cousin's boyfriend got it for me once at the carnival downtown and brought it to me for no reason other than to be nice. I wiped my nose up with the butt of my hand, and sniffed in deeply.

"Mom, can I?" I asked.

"No. Leave it. It's too big to fit in the car."

I cried quietly, keeping my head turned away from her as she drove.

When I gathered up enough courage to do it, I reached into my purse and pulled out a half-smoked cigarette and a lighter and lit it.

"You've got some nerve, young lady, smokin' in front of me like that."

"You've got some nerve actin' like you do in front of your daughter like that," I said.

"Really? You sayin' you think I'm a bad mother?"

"Hey, like dad says, if the shoe fits," I said.

She started to cry as she drove.

"I can't believe all I do for you and you treat me like this? That's some thanks I get," she said.

"What do you do for me? You can't pay the bills, keep the water or electric on, you never have lunch money and you just bail by going back to Wayne when the goin' gets tough," I said.

"Unreal. Like you know anything that's goin' on," she said.

"You know, Mom, that might just be your problem. You just never think I know what's goin' on. You and dad think I never know what's goin' on. I'm not stupid, you know. I hear you talk. Do you not think of what my life's been like? How you and Dad have acted in front of me: all the fighting, the arguing, drinking, screaming, beatings... come on, gimme a break. I'm sick of it all."

It got quiet when we crossed the Steubenville Bridge that delivered us to Ohio. All I heard was the hum of our tires as we crossed her. She was scary, but her sound was mesmerizing. I looked out over the side of the bridge into the chocolate-milk-colored water and sobbed. I hated this bridge, but because she was familiar I'd miss seeing her too. It was just all so confusing.

Silent tears rolled down my face from time to time in the three hours it took to arrive at our new place, a place I'd not even seen yet but would be called my new home. I thought of the new school I had to go to and how I hated being the new kid in town.

It stayed quiet until we got to Route 11.

"You know... I know your life hasn't been easy and you've gone through a lot for your young age. But, honey... This may be a whole new life for you up here. Not just for me. You may one day meet a boy, fall in love and have children from meeting someone up here one day that you wouldn't have met otherwise. Ever think of that?"

"Yeah. I guess," I said shrugging my shoulders.

I looked out the window at the trees quickly passing by and knew that's what my life felt like. I smiled a bit at the thought of a new life, a good one this time. But I secretly hated that I could so easily be talked into hope. I hated hope. It wasn't the thing with wings that perched itself in your soul. It was the thing with horns that clawed your guts out as it laughed in your face for being stupid enough to be hopeful in the first place. And I felt much too old for this. I didn't have much life left in me. I was worn out.

"God, please — let it be a good move this time," I said in my mind as I looked up at the sky.

And just as easily as I prayed that prayer, I lied.

I reached into my book bag lying at my feet and grabbed the blue ribbon. "Here, I won this today," I said.

"Honey, I couldn't be more proud of you," she said.

I wasn't proud of myself. I was disgusted. She taught me to lie for her and now I was learning to lie to her to get attention.

She squeezed my hand.

"Real proud of you, honey, you did good."

I didn't say anything. I turned and sat staring out the window the rest of the way. And just as I thought I would surely muster up the courage to turn to face her and confess my sins of the stolen first-place blue ribbon, I didn't.

I wasn't bold. I wasn't fearless. And for as old as I felt, I realized as I gazed at my reflection in the passenger side window, I was still very much a little girl that would do anything for her mother's attention.

And I hated myself for it.

Part 7

Strongsville, Ohio

Chapter 31

I stood at the bus stop at the end our new street surrounded by kids I'd never met who were curious about the new girl who stood among them this year.

"You have an accent, where are you from?" Melissa asked.

"West Virginia," I said coldly.

"West Virginia?" she said with raised eyebrows. "I thought you were from England."

"England?" I said, laughing.

"Yeah, I heard you talking earlier and swore I heard an English accent," she said as she recited back to me what I just said in a terrible English accent.

They all proceeded to take turns imitating how I sounded to them, my long O's versus their short ones. When I said 'box' they said it came out "bauchs." When they said 'box' it sounded to me like they were saying "backs."

I was only three hours away from my home, but it felt like a world away. I was always the new kid in town, odd man out. I wanted to be accepted, but never quite fit in anywhere I was. I didn't know it then, and I'm glad I didn't, or I might not have made it through, but not being accepted for who I was and never fitting in anywhere would become my life.

"Hey... you wanna sneak out with us tonight?" she asked.

"Sneak out? What do you mean sneak out? Sneak out where?" I asked.

"We have a fort in the woods, we go out there at night and smoke and drink... make out with boys. You in?" she asked.

"I can't sneak out. I've never done anything like that, so I'm not sure how I'd get out of my house without getting caught." I said.

"So, you just stay overnight with me. Simple," she said as if she just solved everything. I didn't even know her well, but just knew I had to ask my mom if I could.

After school that night, I asked if I could go stay at Melissa's house.

"Melissa's house, huh?" my mom asked.

"Yeah, she lives just across the street," I said as I pointed up the street.

"What do you know about this Melissa?" she asked.

"Just that she goes to my school, is a year younger than me and rides my bus, really. I know she has a brother named Michael and her mother is really religious," I said.

"I see," she said as she eyed me suspiciously.

"Can I, please?" I added quickly.

"I guess it wouldn't hurt, right, Wayne?" she asked.

He looked at me suspiciously.

"Can I?" I asked enthusiastically but was aware not to overdo my enthusiasm too much.

"What're you going to do for me?" he asked.

"What? What do you mean?" I asked.

"What are you going to do for us?" he said as he shot a glance at my mom.

"Um, the dishes?"

"Oh, you're doing the dishes anyway, young lady, what else?" he said.

"Uh... mop the floor? Vacuum? What?" I asked exasperated.

"She can go, without doing any of that if she wants. I got the dishes," my mom said, and with that she shooed me to my room.

"Go get your stuff to stay over..." and I was off like a shot.

This was so exciting and unusual to me. I was making new friends on the street and my mom was doing mom stuff, and asking mom questions, and making mom decisions without letting Wayne make them. Maybe there was hope yet to have a new life and be happy.

Later that night at Melissa's house we devised our plan.

"Look," she said, "my mom falls asleep in her chair every night in the living room and it's the garage door we need to sneak out of." She pointed with her finger down the hall.

"But... the garage door is only feet away from her chair!" I whispered.

"Shhhh!" she said with her index finger to her lips. "I know, I know, but trust me, I've done this before. You just have to follow my lead tonight and do everything I do. O.K?"

"O.k. I will," I said.

We excused ourselves after watching TV later that evening to Melissa's bedroom, saying goodnight to her mother and father as we went.

"Sweet dreams, my angel," her mother said.

"Night, my darling," her dad said as she bent down and he kissed her forehead.

"Night, everyone," I said sheepishly, smiling. I already felt bad about sneaking out and lying to such nice parents. Their lavish words and affection made me squirm yet made me feel jealous.

We got to her room and turned out the lights. We laid there in the dark whispering and plotting and waiting for time to pass.

Later that night, Melissa cracked her door to check on her mother's progress of falling asleep and sure enough there was her mother sacked out in her oversized recliner, feet up, head drooped to the side, snoring loudly with the TV going in the background. The dad had long since gone to bed.

She shut the door, came back into the room where we quickly changed out of our pajamas and got into our jeans, T-shirts and tennis shoes.

We snuck out the bedroom door. Melissa showed the way and I followed behind, imitating her every move. Melissa turned to me and instructed me to close the door tight behind me. We got through the kitchen, avoiding the creaky spots, me stepping exactly where Melissa had stepped before me. My stomach was in knots and I felt like I'd be sick, but I was excited too. I wasn't quite sure if I was having fun yet or not.

We were almost to the garage door when her mother started to stir in the chair; snorting, coughing and rearranging herself. We stopped. Bent down and held our positions until Melissa felt the coast was clear.

We reached the garage door, went down a few steps, avoided some yard tools and things that made noise and with the turn of the knob on the door leading out, we were outside into the summer night's star-filled sky.

Melissa turned to me again.

"Don't talk until we get to the fort. Sound carries in the woods and she could hear us," she said.

I shook my head up and down. I knew a thing or two about sound carrying in the woods.

We walked bent over as fast as we could, then off running as fast as we could. Heavy breathing turned to quiet giggling then to full-blown laughter as we reached the fort deep in the woods.

We embraced. We had made it!

"Hey," Michael said.

"You snuck out too?" I said in amazement.

"Yep. We do it all the time," he said as he continued to build the fire.

Once we climbed into the fort, we were offered a beer by Michael and we both lit cigarettes from the pack she had. We felt cool, in control.

"So... let me get this straight," I said as I blew my smoke out. "Your family is Catholic and very religious, and you two sneak out all the time and smoke and drink?" I recounted for them.

"You should see what else we do," Melissa said.

"What?" I asked.

She patted her index finger up to her lips as she gave a quick glance to her brother nearby. She didn't want to divulge it in front of him.

"She lets boys finger her," he jabbed.

"I do not!" she laughed and threw her sweatshirt at him.

When he left, she admitted that yes she indeed let boys finger her.

Michael left us there and later returned with some much older boys that night and I took a few tokes off of my very first joint. I remember feeling mellow, just sitting for what seemed like hours watching the small fire they built and how cool I thought it was to be that close to fire watching it dance, pop and hiss as it licked the night sky.

When it was time to go and the sun was close to rising, we cleaned up the area, made sure the fire was out by dousing it with water and walked to the edge of the woods. As we got to the edge of the woods that led to her house, we stopped. There, underneath the light of their kitchen window, stood her mom at the sink getting a drink of water.

"Shit!" Michael said.

"Holy shit!" Melissa said.

"I am so fucked," I said. "If my mom and her boyfriend find out about this, I am dead meat."

"Shhhh! No one's gonna know. Let's just stay out here and watch what she does. Maybe she's just up for a drink of water and will go back to bed soon," Michael said.

"Yeah, let's hope," Melissa said.

I was speechless and not able to articulate the panic that I felt.

And just like Michael said, after some time had gone by, the mother did just that. She went back to her recliner and laid down. We couldn't see if she was asleep, so we waited some more.

The door going into the garage was squeaky and trying to get through it gave me what I can only remember as a fluttery heartbeat. I was short of breath. My heart felt like it was rolling around in my chest, and at any minute I might faint. I didn't like this kind of excitement. I liked calm. Sneaking out for me was too stressful and I vowed then and there that if we got back in her house without getting caught, I'd never do it again.

Once back in her room, I let out a huge sigh of relief, quickly got my pajamas back on and jumped in her bed. I sat up like a shot when I could no longer ignore the feeling in my stomach, excused myself to the bathroom and got sick.

My nerves were too shot for this.

Chapter 32

When my mom and her boyfriend fought she'd drive us back to West Virginia and stay with her sister Della for the weekend with my brother, who my dad said was still too little to stay the whole weekend. One day, as I was outside riding my bike in front of his house, he called to me from the glass sliding door in the den.

"Robin... Robin!" he yelled.

"Yeah?" I said breathless as I drove my bike up to the house on the grass.

"I want you to come on in here, we have some things we want to discuss with you."

"O.k." I got off my bike and laid it down on its side on the grass outside the sliding door wondering what I did now.

I walked over to the yellow beige velvet rocking recliner and sat down.

"What's wrong?" I asked.

"Nothin's wrong, I just wanna get some stuff straight around here so there's no confusion from the get-go," he said.

"O.k.," I said.

"I called you in here to let you know Lana and I are getting married. And..." he held up his hand, "before you go gettin' all excited and go dancin' around and tellin' the world now... you need to know that from here on out, whatever she says goes. You understand?"

"Yes, I understand," I said.

"And, if I hear of you so much as smart-mouthin' her one bit, you'll go back to your mother's house and you won't be visitin' here no more. And while we're on the subject, I want you to know right here, right now, from this moment on, that I will choose Lana over you any day, ya hear me?"

"Yes, I hear you," I said.

"You sure you got all that?"

"Yes," I said.

"That means that at *any time* she says you did anything, I believe her, not you. And if it ever comes to ever choosin' between you two, you're out. You read me?"

"Yes," I said. My heart felt hurt and my eyes were getting misty.

She just sat next to him not saying a word, but looking like she wanted to crawl in a hole with her hands folded in her lap.

I didn't trust her, but I wanted to.

"Don't start crying on me now and don't get all teary-eyed over it," he said. "I just don't want another repeat like what happened when you flipped Tammy off, ya hear?"

"But, Dad..." I wanted to remind him that I didn't flip her off, even though she said I flipped her off. I wanted to remind him that she admitted she made the whole thing up to see if he would believe her over me.

"I don't want to hear it now," he stopped me. "You flip Lana off or do anything like that, you'll be outta here so fast your head will spin. You got it?"

"I got it."

"I'm makin' myself crystal clear?"

"Yes, I'm clear," I said.

"Now make yourself scarce," he said as he motioned for me to get my ass outside and play.

When I told my mom they were getting married, she said, "See, told you, he'd finagle his way in there."

So, in the summer of 1983, my dad and Lana got married. I was happy about that.

It started out good. They started out good. But, no matter how hard my dad tried, he could not, for whatever reason, control his temper for very long. Sometimes she was there during my visits, sometimes she wasn't. I never knew from one minute to the next what exactly was going on, why someone was or wasn't around or what to expect next.

When I told my mom that I was worried about some things that had started happening shortly after they were married, she said he'd just boohoo his way back into her good graces and she'd take him back until one day, she'd have enough of his shit and leave for good.

"I wouldn't get too attached to her if I were you. Before you know it, she'll be gone too," she warned.

On one of my visitation weekends Lana took me driving in one of Brooke High's parking lots, after being told not to by my dad.

She was working with me on my coordination, explaining that if I listened to the car and the engine, it would tell me what needed to be done next. Steering, moving my feet, and shifting gears around the parking lot was sensory overload for me. Getting out of first gear without the herky-jerky starts and getting it in reverse by myself were my goals for that day, she said.

She took it on a straightaway driving it fast enough to get it up to fourth gear.

"You hear that?" she said. "That's the engine revving up, that means shift," she said. "You'll see the RPM needle over here shoot up to the right. You never want to see it in the red for long, if ever, because it's not good for the engine."

Then, we pulled over and switched seats.

"So, it's in neutral right now, just depress the clutch, put your foot on the brake and start it up," she said.

"You feel that jerkiness when you take off? You just have to push the gas pedal the same depth and speed as you let out your clutch," she said. "But, that's good you didn't stall it."

"O.k. now, for reverse you push the gear shifter all the way over to the right, push down a little to get in reverse," she instructed as she took my hand and placed it on top of hers. "Feel that little notch it catches in there?" she asked. "That's reverse."

As we talked, listened to the car and occasionally looked down at my feet and hands and gear shifter, I hit the curb in the parking lot. I hit slowly, but still fast enough to bust the right front tire. As she changed the tire, she told me not to worry about it, but I could see the dread in her face. He told her not to.

But, she calmed me saying she'd say she did it and everything would be fine.

When we got home with the tiny donut tire on the right front side of the car, she said it was her fault and recited the story we came up with.

And he knew we were lying.

But neither one of us would crack no matter how hard he pushed for us to admit it. He grew furious that he couldn't pit us against the other and we stuck firm to our stories. For hours he prodded us, trying to trip us up with the same questions over and over, worded just a slightly different way.

This was all right before my dad was leaving for work that night and he was enraged to have to end his line of questioning and his reign of terror. He was working the eleven-to-seven shift that night at Weirton Steel and gave Lana strict instructions to not let me out of my room, or else she'd regret it.

"You let me catch her out of her room and I'll beat BOTH your asses. You hear me?" he said to Lana.

"Yes," she said.

"Yes, what?" he asked.

"Yes, I hear you and I won't let her out of her room," she said.

"Yes, I won't let her out of her room, what?" he said.

"Yes, I hear you and won't let her out of her room, SIR," she said.

"Good," he said as he left through the door.

It was the same 'SIR' spiel he went through with me every time he wanted to intimidate me.

I ran to the bathroom and watched him pull away from the window inside the shower until his red taillights were gone.

"Is it safe to come out?" I said around the bathroom door.

"No, not yet, let's give him some time to be gone for awhile, o.k.? You know how he is and if he finds you out of your room, I'm afraid what he might do," she said.

"O.k.," I said.

I sat in the hallway outside the bathroom door, out of sight, watching the TV that sat straight out in front of me in the living room. Lana sat on the love seat to the side of the window. About a half hour or so had gone by and she got up to walk into the bathroom.

"Get up, get up now and go back to your room," she said quickly and in a whisper. "Your dad is in the front yard. He climbed up in the big tree with the floodlight on it and he's looking down into the living room right now. He thinks I can't see him and am probably just going to the bathroom. Hurry."

I crawled back to my room on my hands and knees and stayed there for the rest of the night while Lana sat out in the living room pretending to go about her routine and act like she didn't know he was there.

Later that night when she went to their bedroom across from mine, she said, "Just stay in your room. Don't go out in the living room, don't even crawl because he's up high and will see you on the floor. Just stay in bed now, o.k.?"

"I am," I said, too scared to leave.

I pulled the covers up to my chin and laid there wondering if he was just gonna stay out there all night long or actually go to work.

Something about this just said crazy to me. And, I feared the ally I had in Lana would be coming to an end soon. I knew she'd turn on me, or leave him, or both.

Chapter 33

She was small, unkempt and shy, and lived across the street from me at my mom's. If her eyes met yours she'd look away quickly as if she was hideous. She swayed back and forth nervously as she talked, wore long sleeves in the middle of summer, and would sit on the front steps of her house in all kinds of weather for hours on end. I knew instantly she was an abused kid.

One day I got up enough courage to ask her about my suspicions.

"Lisa," I said. "You can tell me. Are you being abused? You don't have to be afraid."

She nodded, her bottom lip purple and quivering. "Please don't say anything," she begged.

"I won't, I won't, that's not why I asked," I assured her.

"Then why did you?" she asked.

"Because I've never met another abused kid like myself," I said.

"You're abused too?" she asked wide eyed.

"Mmmhmm."

"But… you're so... strong. Tough. Like steel," she said.

"I am. And you have to be too," I told her.

"All I do is try not to cry every second," she quickly confessed.

"I know. But, you gotta get tough," I told her.

"But how?" she begged to know.

"I'm not sure exactly how, but you just need to," I said.

She nodded like she understood.

"I wasn't *always* tough, and I don't always *feel* tough, but you gotta *act* like you are," I said. "If you tell yourself 'I'm tough,' pretty soon you feel tough." I went on to explain further. "Or like sometimes I pretend I'm playing a part in a movie, and I'm the tough girl in the movie. Ya know? And that's kinda how I get through my day. My mom tells me I'm my own best friend, but I'm more than that. Is your mom religious?" I asked.

She shook her head yes.

"Well, you know how they call Jesus their Savior?" I asked.

She nodded.

"I think we save ourselves," I said.

"Why do you think that?" she asked.

"Believe me, I've prayed a million times, and ain't no one comin' to save you but yourself, and by not answering us that's what he's telling us, right? Believe in yourselves, fix stuff yourself, right?"

She shrugged her shoulders.

"Anyway, we'll get through this and not have to live like this anymore once we're old enough to be out on our own. You gotta hold your head up high for now and just get tough," I said. And as I said these things to her, I had the feeling I was saying it to convince myself.

"Can I ask… What does your mother do to you?"

"Beats me with her hands, belts, sticks, throws things at me, calls me names like bitch, ugly, asshole, pulls my hair, blames me for everything, kicks me, tells me I have the devil in me... She trailed off for a second looking away. "Forgets to feed me, or forces me to eat things I don't like to make me sick. She gives all the good food to my little sister. She lets all her boyfriends beat me too," she added.

"Where is your dad? I asked.

"I don't know, my mom won't let us see him," she said. "What about you? What do your parents do?"

"My parents used to do some of that same stuff to me. They still favor my little brother, but whatever. And I hate the guy my mom's with now. We fight all the time and he hits me and still beats my mother. I love my dad's new wife, but doubt they'll be together long. I try to have faith it will all work out, but I cry alone at night and act tough all the rest of the time," I said. "My mom's seemed to change some now that we moved here, she's at least trying to be motherly. Maybe your mom will change too," I said shooting her a grin.

She shook her head no.

"Lisa. I'm not even kidding. The next time you need someone, just knock on my door. If you're hungry, come over and eat with me. I'll be there for you, o.k.?"

She smiled and nodded and excused herself to leave for home quickly so her mom didn't get mad.

I watched out the window everyday for her after that.

Weeks went by and I noticed that she hadn't been outside to the bus stop since our talk. I worried for her.

"Why do you keep lookin' out the window?" my mom asked.

"Just watching for that little blond-headed girl Lisa," I said.

"Why you doin' that?" she asked.

"Because her mother abuses her and I want to make sure she's alright. I told her to come over here if she ever needs anything."

"Abuses her?" she asked. "Like how? Spanks her for not listening?" she added.

"Beats her ... pulls her hair out, calls her names like bitch, kicks her, forgets to feed her, favors the little sister.... allows her boyfriends to beat her too," I said as I continued to look across the street.

"I highly doubt her mother does that stuff to her. She's probably a brat that doesn't listen and back talks," she said.

"That's just stuff abusers say," I quickly shot back. "There's a huge difference between a spanking and a beating."

I knew what she was doing. If she made me doubt that Lisa was abused, then I'd doubt I was abused. If she was able to do that then she didn't have to take responsibility for her abuse, and allowing others to abuse me. She'd be off the hook as if it was poor Starlah, who had it so rough. She liked playing the victim. I found out at a very young age, I'd rather die first, than play that role. I grew up seeing the victim card played again and again by her and I despised it.

"So, I take it you think you're going to be her protector from now on, right?" she asked.

"Sure am," I said defiantly. "She so much as has a bruise on her the next time I see her and I'll call the police myself," I said without taking my eyes off Lisa's house.

There were no more questions as to why I was looking out the window after that. And I got the feeling my mom was reading between the lines.

I ended up liking Janie best. She also lived on that same street directly across from Michael and Melissa and was three years older than the rest of us. I remember her riding the bus with us and acting disgusted by having to do so. She'd stand at the bus stop, never speaking to any of us, off by herself. Then one day she just disappeared.

When she reappeared she was driving a little red Maverick with white interior her parents bought her that we all thought so cool.

"Hey, cool car!" I yelled.

"Thanks. You wanna ride home?"

"Sure!"

I climbed in the passenger seat over the thick white vinyl seats and was glad to be acknowledged by someone older than me.

"You live on my street," she said to me as if I didn't know.

"Yep."

"You're pretty new here, huh?"

"Yeah."

Her long, brown, frizzy hair flew in the wind as she smoked.

"You want one?" she said as she held her pack out to me

"Yeah, sure," I said as I took one.

"Don't get used to it, I can't give out smokes all the time, they're expensive."

"Sure, I understand." I nodded.

She wore brown corduroys and a yellow top with a small ruffle on the rounded neckline, hiking boots with red strings, and carried a large, brown grandma pocketbook with her at all times. I went through pocketbooks like hers when I was little and only wondered what in the world she could be carrying in that big thing.

"So, what do you like to do for fun?" she asked. "I mean, I know you're younger than me by a few years, but I was hoping to find someone cool to hang out with, ya know?" she said.

"Yeah, I know. Michael and Melissa are cool. I hung out with them once," I said.

"Yeah, you hung out? Where?"

"In a fort they have in the woods behind their house," I said. "But don't say anything about that to anyone else."

"Nah, I'm cool," she reminded me.

"Yeah. Me too," I shot back.

"How cool?" she asked.

"How cool do you want me to be?" I asked.

"Just cool enough to try things with me and keep your mouth shut about it."

"Well, I have no close friends here so who would I tell and yeah, I've tried some things in my day," I said.

"Yeah, like what?"

"Pot," I said proudly.

"Really?" she asked.

"Yeah," I said.

"You know how to get some?" she asked.

"That I don't," I said.

"I think I do," she said.

"Cool."

She pulled down our street slowly as we talked. She passed up her house, then mine, drove all the way to the dead end, pointed to where to meet her later off in the woods, and turned the car around facing back toward our homes.

She stopped the car.

"Hey. You're pretty cool," she said. "I think I can trust you."

"You can," I added quickly.

"Meet me here tonight after dinner," she instructed.

"I will," I assured her.

She drove up to my house and stopped at my driveway and I got out.

"Thanks for everything," I said bent down in the window. "See ya later."

"Yeah, you will. But remember. Shhh! And do not tell any of the other neighborhood kids, especially them," she said as she pointed to Michael and Melissa's house.

"Nope. I won't."

I shut the door to her red Maverick and walked up my drive. I wasn't even up to my door and she was already pulled up in her driveway getting out and waving at me.

"Who's your new friend?" Wayne asked as soon as I got in the house.

"Janie," I said coldly.

"Janie? She's a bit older than you, isn't she?"

"Yeah, just by a bit," I said.

He proceeded to gawk out the window, trying to see where this little red car that dropped me off went.

All I wanted was for him to forget about her, where she lived, and mind his own business, and maybe just go parent the seven kids he never saw and stop acting like he cared about what I did.

"Dinner's good, Mom."

"Good, glad you like it. Is the corn sweet?" she asked as she was sitting down.

"Mmmhmm," I said as I was eating my corn on the cob.

"Hey," Wayne said, "when you eat your corn on the cob, do you move it back and forth like a typewriter or around and around in a circle?"

I could tell by the tone he had that he was trying to pick a fight with my mother or me. And unlike my grandma Edith who picked and chose her battles with care, I tended to every last one of them and always took the bait by fighting back.

I answered.

"Around and around like this." I demonstrated.

Moving his corn on the cob back and forth and moving his bottom lip in and away from his upper teeth to exaggerate buckteeth, he started to eat.

"This is Robin eating corn," he laughed with his mouth full.

"You are so not funny," I said.

"Stop it, you two," my mom said.

"What? You don't think your daughter's Bucky Beaver teeth are funny?"

"Stop it, Wayne," she said. "She's not doing anything to you. Just leave her alone."

I wrinkled up my nose to him, like "There!" I guess she told you.

"Don't you tell me how to be in my own god damn house. I don't know who you think you are," he said leaning closer to her face.

She backed down.

"You think you're somethin' else, gettin' your mommy to stick up for you, don't you?" he asked.

"No, I don't. But, it's about time she does," I said.

"Whoa! Did you hear that, Starlah?" he said. "She thinks you suck as a mother."

"I didn't say that, and no, I don't," I said.

"Stop back talking, Robin Lynn," she warned.

"I'm not back talking, I'm explaining myself and what I meant."

"You'll not do any such thing in my house," he said as he rose from the table. "Don't you make me take this belt off," he said as he reached for his belt buckle.

"Robin, go to your room," my mom said quickly.

"But —" I said.

"Just do it!" she yelled and pointed to my room.

I lay in my room and listened to them fight for the next hour until he finally had to get ready for work. To pass the time I drew pictures of him. I'd draw the profile of his big nose first. A large nose that took up almost the whole page, with small beady eyes on top of it, with the saying, "Who the fuck used my razor!" coming out of a speaking bubble out over his head.

I remember my mom finding them and laughing hysterically, saying, "Oh Robin Lynn, you'd take on Godzilla before you even thought of the consequences."

"Whatever," I'd say. "Fuck Godzilla."

I heard him in the bathroom getting ready while I drew.

"What the fuck is going on with this razor? I just changed it," I heard him yell to my mother.

"I don't know," I heard her say.

"Did Robin use it?" he asked my mom.

"How the hell should I know? Ask her," she said.

My bedroom door opened and there was his nose and beady eyes with small pieces of toilet paper with red dots all over his face.

"Did you use my razor again?" he asked.

"I used *a* razor, I'm not sure I used *your* razor? Why?" I said.

"Why? Why! WHY! She wants to know why!" he yelled as he slammed my door.

"Fucking little bitch!" he screamed.

I went back to drawing.

If you didn't want people using your razor then don't leave it in the fucking shower, it's that simple, I thought.

All I wanted to do was meet Janie at the end of the street in the woods and see what was in her big, fat grandma pocketbook. And that's exactly what I did once Wayne left for work.

When I got to the end of the street the sun was just setting. I walked by all the neighbors' houses as nonchalantly as I could, hoping not to give off any vibes that we were up to no good, although I wasn't sure what exactly we were up to? But whatever it was, I could hear my dad preaching now.

"Forbidden fruit is the sweetest."

Sure is, I thought.

We sat in the woods at the end of the street that ironically faced a church parking lot and got stoned out of our minds on pot.

I walked home, and sat stoned, flying high as a kite right in front of my mom and she was either too busy with her own shit to notice, or didn't even care.

It went on like this for a while. And in spite of my nerves, I snuck out of the house again and again to meet Michael and Melissa, the Swanson boys and Janie and her old lady pocketbook in the woods. I even got a much older boyfriend who had a car my mom knew nothing about who hung around the fort in the woods. He said he wanted to marry me and kill my mom's boyfriend if he ever touched me again after I told him about the abuse.

I cussed, smoked, drank, fought with other kids, snuck out of the house, defended my mom, defended my neighbor, lied, made out with boys, and took on my mom's boyfriend every time he threw the bait. I fought ferociously. People called it rebelling. I called it speaking up for myself, trying to be heard, explaining myself, and fighting to be seen in my own life. I was sick of people using me as a punching bag.

One time, my mom had over one of the new friends she'd recently made from the new beauty college she was attending. They were sitting around smoking, drinking beer and doing each other's hair when my mom and I started arguing about whether or not I could go to a sleepover. After some back and forth between my mom, her saying no and me pleading, which was our usual, her friend got up, walked right up to me and slapped me across the face for talking to my mom with a tone. I couldn't believe it. My mom just sat there and had no reaction to it at all.

"What's that on your neck?" Janie's mom asked me.

I couldn't feel the red blotchy area because it was flat. She took me to the mirror in their bathroom and flipped on the light.

"It's a red, rashy-looking area," she said as she showed it to me. "Does it itch?"

"No, I didn't even know I had it," I said.

It looked like splotchy sunburn.

"I get this way sometimes, my mom says it's from my nerves," I said as I looked at it in the mirror.

"You know, you have been making that noise in the back of your throat again," she said.

"I have?" I asked.

"Yes, and I've noticed you've started stuttering a bit here and there again." she said. "It's not bad, no one but me probably even notices it." "You o.k. at home?"

"Yeah, everything's normal," I said.

"If you're not, I can call someone," she added.

"No. Please. Don't do that," I said.

"Janie told me it's not… so pleasant for you at home with your mom's boyfriend," she said.

"No, it's not anywhere near pleasant," I said.

Not really knowing where their life ended and mine began, and what a call to someone about all of this would do, exactly, I said, "But, I'm fine, really." And smiled.

Janie was lucky to have a mother like her. She had some sort of childhood development background and a degree in something related to children and their welfare. She was kind, mature, and very motherly to her children. When Janie told me she and her sister were adopted, I was amazed. I wanted to know more. "Tell me everything about it," I said.

Her mother would let me stay over and bring snacks into the bedroom on a tray to us. She'd let us know she was there if we needed anything. It was cool. She was there, but gave us enough room to be kids. I wished she were my mom.

Her mother delivered the tray and left with a smile, pulling the door behind her.

"If she's the kind of mom you get when you're adopted, then I wanted to be adopted too," I said.

"I get anything I want because of it," she said.

"Because of what?" I asked.

"Because I'm adopted," Janie said when her mother left. "All I have to do is throw a fit and voila, I get what I want."

"Really?"

"Yep. See that car?" she said as she parted the sheers in her bedroom window that looked out on to the driveway.

"Yeah?"

"Cost: One royal fit," she said.

"So, you just throw a fit and get what you want?" I asked.

"Pretty much," she said proudly.

Her sister confirmed this story as she sat and listened grinning ear to ear, nodding her head about the royal fit thing.

This, I thought, is what a spoiled brat is, as I walked over to her makeup mirror on her vanity.

"Hey, do you think I have buck teeth?"

"No, not at all." she said.

"Hey," I said as I swiveled away from the mirror, "would your mom allow one of her friends to hit you?"

"Oh my god, no, why?" she asked.

"I don't know." I said.

Later that night, against my promises not to speak a word to anyone, I told Janie about the abuse Lisa was going through across the street. I think I did that to take her mom's eyes off my life, and derail her mom's attempt at wanting to call someone for me.

On weekends when my mom and Wayne went out and Janie knew we'd be alone all night to smoke and do what we wanted, she'd beg and plead to be able to sleepover my house. Her mother would cave every time and we'd order pizza to Lisa's house. We hoped it would serve two purposes. We'd see Lisa come to the door and know she was o.k, and we hoped the mom would decide to buy the pizza and Lisa would get to eat. Each time she sent the pizza guy away and each time he carried the pizza box back to the car with him. Eventually no matter how we disguised our voices over the phone, they would not deliver to that house anymore.

I knew Janie used me in order to stay over and talk on the phone with her boyfriend who was much older than her. She was seventeen and he was in his thirties.

One night when she was over, my mom and her boyfriend woke us with the sound of screaming and fighting and things breaking out in the living room. My mom was acting like a wild animal trying to be caged. When I came out of my room to see what was going on, he was on top of her on the couch trying to catch her flailing arms and legs. I screamed for him to get the fuck off of her and ran back to my room stepping off to the side just inside the door. With that, I knew he'd come barreling after me into my room. The room was dark and as he reared his hand back to hit me across the face for screaming and cussing at him. I turned on the light to let him know I had company.

The second the light went on, he realized he was about to deck my friend Janie in the face. He lost all color in his face, lowered his hand from high above his head, turned to face me, unclenched his fist and quietly left the room.

Needless to say, Janie couldn't gather her belongings and scurry home fast enough. I could tell by her face she had never encountered such a mess in all her life. And for as much of a spoiled brat she was, I think she got home that night and thanked her lucky stars she didn't have to live like that.

Days later when trying to figure out what happened, my mom said she thought someone must have tampered with her drink while they danced that night. She recounted never feeling quite that out of her mind in all her life, but couldn't quite remember all the details.

Story of her life, I thought.

And just like that, we left Ohio and went back to the trailer on Rabbit Hill.

Part 8

Rabbit Hill/Manner Ridge

Wellsburg, West Virginia

Chapter 34

One night when it was just me and my dad at the house, I asked to use his Nova to go to the drive-in. I didn't officially have my license yet, but my dad never cared about such things. I liked the Nova better because it wasn't a stick shift. A "D" for drive and an "R" for reverse. Simple.

"Dad, can I use your car tonight so we can go to the drive-in?"

"Drive-in?" he asked

"Yeah, Blue Moon Drive-In."

"We?" he asked.

"Ah, Karen, who else?"

"What's playin'?" he asked.

"*Flashdance* and *Stayin' Alive*. Dance movies. You know… Karen's going to be a dancer when she gets older, and loves dance movies," I said like that would make him remember.

"Oh, I see. Girl movies and junk, huh?" he said.

"Yeah. Can I?"

"Will there be boys there with you two?"

"No. No boys, Dad. Why?" I said.

"Just askin', you know how I feel about the types of boys you like."

"No, Dad, no boys will be there, now can we go?"

"Sure, I guess," he said.

"Yay!" I said, excited.

I turned around, excited, and ran to call Karen.

I grabbed my purse, yelled, "See ya, Dad!" over my shoulder as I left, and went to get Karen who was already standing outside on her porch waiting for me.

Once at the drive-in, we went to the concession stand before the movie to get our food. Two hot dogs, a small pizza to share, a large popcorn, and two pops. It was still a little bit light out once we got back to the car.

I rolled my window down but left just enough of it up to hang the big metal speaker on. Down in front of the large white drive-in screen were kids swinging on the swings and little kids running around as their parents watched.

We watched the movie, passing small talk between us.

"Look at their bodies and all those great costumes," she said. "I can't wait to be a dancer someday," she said as if I didn't already know.

"You're gonna be a great dancer. You were awesome in the talent show at school last year. Blew Candice-what's-her-name out of the water, if you ask me," I said.

"Do you believe she had the nerve to tell me that I should give her the outfit I wore that day on stage because it would look better on her?" she asked.

"I can believe it. I've never seen anyone so stuck on themselves as she is. Besides, she's a redhead," I said.

Karen looked at me confused.

"Your top was hot pink. Not the right color combo. It looked *way* better on you with your dark brunette hair," I said, watching the screen.

It felt good to be independent and to be trusted with the car out at night, especially that late at night when the last movie ended around one-thirty in the morning. And, by the time I drove Karen home and got home myself, it would be well after two in the morning. I loved spending my own money earned from mowing the grass, doing chores and selling things I no longer wanted or used for buying food I wanted to eat and seeing movies I wanted to see. I loved doing things my way and paying my own way.

Something caught my eye in the rearview mirror. I thought I saw the trunk lid move. I nudged Karen to turn around and look too.

Just then it started to rise slowly, then lifted with a thud. Karen and I both screamed. Popcorn went flying around the inside of the car and drinks spilled.

Before I knew it, he had his head in my window, laughing like a madman.

We both grabbed our chests.

"Dad! What are you doing?!" I said, holding my chest.

"Eh, just messin' with ya, kid, and seein' if you were lyin' to me about havin' any boys in here. Thought I'd sneak in and check things out and scare the hell out of you two at the same time. Kinda like killin' two birds with one stone. How'd I do? Did I get you?" he said as he bent down to see Karen's reaction.

"Well, Mr. Jessup, you scared the crap out of me!" Karen said as her widened eyes looked over from the other side of the car.

"Yeah, you managed to scare me pretty bad too," I said, slunk back in the seat, looking forward, continuing to hold my chest.

"Well, the movie's about over. I'll just sit out here on this blanket that was in the trunk," he said.

He made himself a sitting area with a blanket and watched the rest of the movie while sitting off to the left side of the car.

My mouth hung open and I was speechless. All I could do was look at Karen while I still held my chest. She looked back but with really big, round eyes as she shook her head back and forth and mouthed the word, "WOW!"

Chapter 35

There was a boy I liked, but he didn't live in our town. He visited his dad for summers, because he lived in another state with his mom. I had a major crush on him. He was tan, had super-white teeth, and wore a windbreaker when it was seventy degrees out.

Over the course of several summers, he'd come to our house and swim in our pool. And my dad actually started to like him. So, when the invitation to visit him was extended to me one evening as we sat at the picnic table outside, and he even invited my friend Karen if she wanted, I nervously awaited the resounding no from my dad.

But, after a slight interrogation of who would be with us at the house, what we'd be doing, when, and where I'd be, my dad said it would be o.k. to go stay with him at his house with no problem whatsoever. When he even gave me spending money to enjoy myself while I was there, I decided the heavens above had parted and it was meant to be. To have my dad approve of a boy was surreal.

Karen and I spent hours in the back seat singing to every song that played on the radio on the way there while her sister and her friend drove. Since none of us had the money to get a hotel, we drove all the way through.

Never having seen the ocean before, we were excited that my boyfriend had planned to take us to the beach while there. On the day Karen's sister and her friend dropped off at his house, his mom was welcoming to us. She was as short as my grandma and as tanned as my dad with white hair and wore an all white golf skirt outfit that day. She warmly reminded us that we could help ourselves to anything we wanted in the refrigerator and that she wouldn't be home until later in the evening. She reminded her son on the way out the door that the sheets to the guest bed were in the dryer and asked him to please make the bed up when they were finished drying.

We all watched TV, listened to music and planned what we'd do the next day as we ate snacks out in the living room that evening.

When my boyfriend went in the guest bedroom to make the bed for us with the clean sheets, Karen nudged me to go in there with him.

"Fitted sheets suck to put on a bed," I said.

"Yeah, they do," he said on the other side of the bed, pulling the sheet.

We laughed and pulled a tug of war of white sheets between us while trying to get the bed made until at one point he came around the bed and planted a long kiss on me. Liking him for two years, I kissed him back. He slowly lowered me to the bed and got on top of me, kissing and kissing.

"We gotta get up, we can't leave Karen out there all by herself for long," I said.

"She's fine," he said.

We went back to kissing. He fumbled with the snap on my jean shorts while still kissing my mouth and my neck.

"We can't," I said. "She's gonna know."

"So what?" he said as he kissed at me and fumbled with my pants.

"I care," I said. "I don't want to."

He had my pants unbuttoned and was pulling at the waistband of them and my underwear. I liked him so it was all so confusing. Yes, I liked him. But did I want this? I wondered. My body said I did. My mouth said I didn't. He had managed to get my pants unsnapped and wiggled them down to my ankles, and removed one leg. His pink-tipped, hard penis peeked out the top of his underwear band.

"No, really," I said. "I can't," I said as I tried to close my legs.

He pulled my legs apart forcefully with both hands, landing forcefully with his waist between them. He pulled just his penis out of his underwear with one hand and placed his other hand over my mouth while trying to guide his penis to enter me.

"Shhhhh," he said. "Just lay back and relax."

"Stop!" I yelled through his hand.

"Shhhhh. You want it. You like me, I know you do," he said. "It may hurt some."

"No! I don't!" I yelled. It felt like a piercing knife going in and I squinted my eyes in pain. He thrust his body into me several times, groaning while trying to be quiet. He lay writhing on top of me, and then his body went limp, further pushing me hard into the bed.

I pushed him off, got off the bed and struggled to untangle my underwear and pants that were around my ankle. When I turned around to look at him lying on the bed, I was startled to see a round circular area of bright red blood on the white sheets we had just put on the bed.

He looked at it too.

"You're a virgin?" he asked.

"Was. Was a virgin. 'Was' being the key word here. And yes, that's why I told you I couldn't... that I didn't want to. Asshole," I said.

"So, I got your cherry, huh?" he said, proud of himself. He got up, walked around the bed to kiss me and stood there holding me.

"Yeah," I said, confused as I stood there inside his arms, not knowing what to make of how I was feeling.

"Awww. Don't be mad. We've liked each other for so long. Don't make it out to be something bad. Guys never forget a girl who give up their cherries to them," he said.

So, this was losing your virginity. This was sex, I thought. All I knew is it hurt like hell. How anyone could enjoy this, I wondered, was beyond me as I looked at the blood. And I didn't give up anything. He took it.

"Well, let's strip the sheets and put them in the wash before my mom gets home," he said.

When we walked out of the bedroom, into the living room, Karen was still there listening to music.

"What happened?" she asked as she saw him taking the sheet and putting it in the washer.

I just shook my head that nothing happened.

Karen mentioned how quiet I seemed that night. I said I didn't know why I was. But I was trying to process why after liking this boy for so long, I felt so weird about what just happened. It was hard to process this while in their company so I just decided to think about it another time.

Karen and I slept together in that same bed that night. The clean, white sheets washed before the stain set in reminded me that nothing happened here today.

She talked excitedly about going to the beach the next day while I just nodded and agreed, just listening.

Afraid of the ocean after seeing *Jaws*, and knowing sharks, like boys, could smell blood, Karen finally coaxed me out to play ball on the first sand barge we came to that day. We talked about how neat it was to be that far out from the beach, yet be able to stand up in water that was only knee high. We played ball there until the skies grew dark and you could hear thunder rolling in the distance.

Soon, a man, made leathery and brown from the sun, came to the edge of the water, wearing a large hat with a string around his neck and cut off shorts. He was yelling at us and motioning with his hand for us to get out of the water, emphasizing the word, "now."

I saw the movie, so I swam like my life depended on it.

We got out, breathless. When we got up to him, asking what the problem was, he said he had spotted a shark not fifty feet from where we were playing ball. We thought he was joking, but he took the time to explain that as storms rolled in, everything living in the sea swims closer to shore for safety and to never stay in the ocean when a storm was coming for that reason.

"Had that shark been much closer, someone could've quickly been attacked," he said.

I thought about that and shuddered. Attacked. Wow. Like in the movie. Blood everywhere.

Then, the scene from the day before came flooding back. My pants twisted up at my ankle, his hand over my mouth, my legs pried apart, him landing between them with a thud and the piercing pain I felt. I was still sore down there today and wondered if it was because of me the shark came.

On the drive back to West Virginia, as Karen napped, I thought about what had happened over and over. I felt a kind of weirdness I couldn't explain. I liked this boy and yet I now felt like I didn't. What was wrong with me?

I rolled the word *attacked* around in my mind and knew I hadn't been attacked. I wasn't dragged back to an alley, I thought. I was in his bedroom and it just happened. Some of it I wanted and didn't fight and some of it I didn't want and fought. And I said no. But it still happened.

When I got back to the trailer on Rabbit Hill, I gathered enough courage to tell my mom about it. I told her I thought this boy forced himself on me and that I used to think I liked him, but now did not. I wanted to know why I couldn't stop feeling weird about it.

"Were you in his bedroom?" she asked.

"Yeah, why?" I asked.

"Well, you can't go around saying a boy forced himself on you when you willingly go waltzing into their bedroom with them," she said.

"So, even if I say no, it's my fault?" I asked.

"You put yourself in a boy's room, that's what happens. You should know by now how boys are," she said.

Well, I thought, that's that. It was my fault. I was stupid enough to go into the bedroom with him and that's what happened. This is what my dad had been warning me about all this time. So, I never told another soul about it and I went on with my life and tried to forget about it.

It wasn't until I was in my twenties the term "date rape" came out in the news. I knew instantly after hearing it that that's what happened to me that day back in 1983 when I was sixteen years old. And I finally figured out why the whole thing made me feel so weird and why I no longer liked the boy who visited our neighborhood for summers.

I may have been in his room, but I certainly didn't deserve that. I was "on a date" but I was also "raped." One was not an invitation for the other. How ironic to me now, that he was the only boy my dad approved of for me. And how sad, I thought, the only time I ever went to my mom for motherly advice, she blamed me.

I still have the pictures from this day of us at the beach. There I was with my Pat Benatar haircut smiling on the pier posing with my friend Karen. Pictures of us running in and out of the water, taking extreme close-up photos of pelicans, and there are even a few of me embracing this boy on the pier for the camera. I'm acting as if I'm glad he is mine and I hold him in what looks like a chokehold around his neck. He is acting shy as if he's embarrassed by it all.

There I was, putting on that happy-girl smile again and acting as if I was the Happiest Girl in the whole U.S.A. But, only Pat Benatar got it right. Hell was for children.

Chapter 36

I got my driver's license shortly after getting home that same summer and my dad wanted me to get better at driving Lana's stick shift. No daughter of his was going to break down only to have the wrecker deliver her a stick shift to drive home and her not know how to drive it. I hated having him teach me anything and preferred learning with Lana or actually anyone else. But there I sat one day, at the bottom of Washington Pike in Lana's silver Honda Prelude 5-speed stick shift, with my dad in the passenger seat. I white knuckled the steering wheel. I was sweating, my heartbeat pounding in my ears, my palms wet as I death-gripped the wheel.

"Whatever you do… don't drift backwards," he said. "There's a car behind us and he's so far up your ass right now, you'll hit him if you drift."

The light was red. My feet were pressing so hard on the clutch and the brake; I thought I might push them through the floorboard.

Remember everything he taught you, Robin, I said to myself. Let up on the brake and release the clutch, as you press down the gas at the same time, even-steven, like you were taught.

I looked over at my dad. Everything seemed to be in slow motion. He was holding onto the handle of the car door and the dash looking in his side-view mirror at how close the car was behind us, nervous.

"Girl… you better not hit that guy's car behind us. I don't care what you gotta do, don't you fucking drift… don't do it, you hear me, girl?" he said, not even looking at me.

God, this light is long, I thought.

Please don't turn green, I said in my head. I can just sit here for the rest of my life like this. Please don't turn green. If I drift, I'm dead meat. If I hit that guy's car, I'll be grounded, I'll be… Oh, Please God, please… help me NOT TO DRIFT! I prayed, no, I yelled at God in my head.

The light turned green.

My feet were as fast as lightning. I pulled my foot off the brake and pressed it down on the gas, and let the clutch up halfway even-steven like, squealing the tires. I pulled the gearshift hard into second gear. I was so relieved. I had done it. And for the quick millisecond I was about to feel proud of myself, I realized that in my breathless, sweaty, laser-focused concentration on what to do with my feet, I forgot I needed to continue to shift gears.

I was halfway up the first hill of Washington Pike and still in second gear with the engine revving and the RPM needle in the red.

Finally, it clicked. "SHIFT!" I thought to myself.

I depressed that clutch again, yanking and pushing the stick up into third, and gassed it up some more, the tires screaming and chirping behind me, the smell of burnt rubber filled the air.

I looked behind me in the rearview mirror to see how close the guy was behind me, but he wasn't. Not even close.

I flew up Washington Pike, not thinking anymore, but shifting again and again, not looking over at my dad even once, finally in fifth gear. When it felt safe to look away from the road, I finally looked over at my dad. His stiff concerned body, that was all hunched up around the dash, was now less stiff. He was sitting back in the seat, hand up on the roof through the window, holding on, not saying a word, our hair spilling around our faces as the air swirled in around our heads.

He turned to look at me and when his eyes met mine, he broke out into a fit of laughter. He was laughing so hard tears were rolling down his face. I continued nervously to hold on to the steering wheel. And after a bit, I laughed so hard nothing came out of my mouth and my nostrils flared in my contained laughter.

"Well, I told you not to drift and you sure as hell didn't drift, did ya?" he said, wide eyed and amazed as he ruffled the hair on my head. "I didn't say a god damned word about laying rubber for miles, did I?" he said as he laughed and laughed.

He seemed proud, laughing, telling someone later on the phone how I laid rubber and he might need to buy Lana new tires now.

"You're alright, kid. You're alright," he said as he patted my shoulders as I parked the car in the garage. "Now get your ass outside and play," he said.

And just like that I was outside and happy to be on my trusty ten-speed. I definitely knew how to shift gears on that.

Chapter 37

Unbelievably, after all the beatings my mom and I had taken from Wayne, and all the times my mom caught him cheating on her, he coaxed her into marrying him.

When I protested to another move, my mom said she had a chance at a new life and pointed out that he even bought her a house with a pool this time, and she'd be damned if she was gonna pass that up because I didn't want to move.

But somehow, some way, I got my mom, dad and step mom Lana to agree that I would stay with my dad and Lana until I graduated from Brooke High.

So, with Lana's help, I started driving more and more, and spent more time being independent. And the older and more independent I became, the more suspicious my dad was of me doing something I shouldn't be.

And if following me to the drive-in hidden in the trunk of the car or climbing trees to catch me out of my room weren't going to yield results, he'd put Lana up to tracking me while he worked. So, just like that he had her tailing me to friends' houses. But she never once tried to hide herself.

I was at my friend John's house one day. He was the boy that gave me the blue ribbon and lit up like a Christmas tree when he saw me. We were sitting on his front porch smoking cigarettes and listening to "Stroke Me" by Billy Squire, and here Lana came driving down the steep dirt road in the tiny silver Honda Prelude. She waved back as I waved. I went up to the car and she rolled down her window.

"Sorry, kiddo, I had to. He checks the mileage on the car," she said before I could ask.

"Wow. This is getting ridiculous," I said.

"Yep. It is. And it's coming to an end on my end soon. I'm not putting up with this shit much longer. You, on the other hand, I feel sorry for. It's not like you can just leave like I can," she said.

I watched her drive back up the steep dirt road and broke into tears. I knew without her in my life, I would lose the only person who would never turn on me.

I downed a shot of Wild Turkey, opened a beer and John lit my next cigarette. If I was gonna be in trouble or get killed for something I shouldn't be doing, I better do it up right, I thought.

"I love you, Robin. You know I do. I can protect you, care for you," John said as he came up behind me and wrapped his arms around me.

I knew he wasn't like other boys. He was tender with me, never forceful and yet wild and fun. And we never had sex or even made out, even when we sat together in his room. I loved him for that alone.

"John. We're kids," I said. "You can't protect me. No one can."

When Karen's sixteenth birthday rolled around that May, one of the guys at DiCarlo's Pizza gave us a small joint to celebrate. After getting our pizza — four pieces with extra cheese and mushrooms for me, and for her two corners and two regular with extra cheese and extra pepperoni — we headed up the pike to Parson's Run Road. It was the only place I could think of that was almost always deserted and if there was the occasional car, it meant you lived down there and probably wouldn't be the cops.

I put the Nova in park on the dark dirt road, and turned the ignition off and backwards to still hear the radio, rolled down the window and lit the joint she rummaged from her purse.

Now, DiCarlo's pizza is a delicious treat by itself, it's the hot pizza with cold toppings that is all the rage in the area, but when you're high, it's an orgasmic delight to the taste buds. You close your eyelids over the eyes you're rolling back in your head as you take your first bite. Saliva floods your mouth and you want more and more. The heightened taste we both experienced from the joint made us giggle as we continued to eat pizza, drink our favorite pop Mello Yello and smoke a doobie. As the high kicked in, we laughed as we said "dooooobie" over and over, crossing our eyes as we looked down at our lips.

Laughing and enjoying ourselves soon gave way to the feeling as if we were being watched. We talked about my dad being in the trunk and then the cemetery at the start of the road, and that made us even more paranoid.

"Stop. You're freaking me out," Karen said.

"Shhh," I said.

I quickly pulled the headlight knob out toward me to turn on the headlights. Nothing there. So I turned them off. Relieved, we continued to smoke and eat and talk.

Then, Karen shushed me. She thought she heard someone talking so we turned off the radio that was playing softly and sat listening.

Nope. Nothing. No one but us.

"Do you think your dad's in the trunk?" she asked.

It was quiet except for the crickets chirping and an occasional frog croaking in the distance under the starless country night.

"Nah, he's at work," I assured her.

We giggled at our silliness and continued on while dismissing our feelings of someone or something being close by.

The pizza was finally gone.

I didn't want to drive this stoned and voiced my concern for how we were going to get home.

"You'll do great. I'll let you know how you're doing and if you start to go off the road, we'll stop and start again. There's no one out here this time of night anyway," she said.

Had I heard this somewhere before? Weird, I thought as I shook it off. Anyway, it made perfect sense to me now.

So, I turned the car around and we started home.

It felt as if I was driving sporadically and faster than I had ever driven before. I felt at any moment I'd lose control and for the first time in my short driving experience, I was terrified.

"Maybe I should slow down a bit!" I yelled.

"I'm right here. You don't have to yell," she reminded me. "And you're doing fine," she said as she stuck her head up higher than normal to look out over the hood of the car.

I trusted her judgment. She was my longest, closest, dearest friend, ever, and had been through a lot of my hell with me, and kept being my friend in spite of it all, so I kept driving.

God, this is taking forever, I thought.

"Feels like we're flying but not going anywhere? The road seems to stretch out further and further in front of me," I said, puzzled.

The speed at which we rounded the curves of the mountain roads felt as if we'd flip the car at any moment. I'd feel over too far to the right one second, then too far left the next. I was losing control.

The speed scared me and I just knew it was going to hurt when we got into the accident I was sure we were going to have. I knew my dad was going to flip out, and punish me unlike anything I'd experienced before, if I even lived.

I looked down at the speedometer.

I was going 5 miles an hour.

We eventually got back to my dad's that night. There was no way I could drive her home clear out onto Rabbit Hill like this, so she agreed to stay overnight. Karen agreed to get out and guide me in the garage to be sure I wouldn't scrape the sides of the car as we pulled in.

"Whew! We're safe," we said, as we made it into the house.

In the morning, my dad came in my room, ripping open the blinds and windows to let the sunlight and fresh air in.

"Dad, what time is it?" I said squinting.

"Time for Up and At 'Em," he said. "And to blow that stink off you two lushes. This whole god damn room reeks of alcohol, cigarettes and reefer."

"Ugh!" I said. He knows! I thought. Oh shit!

"When you two ladies are awake, I need you to meet me out in the kitchen," he said.

We walked to the end of the hall where we could see the kitchen and just stood there baffled. Just about every dish, pan and utensil we owned was piled high in the sink or on the counter. We had made chicken and waffles, spaghetti with meatballs, ate all the Doritos, and various bags of cookies and wrappers now lay empty on the counters.

"You drunk asses are gonna clean this shit up," he said.

So, per our unspoken arrangements, I washed and rinsed, Karen dried and put away.

"Do you remember making all this food?" I asked.

"I don't even remember eating all this food," she said.

"Me either," I said.

As we did the dishes and cleaned up the kitchen, we couldn't help but see my dad out the little window over the sink. He was down over the hill, walking in and out of the garage. From time to time I'd see him just standing there looking in at something in the garage, scratching his head.

"What do you think he's doing?" I asked Karen.

"With him? Who the hell knows?" she said. "Do you believe he knows we smoked a joint last night?" she added.

"I know. But he didn't say anything else about it? He must be in a good mood today," I said, confused.

"Let's hope," she said.

We watched him walk back up the hill and he spoke to us through the screen door in the breezeway.

"Hey, can you two ladies come down here for a minute?" he said.

We dried our hands off and went down over the hill where the garage doors were open, afraid of what we might see.

And there was my dad's silver Nova pulled in the garage, precisely, sideways.

"You mind tellin' me just how the hell you managed this?" he said.

"I don't know," I said. "I did that?" I asked.

"Yep. I don't even know how to get it out now. That's what I been out here trying to figure out," he said.

We all three stood there just staring, baffled. I was terrified of the punishment that I would get for the reefer and now this.

No one spoke.

Then my dad started laughing.

"All I'm gonna say is, I wanna party with you girls! I mean, what the hell did you two drink and smoke last night?" He bent over to slap his leg. "Your grandpap's not going to believe his eyes when he sees this one."

We started to laugh too, nervously.

He stood up and put an arm around each of us.

"I'll tell ya, sometimes," he said, "I don't know what to do with you two. But, I figure, I'm gonna keep ya around, cuz you two twerps make me laugh like no one else does."

He wrapped his arm around my neck, gave me a noogie on my head, slapped at Karen's shoulder and told us to get our asses back up to the house and make sure the kitchen was cleaned.

Chapter 38

It was now the middle of winter, and after a fight with Lana one night, my dad pulled down the steps leading up onto the deck of the pool, and walked out onto the frozen pool with his sawed-off shotgun and was threatening to kill himself.

I can't remember exactly what the fight was about, I can only now speculate it was probably about her telling him she couldn't take his shit anymore and was finally leaving him for good this time. And it was always the same cycle.

First came suicide threats,

then came stalking,

then came a restraining order,

then divorce papers.

"Dad! Stop this!" I yelled. "Dad, please… please come down and just talk about it," I pleaded.

"Harland, this is what I'm talking about," Lana tried to explain. "This is just nuts and I can't and I won't live like this anymore. I'm going to my parents' house tonight." And she walked back inside.

"Please, Lana, please don't leave me here alone with him tonight," I said.

"I can't take it anymore, Robin. I feel sorry for you, I really do," she said as she filled up a bag with clothes.

"What am I supposed to do?" I asked.

"I don't know, he's your dad, maybe you can talk some sense into him, but I just can't anymore," she said. "I'd move in with your mother if I were you. It can't be any worse than this."

I felt helpless as I watched the red taillights of her silver Honda Prelude slip away into the cold, dark night. The steam from the exhaust danced excitedly behind the car and tailpipe as if it to say goodbyes can also be fresh starts.

And that was the last time I ever saw Lana.

I had learned over time not to get too attached to people, places or outcomes, never hanging my hat in any one place for very long. I'd made friends everywhere I ever moved, only to move again and never see them again. I had to learn to roll with the tides, fighting against it just made it harder. And I was so tired. Now, one of the most pivotal people in my life, my biggest defender and ally, Lana was gone from my life, just like that. There were no goodbyes, no hugs, no telling her just how much her kindness meant to me.

But I couldn't spend time crying. Right now, I had to get back to talking some sense into my dad.

You can see your parents do a lot of shit that's awful, to animals, to others and to you. Your mind can be tangled up in the confusion of their actions, but you still love them because they're all you know. And when they grab a loaded sawed-off shotgun and are threatening to kill themselves, you tell them from your heart, anything and everything that comes to mind, to make them laugh, and let them know they are loved and wanted and beg them to please come down off there this instant. And everything you say at that moment, no matter how trivial, are the truest words you'll ever speak in your life.

"Dad. Please. Stop it and come in the house," I said.

He was sobbing.

"I should just end it all, right here, like this. They can find my dead body on top of a frozen swimming pool in the morning and all this hell will be over and everyone can go on living their lives without me since I'm such a fuck-up," he said.

"You're not, Dad. People actually love you. A lot. When you let them. You make people laugh like no one else. I'm not saying you can't have your feelings and get upset, but you get so mad… about the littlest things. When you're in a good mood, you're a blast to be around," I said. "Remember the time you set off that huge bundle of M-80's during the neighbors' Jehovah Witness meetings?" I asked.

I was at that particular meeting, just to be with a friend of mine from the neighborhood, and we did everything we could not to enter into fits of laughter, making it that much funnier to us. It was a solid few minutes of M-80's going off in her breezeway. Every time the next person would start to read, they'd go off again. The whole room would stop. We'd cover our faces with our books trying to conceal our laughter. They'd think the coast was clear, start to read, and it would start all over and go on and on… and on. When I got home that evening, my dad asked, "So how was Jehovah today over there in the Kingdom Hall?" as he held his hand over his mouth and laughed like a little boy.

"And, whether you like it or not, you have a good heart," I continued, "a heart of gold, under there somewhere, because I've seen it. You're generous and caring and would give people the shirt off your back if they needed it."

I reminded him of his goodness by talking about an impromptu yard sale I had once to make some money. After hours of him watching me sit in the front yard and not making a lot of money, here he came walking out of the house with these huge air-conditioning window units from all the bedroom windows, a vacuum cleaner he'd had since I was a baby, and tools from the garage so I could sell more and make more money. When he brought out the last utensil from the kitchen he didn't think he'd use, he remembered and hurriedly ran back in to grab some canned food from the cabinets I could sell too.

I went on.

"And no one wants to go on with their lives without you in it," I said. "But, you gotta get control of yourself and your rage. I don't know where it comes from, but it's ruining your life and runs off every woman you've ever dated or married," I said. "Why can't you just let people love you and stop getting so irate over things?" I asked.

I'm not sure how long I was outside in the cold talking him down that night, but eventually he came inside, put the shotgun back in his closet and settled down.

I can vividly see him in my mind's eye standing up on the frozen pool, the warmth of his words and breath filling the cold air as he spoke and sobbed. The white steam rose from his mouth through the starless winter night sky and I felt sorry for the tortured soul that he was. I was trying to help him, but I was up against something much more powerful than I could ever know about or even fix. It was a war of some kind that had nothing to do with me. And, as I stood there listening to him rant and rave against his demons something told me we can be 'from' a family, but we don't need to be 'of' their issues. And even though I meant all the words I said to my dad that night and I did love him then and love him now, I remember what a huge difference those two little words "from" and "of" made for me from that moment on.

I knew I was a lot like both my parents and my family. I could rage and fight like my father, check out and become selfish like my mother, cover my pain in a warped sense of humor like my cousin, and smile widely as if my life wasn't falling apart like my grandma.

But, I was me.

I knew as I watched him that night that our minds believed what we told it. If we told it we were messed up, and couldn't do anything right, then we were and we couldn't. If we told ourselves no one loved us, then no one did. Not because it's true, but because our bodies can only react to the thoughts we feed it, even if it's an untrue thought. He wasn't able to control the thoughts that flooded his mind and when they got too bad, he tried to project them onto me. He didn't want to change his behavior. It was his excuse to do bad things.

But my family and all their dysfunction didn't have to be the rest of my life. I saw that there was a whole world out there for me outside the world my parents had created for me as a child, and soon, I didn't have to live like this anymore.

My mom came to pick me up shortly after this incident, and I no longer lived with my dad or visited him as a minor again. I was in tenth grade when I left. When I told her I talked my dad out of killing himself that night, she said I didn't. It was a manipulation he used to get people to do or not do what he wanted.

Whatever his problem, I knew I couldn't go back for a long while. My nerves just wouldn't allow it. I just couldn't do this anymore, and without an ally, I wasn't sure I wanted to.

As we approached the Steubenville Bridge to go back to Ohio, I made sure to take a good long look once inside her to soak it all in. I saw the damage, but I also saw the strength and beauty. I was in awe of her and yet still so afraid. I somehow knew that being scared of her was an insult to her beauty, but I just couldn't help it. She meant something to me, and I just knew she was trying to teach me something about myself. Why else did she evoke such strong emotions in me? Why did she visit me in my dreams? What was she saying?

I just didn't know.

Part 9

Valley City, Ohio

Chapter 39

My mom had graduated from beauty school, and was now doing hair at Fantastic Sam's. When she was off, she allowed me to take her 1983 gray Buick Regal to get out of the house. She did anything and everything to keep Wayne and I separated because it was apparent at this stage that we both hated each other's guts.

So, I met kids my age, got a job at Dairy Queen and stayed gone as much as possible. When I started working more, my mom called and convinced my dad to send her five hundred dollars to help her get me a car. With his five hundred, she'd add five hundred and I could get a thousand-dollar car for work.

Only she didn't add five hundred dollars to his money, so I got a five hundred dollar car. It was a white 1974 Plymouth Duster. The day I drove it out of the driveway, I wasn't but ten feet up Route 303 in front of our house and the torsion bar broke. The ass end of the car fell to the right and wobbled and swayed as I continued to drive to my job at Dairy Queen. My boss at Dairy Queen called it a Rolls G'narly. When I asked what that was, he said, "It rolls down one hill, g'narly get up the next."

It never was fixed, and pretty soon I just no longer had it.

On days my mom worked, and I was off, I remember hating being left home alone with my stepdad. I'd hear him down in the basement, huffing and puffing, and see him lifting weights while admiring himself in the mirrors when I had to go to the basement for my laundry. I used to think what a wuss he was for making such a racket when he was only lifting ten-pound weights. I'd laugh at what a buffoon I thought he was when he did more walking around looking at himself in his spandex workout pants than he did working out. He'd flex in the mirror and inspect his body while twirling his mustache.

"What are you laughin' about?" he'd ask.

"Nothing," I'd say as I walked away, rolling my eyes. Remembering my mom saying not to provoke him.

"While you're up there doing nothing, why don't you earn your keep and make me some fried potatoes," he'd say.

"Why can't Mom make them for you?" I'd say.

"Because I asked YOU to do it, that's why."

I remember worrying that he kept his loaded police-issued gun in its holster on the bar in the house. Loaded gun plus alcohol, what could go wrong, I thought.

Plus, I wasn't entirely sure if I trusted him not to shoot us or me not to shoot him. A loaded gun out in plain sight with kids in the house, good parenting, I thought.

Sometimes I thought I was the only one on the planet with any sense and I was the seventeen-year-old.

I peeled a five-pound bag of potatoes, got out the big silver electric skillet, coated the bottom with oil and piled it high with the sliced potatoes I wished I could poison.

He was grunting from lifting weights to Bruce Springsteen. "I'm on Fire" came through the floor from the basement. The words made me think of my dad. He'd never called to check on me. He and my mom rarely talked, and I wasn't allowed to make long-distance calls.

"Potatoes are done," I said down the basement steps.

"I'll be up in a minute."

He'd stop to look at himself in the wall of floor-to-ceiling mirrors in the basement one more time, admiring his biceps and physique.

"This is it?" he said as he came into the kitchen.

"What do you mean?" I said.

"You just made potatoes, nothing else with it?"

"You just asked for potatoes," I said. "I can open a can of baked beans and make a hot dog for you, if you want," I added quickly.

"Sure, do that, then," he said.

He sat in the kitchen and ate. I went to my room. I couldn't stand being in the same room as him, I hated even looking at him. I thought he was gross.

"Hey," he said as he knocked on my bedroom door.

"Yeah?" I said, not opening the door.

"You need to get in there and clean up the kitchen before your mom gets home," he said.

"She'll want to eat when she gets home, so why don't I leave it for her, then I'll clean up."

He opened the door.

"You have something to say about everything, don't ya?"

"Because I'm the only one around here that thinks, that's why!"

"You fuckin' little bitch! You get your ass in there and do what the hell I tell you to do before I ground you to your room for a month," he said.

"Oh, please… by all means… do that, because I'm tired of being your stand-in wife when my mom's not here, then being punished for nothing every time I turn around. Ground me to my room and do this shit yourselves, then!" I yelled.

And with that, his face changed.

My mom had just come in the front door from work and by the time she had gotten to my room, he was carrying me past her in the hall by one arm and one leg.

"What is going on?" she asked.

"Mom!" I yelled

"Wayne, what is going on?" she asked again.

"I'm sick of this god damned kid's mouth and not doing what I tell her!" he screamed.

He struggled to contain my flailing, fighting body as he carried me through the kitchen, dropping my arm long enough to open the front screen door. He picked my arm back up and swung me out the front door as if throwing someone in a pool. I went down four concrete steps and landed in the gravel driveway. He and my mom stood in the doorway looking down at me as I lay there.

"Robin Lynn, I don't know why you have to provoke him all the time!? Why on earth can't you just listen, for Christ's sake? I don't know why it's so hard to do as you're told?"

"Mom! You have got to be kidding me right now! I am sick of this! Of YOU! I'm not his fucking wife when you're not home. I'm leaving," I said.

"Good! Get your shit and get out!" he yelled.

"Where are you going, young lady?" my mom asked as I packed a bag.

"Like you care," I said as I walked past her with my bag and left out the door.

I walked down Route 303 as far away from the house I could get before I walked up to a house and asked to use their phone.

I called a new friend I had made, and she and her boyfriend came to take me to New Horizons in Medina.

New Horizons was a runaway shelter.

They were the same two that had not just a few weeks before brought three bags of groceries to the house one day after I told them how Wayne had taken the keys from my mom and refused to let her go to the store for several days. They just rang the doorbell, left the groceries on the doorstep, and took off. When I brought them into the house and sat them on the counter, my mom stood in her embarrassment. And just as surely as I thought she'd say how stupid it was of her to allow a man to prevent her from grocery shopping, and she was leaving this mess, she didn't say that at all.

"Jesus Christ, Robin Lynn, you need to learn to keep your mouth shut about your business," she warned.

"Why do I need to keep my mouth shut? I'm not the one being an asshole, he is," I reminded her.

When I got to the shelter that evening I was interviewed by a counselor about the issues going on at home. She asked questions, and I answered, as she took notes. I reminded her that she needed the records from Child Protective Services when they had been called out to take pictures of me at school one day after Wayne had busted my lip, bruised my face and pulled a wad of hair out of my scalp during a fight.

"Hi, I'm Robin. I guess I'll be your roommate for a few days or whatever," I said to the girl in the shelter.

"Good, another girl. This house is full of runaway boys; I was the only girl till you got here. Well, the shower is over there," she said. "You can put your stuff over there, that bed is yours, and you can take your shower now if you want, I already took mine."

"O.k., thanks," I said.

I took my stuff out of my bag, put it in the drawers and went in to take a shower. When I came out, I realized the girl had taken money from my bag and was gone. She'd been cleared to go home with her parent, the counselor told me.

I just didn't know how much longer I could take the unfairness that was my life. No matter what I did, I couldn't seem to earn my way out from under all this agony. I laid down on the twin bed on a metal frame inside the room for girls at the runaway shelter and stared off in my misery like the bust of Jesus with the bleeding crown of thorns.

During one of the counseling sessions my mom and stepdad had to attend, they turned on each other and started to fight right in the office in front of the counselor.

The counselor listened to them for a while and said, "So, this is kind of an example of what Robin has to listen to at home?"

"Um, no. I mean, yeah, I guess. We fight. Who doesn't?" my mom said.

"Well, that may indeed be true that everyone fights, but adult issues should be kept between adults and not discussed in front of children. It causes anxiety and stress for them. And," she added, "with the stress of having to get through all their school classes and extra-curricular activities and functions, well, it's not healthy nor easy for them."

"But, she's seventeen years old, she's not exactly a child," she said as she made air quotes around the word child.

"It doesn't matter if she is seventeen, she's still a minor and needs a place to feel safe and secure. With all the places she's lived and the schools she's gone to — not seeing her father, having been hospitalized for anxiety at age seven, not having you to lean on during it all — that's a lot of nervousness for her to deal with all her life. It's one thing to move a lot, but why can't she feel safe in her own home? Why is she always worried that someone will put their hands on her or that she'll have to watch her mother be abused?" she asked.

My mother started to cry as she always did when confronted. Wayne looked surprised and then disgusted by her show of emotions. He started to squirm in his seat. Crossing his legs to get comfortable and then uncrossing them and re-crossing them the other way. Fidgeting in his seat, looking down at his hands and finally reaching up to twist one side of his mustache.

"Do you want him to leave so we can talk?" the counselor asked.

She didn't answer, but shook her head up and down.

In a huff he got up and walked to the door. As he closed it he looked at my mom as if she better not say anything about him or else. When he caught me looking at his expression, he quickly shut the door.

"O.k., Starlah. Can you tell me what's going on? What is it you're feeling?" she asked looking down at the pad of paper in her lap.

My mom couldn't speak. She was sobbing. I got up, grabbed a tissue from a small wooden table next to us, and handed it to my mother and sat back down in my seat.

"I don't know your daughter very well, she's only been with us a few days, but I can tell you for all she's told me she's been through, she has a very good heart for other people. Do you find this to be true?"

My mom shook her head up and down and the tears flowed more.

"Why are you so upset?" the counselor asked.

"Because. Because she does have a good heart and I'm just a shitty mother."

"No, you're not," I said quickly.

"See, even your daughter doesn't think you're a terrible mother. Why do you say this about yourself?"

"Because I can't do anything for myself. I've always had to depend on a man. I've been abused, and I've turned around and taken it out on my biggest defender, Robin Lynn," she cried.

"So, if she's your biggest defender, why do you allow the abuse you get to affect your relationship with your daughter?" she asked.

"I'm just mad and sometimes I don't think. I don't realize I'm hurting her or that it's affecting us when I do it," she said.

"Well, you're a thirty-six-year-old woman with a daughter who's almost eighteen-years-old, it's about time you start thinking and acting like an adult and work through that anger before you alienate yourself from your daughter for good," she said.

My mom shook her head, wiping her nose and looking at me like she was sorry.

"Robin's been here for only a few days and can stay up to a few weeks. Do you want that?" she asked.

"No. I want her to come home and feel safe."

"And how is that going to happen?" she asked.

"I guess I'm going to have to put my foot down about things before she comes home," my mom said.

"Put your foot down. Exactly what does putting your foot down look like?" she asked.

"I just need to lay it all out. Tell him what I won't put up with anymore," she said.

"And what is it that you won't tolerate anymore?" she asked.

My mom looked down at her crumpled tissue in her hand twirling it around and around. She said nothing.

"Starlah, if you can't tell us what you won't tolerate anymore, how are you going to muster up the courage to tell him?" she asked.

"You're right," she admitted and took a big breath in. "I need to tell him if he ever touches my daughter again that I will leave him."

"Are you prepared to leave if it comes down to it?" she asked.

"Not at the moment, but I'll have to figure it out," she said.

"I'd like to hear more about this 'figuring it out' the next time we meet," she said. "But, time is just about up. Anything else you two want to say?" She passed a look between the two of us.

"I love you, Mom. I know you are stronger than this but you continue to let men abuse you and abuse your kids," I said. "You need to speak up and put a stop to it and if you can't stop it, you need to leave it."

My mom smiled, wiped her snotty nose.

"You know... they say kids are smarter than us parents like to believe," she said. "Sounds like that one has this guy's number."

She pointed to me then out to the waiting room. "And he doesn't like it one bit," she said.

"Well, then, maybe it's time you listen to her. She makes a lot of sense. Very mature for her age," said the counselor as she smiled at me.

"She's a smart girl, yes. I don't know where she gets it from, surely not me," she said.

The rest of the kids at the shelter and I made dinner in the community kitchen that night and then ate it on a large wooden picnic table that served as the kitchen table.

The rules were: girls washed, boys dried and put away. It was like being a part of a big family, each person with their own set of problems, but we were all considered outcasts that were defective. But the truth was we were all in a runaway shelter because people had done things to us that the world turned a blind eye to, yet we had to talk about what those things were behind closed doors. We were there because we were damn mad about it. This kid's father beat him too, this one stole things and got caught, this one was fighting with their siblings too much to stay in their own home, and this one was into drugs and constantly in trouble in school. I was the only girl. Again. The girl who provoked everyone, and who'd take on Godzilla not thinking of the consequences, my mom said. And, in all my confusion and toughness, I still wanted my dad. But he didn't even know where I was.

I needed to process it all, but right now, I felt my most immediate problem was getting my mother to realize she was strong enough not to be abused by a man. She had never been there for me, but I had to be there for her. I could be there for myself later.

Days went by and the counseling sessions continued. I went to my school from the shelter and then back there instead of home each night.

My boyfriend would come by to see me and we'd sit on the porch of New Horizons, holding hands, swinging on the front porch swing. He'd tell me he'd never abuse me like that, assure me I was safe and threaten to go beat Wayne's ass for me.

Before we were intimate, I told him I had something to tell him first.

"What? You can tell me anything," he assured me.

So, I told him about the boy I liked a few years back and what had happened.

"It's o.k.," he said, "we'll just say this is your first time."

"What about you?" I asked.

"I'm a virgin too," he said.

I could see how a girl could get so crazy over a guy but I swore I'd never let a man abuse me or hurt my children no matter how much I thought I loved them. I'd always love my children and myself more than anyone else.

"Well, I feel good about all we've accomplished here the past few weeks," the counselor said. "Anyone have anything they'd like to add?" she asked, looking around the room at the three of us.

"Uh, no, I don't think so," he said, squirming again.

"No, I think we covered everything that needed covering," my mom said.

The counselor looked at me. "Do you have anything to say?"

My mother looked at me like she always has something to add, but I just said, "Nope."

I gathered my belongings, said goodbye to the counselors and the other kids I'd made friends with at the shelter and left with my mom and stepdad to head home.

"Hey, buddy, how'd you like to stop and get something to eat on the way home?" Wayne said.

Buddy? Where was I? A *Leave it to Beaver* episode?

But, I just said, "Sure!" a little too excitedly, hoping we could just get along.

We ate while having superficial chitchat. How's school, how're things with your boyfriend, and who's this new friend you made at the shelter, they wanted to know. I wasn't used to my mom giving a shit about what I did or didn't do, what I thought, or about what was going on in my life so although it made me a bit uncomfortable, I answered as if they cared, even though I knew neither of them did. People being too nice to me made me nervous. I knew their sudden attention was just their way of dealing with being uncomfortable with all the things they'd been learning about each other in our counseling sessions. They were acting. He learned she was vulnerable and too scared to stand on her own two feet, and would take pretty much whatever he dished out no matter what she said in counseling, and she learned her knight in shiny mirrored sunglasses and police officer uniform was nothing but a wife and child beater, and deadbeat dad.

I knew they were now putting on a brave front to act as united parents who had less than a year to go until I was eighteen years old and could move out on my own.

In an attempt to be nicer to me, and show me he had changed from all the therapy, Wayne 'gifted' me a car. That's what he wrote under the dollar amount on the title: "gift."

It was a white 1973 Mercury Montego with a 450 Cleveland engine. It went so fast at barely the touch of the gas pedal, that when my mom followed me somewhere in it once, she said, all she saw was exhaust blow out the back and I completely disappeared in a cloud of black smoke.

The car had so many rust spots that had corroded holes into the white metal, I called it the Dalmatian Dog. And, Dalmatian Dog idled at 3,000 RPM's tearing through gravel with its bare teeth like a beast. My mom told me my stepdad Wayne would sit there twirling the end of his mustache just waiting for me to spit gravel all over the front yard as I pulled out our driveway that went directly onto Route 303. She said before counseling he'd cuss and flip out each time, saying I was doing it on purpose. After counseling, she said he'd just sit there with his nostrils flaring and twirl the end of his mustache trying not to flip his lid. Once when one of his friends had to move my car, he told my stepdad Wayne he couldn't believe he let me drive this piece of shit that idled so high there was no way I was throwing the gravel on purpose. And how dare he call this a gift when it was, in fact, a death trap.

I had to use both feet on the brake to stop this thing that felt like a nine-thousand-pound tank. And because it idled so fast, you could feel it lurching slightly, just waiting to tear ass down the road at stops. At night, I had to flick my lighter in order to read the speedometer because it had no dash lights. The inside door panels were missing and there was so much play in the steering wheel it looked like I was trying to steer a boat down the road. The horn was located on thin rubber tubing that lined the inside of the steering wheel and occasionally, due to a power steering leak, you'd hear an occasional horn beep as I tried to steer this monstrosity around some corner. It was totally embarrassing to say the least.

When I left Dairy Queen and started working at McDonald's, I had left an empty crumpled up bag in the back on the floor, not thinking too much about it. The next morning, I found raccoon paw prints all over the back seat from them climbing up through the rotted floorboards at night to check out the bag they smelled.

One day, as I was washing dishes, some guy pulled in our driveway and came ringing the doorbell wanting to buy the car that sat in the gravel turnaround off the side of the driveway. When I asked him what for, he said for the local demolition derby. When I told him I drove that car to work, thank you very much, he apologized profusely and was so embarrassed he couldn't hightail it out of there fast enough.

Chapter 40

I was picked up around 4:30 p.m. the night of the shooting. My boyfriend and I left for dinner and then planned on going to the drive-in that night.

We had just pulled out of the driveway and were not even a mile up the road when I realized we had passed my stepdad's father driving his big gold Lincoln Continental erratically by us.

"Hey, I think that was Wayne's father we just passed and he's all over the road," I said. And didn't think anymore about it.

We saw *Mad Max Beyond Thunderdome* that night with Tina Turner and Mel Gibson. Tina wore those big metal earrings that looked like round ram horns and Mel was, well… lean and sweaty most of the movie.

When I got home that night, I could see the glass had been broken out of the front window of the door leading into the house and there was yellow Caution: Do Not Enter tape blocking the entry of the door.

There was a note attached to the banister from my mom telling me to not go in the house, but to please come to Medina Hospital and please hurry.

We went through every scenario we could think of on the drive there, but I knew whatever it was, it didn't involve my mom. Then my thoughts turned to my little brother. I hoped and prayed he wasn't hurt and could not for the life of me figure out what might have happened.

Moments after I left that evening Wayne had been shot through our front screen door by his father. He was coming to claim his wife. My stepdad had been letting his mother stay with us to protect her from his terrible abuse. The irony of that was not lost on us. He'd comfort his mother right in front of us, my mom and I passing glances of "give me a break" between us knowing that only weeks before, he'd almost knocked my teeth out by back handing me, for saying I didn't recognize a phone number listed on the phone bill. When he called the number and asked the kid that answered if he knew me, he hung up, thinking I was lying to him and backhanded me right in my mouth.

Months before that, he had broken my mother's nose by cracking her across the face with a plastic bank shaped like a Michelob beer bottle. He claimed that that was all just an accident though, so she stayed. And because he was able to convince her it was an accident his employer would never have to know.

When he refused to allow his mother to come to the door that evening, his father pulled out a pistol and shot four times, each bullet finding its target deep within Wayne's body.

"Oh my God, Robin, I'm so glad you're here. He's in critical condition and they're not sure he's going to live. I don't know what I'm going to do if he doesn't make it," she said as I entered the waiting room.

"What happened?" I asked.

"Wayne's father came ringing the doorbell right after you left, I mean, it was so close to the time you left, we thought it might be you coming back for something and that maybe you had forgotten your key," she said.

"Yeah, I thought we passed him. He was driving erratically like he was drunk," I said.

"Yeah, he was drunk. But all of a sudden we heard pop, pop, pop, pop, four shots, I ran to the front door and Wayne was lying on the floor in a pool of blood," she said.

"Oh my God. Did they arrest his father?" I asked.

"They did. But he got all the way back to his house before they arrested him," she said. "Robin, I need you to pray for Wayne. Put aside whatever issues you have with him and pray. I need you to do this for me. Will you?" she asked.

"Yes, I'll pray, Mom, I'm not a monster. I don't like the guy, but I don't wish him dead," I said.

I lied. But, I prayed for him anyway.

Because right then, I really didn't want him to die. For her sake, not mine. God only knew how'd she take it if he died. I knew she had zero coping skills and I had no idea if she'd be able to get back on her feet without a man in her life.

"I need you to pray like you mean it, not half–assed. Like you mean it," she said as she held my shoulders and looked me square in the eye.

"I will. I will. Don't worry, everything will be alright," I said.

So, I went to be by myself.

Dear God,

Please. If you could... Could you please save Wayne from death? As you know, he's been shot. So, could you please save him for my mom? And of course, you know, his kids? And his mom? And his... never mind. You know what I mean. Anyway. Look... You know I don't like the guy, probably never will, but I don't want to see him suffer or die, or my mom suffer and not know how to go on without him. So, can you please heal him? And, I usually wouldn't add something for myself in a prayer about someone else, but if you could... could you please let this whole thing make him be nicer to me and my mom? Please, just send me an angel to watch over me. Thanks. — In Jesus name I pray, Amen."

And wouldn't you know it, Jesus finally answered me. He saved my abuser.

I visited Wayne in intensive care and he gradually got better, but not without lots of pain, tubes, and beeping machines around him for a very long time. It humbled him some. He would ask for things nicely now and started using words like "please" and "thank you," even smiling more and eventually started talking to me like I was a person. But, no matter how nice he was to me, or my mom now, there was no way around the agony he had to deal with to heal. Jesus might have answered my prayer to save him from death, but when it came to his prayers about getting out of the pain it took to live, Jesus said no dice.

He slowly stepped down from intensive care to critical care to a regular room and I remember him talking about the removal of the chest tube that just about killed him that day. He said he didn't remember it going in, but sure as hell felt every last inch of it come out, he recounted.

Months later when he was back at home, he was a lot more docile than before, as if someone had unplugged him and he'd lost some of the animation that was in him. His once lean, trim body that he tanned at the tanning salon was now pale, weak and looked withered and old. I had to admit, even if to myself, that I did feel sorry for him. The trouble with having a big heart is you tend to feel sorry for assholes, too.

Some months went by and pretty soon my mom received some certified mail that my dad was fighting for custody of my brother, to take him out of the dangerous environment in which he lived. He was ten years old. I was seventeen.

The sad thing? I don't remember much about my little brother once he no longer required my immediate care and he was self-sufficient, I was too busy struggling to survive. I do remember he always looked sad, lost and alone and stayed in his room a lot keeping himself occupied like I did when I was little. Once in awhile he'd giggle at me when we peeked in on each other, but that was about it. I knew he got a kick out of my feistiness and on more than one occasion I knew he realized I saved him from an ass beating of his own.

The courts deemed the situation an emergency and my mother lost custody of my little brother very quickly after the letter came. I remember him being there one day and he was gone the next. She cried more over that than anything I'd ever seen her grieve over. I felt sorry for her too, but had to remind myself that she always chose men over us kids so I blamed her, while she blamed my dad. She'd tell anyone that would listen what a prick he was for taking my brother off of her, saying how ridiculous it was to think my brother could have gotten hurt in the shooting. I thought how ridiculous she was for thinking it was ridiculous that he couldn't have been hurt. What if he'd answered the door, I wondered.

Life went on. My mom worked at a hair salon between crying jags and trying to drink away her pain, and Wayne just existed for a while. I think he was trying to quietly come to terms with having his own father shoot him. Talk about Dysfunction Junction, I thought. Dang.

Chapter 41

It was summer of 1985 and I continued to date my boyfriend. I went to his senior prom, and did all the things kids at my age did. My life was finally becoming more about me. My mom said she couldn't afford a lot so when we went shopping I chose a pink lace prom dress with a high-neck collar I found on the sale rack at the mall for $16.00. The perfectly matched lace and pearl earrings I found were $3.99, making my total cost for prom $19.99 because I wore pink patent leather pumps my mom had. My boyfriend wore a gray tuxedo with pink cummerbund and bow tie that cost much more than my whole outfit did. We posed for pictures out in his yard taken by his parents and although his mother didn't like me, she acted happy and proud of her son anyway. He wasn't the type to go to his prom and she wanted to celebrate that he did. The next day we went to Cedar Point Amusement Park like all kids did.

School was out and summer went on. We went to drive-ins, parties, went on double dates, and I was finally getting my share of some happiness.

As Fall approached and the leaves were just starting to change, I went to my mom and told her I needed to go to the doctor.

"Oh yeah? What for?" she asked.

"I'm pregnant," I said.

"What? Are you really?" she asked in a whisper, getting up to come closer to me.

"Yep," I said confidently.

"Well, how to do you know for certain? Did you take a pregnancy test?"

"No, I just feel I am."

"Feel? Have you missed a period yet?"

"No, not yet," I said.

"Well, then… maybe with all the stress of everything lately, your cycle is just thrown off," she said.

"No, I just know I am," I said. "I felt it the moment it happened. I've been a bit nauseated and light headed lately, I'm tired a lot, so I think that's it," I added.

"What are you going to do if you are?" she asked.

"I'm having it and I'm raising it," I said.

And sure enough, the doctor confirmed I was about six weeks along as his nurse came in while he was checking me and handed him the results. My mom sat in the corner in the chair as the nurse handed her some pamphlets about my options. Young, scared and pregnant? Don't know what to do? You have options.

I was the same age my mother was when she got pregnant with me, but I knew I would be a different mother than the one I had. I'd hug my child and tell them they were good, that they could do whatever they put their minds to and let them know they could always count on me. I'd light up when I saw them, I'd play with them, teach them, celebrate their birth and they'd know they were wanted and loved. I was young, but I was over being scared. I was having this baby.

On my 18th birthday that year, I received a letter from my father. I was excited to hear from him as my mom handed me the envelope with his handwriting on it. I wanted to hear what he and my brother were doing now and hear how they missed me and maybe set up a visit soon.

Robin,

I heard from your mother last week that you are pregnant. I've sat with my feelings over this for the past week and I don't think I can convey to you just how disappointed I am in you.

My heart sank. Tears welled in my eyes. My mother sat across from me at the glass table, watching my every facial reaction to reading the words.

I was so naive. I read on.

I've thought long and hard about what I'm about to say, but I've made the decision to give any and all monies I've saved for your college education, and any and all assistance I was willing to give you during that time, to your brother.

You have ruined your young life and disgraced the Jessup name. It will kill your grandmother and grandfather when I tell them what you've done.

You are nothing but a whore. You are now, and forever will be, a nothing, just like your mother. You won't amount to anything.

I will have nothing to do with you or your bastard child from here on out. Do not contact me, or your brother again. You are no longer welcomed in our lives or our home. You've made your bed, now you have to lie in it.

Signed,

Harland E. Jessup

11/1985.

I folded the letter as the tears slipped from my eyes. It was like being punched in the gut when I was already begging to be seen and heard, valued and loved. Reading this made me feel like I was dying. I'd spent my young life doing everything to make them love me and it was never enough. I could not earn their love.

"He's not happy, is he?" she asked.

I handed her the letter to see for herself and she started to read.

"You know he's not happy and that's why you called him, isn't it?" I said as she tried to read.

"That's not why I called him," she said as she looked up from the letter, "but he's your dad and he needed to know. It's not like you can hide this for long, Robin Lynn." She looked at my stomach as if I didn't know my stomach would get big.

They rarely if ever communicated and he never needed to know anything about me for months at a time, yet she had to run and tell him this within only a few days of me getting a doctor to confirm what I already knew.

"You love it," I said.

"No, I don't," she said. "I don't."

"You know how he is. How dramatic, mean and over-the-top he gets about things." I said.

"I didn't know he was going to write a letter like this," she said as her eyebrows went up.

I walked into my bedroom and she followed me.

"I'm sorry he wrote that stuff to you. You don't deserve it," she said as she hugged me.

I sat on the side of my bed and wept in her arms. And she just let me cry, not saying a word. She held me, pushing her lips into the top of my head, rocking me slightly like a baby. It was only the second time in my life I'd ever sat in my mother's arms crying. The last time being right after she pulled me to the floor by my hair and kicked me in my ribs. It was like seeking respite in the arms of a tsunami. At any moment the tide would turn and you'd be swept away for trying to get too close.

Then she spoke.

"Just tell me again," she said, "you're having the baby and keeping it, right?"

"I already told you, I'm having the baby and, yes, I'm keeping it," I said. "Why?" I asked.

And with that she yelled for Wayne.

"Wayne, can you come in here for a minute!" she called out to the other room.

His weak, pale body with bags under its eyes appeared in my bedroom door.

"Yeah?" he asked.

"I just wanted to tell you something. Robin Lynn here's pregnant and she's keeping it. I just want to tell you right here and now in front of her, so she knows, that if you ever so much as lay a hand on her, for whatever reason, from this moment forward, I will kill you, do you understand me? I will take that revolver you have out there and I will shoot your ass right where you stand. And I'll guarantee you, you won't live through it next time. You got that?" she said.

He nodded and without saying a word, he turned and walked away.

"There. Now you know," she said.

"Know what?" I asked.

"That I'll defend you. Protect you. Protect the baby. Be your mom. Pick you over him," she said.

We hugged.

She stopped hugging me and pushed me back by my shoulders to get a look at my still flat stomach.

"Ooooooh," she said excitedly as she patted my belly. "A grandbaby. So, what're you going to name it?" she asked.

"Jancie, after Grandma, if it's a girl, and Cody if it's a boy," I said.

"Six weeks along and you already have names picked. Seems like you have it all figured out then," she said and hugged me again.

I sat on the side of my bed reading the letter so many times I had it memorized.

As I sat and replayed all I'd been through up to this point in my life, I wasn't sure how I knew, but I did, that I could do this by myself if necessary. I didn't care if anyone loved me or cared about me anymore. I cared about me and loved myself, and now I loved my baby. I had been the only constant in my life and had gotten myself through things up to this point without much help. I lay down on the bed to rest. I was spent. My life replayed in my mind as I drifted off caught between this world and sleep.

I didn't know why my dad hated me so much. But, the answer came to me.—He didn't hate me. He hated himself. If there was anything at all he hated about me, it was my light and his inability to change me into what he was. On one hand, he was attracted to my light like a moth to a flame. He wanted to examine it, play with it, laugh with it. It made him tilt his head to one side trying to understand it and be a part of it. But when he couldn't take it all in and he couldn't leave the confines of his own misery long enough to make sense of it, he wanted to smother it with his darkness. He and my mom fed off one another. And when my light never fully went out and it went on to shine even brighter than before, it infuriated them even more.

Each attempt at extinguishing my light got worse over time and one day you realize that although you love them, it feels painful to be around them. Nothing you do for them is ever right. It was like trying to please Big Berta. Move to the left, move to the right, and no matter how many times you accommodate them, or how much, it's never enough.

I woke up with the letter still in my hand.

"Fuck you," I said to the letter.

He wanted to predict my doom, my failure. Fuck if I was gonna let him do that. He didn't get to say who I was going to be, and where I was going in my life. I did. I wasn't wasting one more tear over this person I called my dad.

I folded the letter and locked it away in a metal box.

I looked at my face in the mirror and knew I was as tough as the steel I grew up around. My dad tried his best to temper, roll and cast me like the steel he worked with at the mill, but still, I would not set. He was physically abusive, emotionally and mentally cruel, and loved terrorizing me as a way to avoid facing his own demons. My mother, although an abuse victim herself, was never there for her children emotionally, never nurtured us, or took accountability for herself or her choices, and later in life became even more cunning, manipulative and cold.

I stayed fluid, unyielding at their attempts to harden me, and so bright they couldn't stand to look at me for very long. And they resented me for it and both eventually discarded me as their daughter.

I took that pain and used it as fuel for this ride.

Months went by and my stomach grew. And with a life growing inside me, I got the sense that like this baby, I too belonged to a much bigger entity than just two people, or a town that made steel and never changed. And when I looked to the sky looking for God, I knew I belonged to a bigger cosmos of things. Maybe I was part of the earth and sky, maybe I was made with the sun, the moon and the stars. Maybe I existed for many hundreds of years and not just eighteen.

It sure as hell felt like that.

"From," not "of." Always remember that," I said as I rubbed my belly and smiled.

Epilogue

February 21, 2012:

I was forty-five years old when they demolished the rickety old Steubenville Bridge that still caused me to wake in the middle of the night.

I had spent my life helping others before myself. I was trying to prove I was good and worthy and the exact opposite of my parents. Sounds like good things, but putting yourself on the back burner in your attempt to not look selfish can become a habit and becomes a way of hiding out. Pretty soon anyone and everyone needs something from you. It's like running from fire to fire. Soon you're running all over the place trying to save people while you're drowning yourself. You look in the mirror one day and you don't even recognize your own reflection.

I learned in counseling I was conditioned in childhood not to need much of anything for myself. I learned to become a caregiver to everyone but myself. And for as much as I fought my way through life, I spent an exorbitant amount of time making myself small enough for others to use and abuse. In my attempts at trying to be seen, valued and loved in my own family, I had become a dumping ground for other people's toxicity. The more I took the more I thought they'd love me. I'm here to tell you, it doesn't work like that.

The Steubenville Bridge had taken eighty-four years of wear and tear and I felt as old as she did. In 2006 a weight restriction was placed on her and in 2009 when a dip in the floor was detected during routine maintenance, she was very shortly afterward deemed impassable by the Ohio Department of Transportation.

While they were figuring out what to do with her she stood defiant for another three years until it was finally decided. Now, in a matter of minutes, she would be gone. Demolished. Like she meant nothing. I screamed in my head as the tears flowed out of me, "But she means something to me! I was scared of her but I loved her too! Please, why can't you just fix her?" my child self asked.

I sat safe and alone in my empty nest as I watched her demolition on TV, and later repeatedly watched YouTube videos of it. I cried like I had just watched my sibling or parent be blown to bits. Why, after all these years, was I having this same reaction to this bridge?

It wasn't until that day, in the last ten seconds of her life, I learned she wasn't trying to scare me in my dreams and she wasn't just delivering me back and forth to Ohio and West Virginia all those years; she was delivering me to myself. And like her, I was slowly being crushed by the mere magnitude of carrying the weight of the stories I'd never told a soul.

She was rigged with explosives now.

She had only ten more second to live.

And she spoke:

10 - Like me, you are scarred from all the abuse

9 - but, still, you refuse to fall.

8 - You stand exhausted, but defiant thinking that is strength

7 - but your real strength comes from your sway.

6 - Sway is what kids learn to do when help doesn't come, and
   bridges do so they don't collapse under the pressure

5 - but our real beauty is in our scars.

4 - You're a steel town girl like me

3 - from a town that never changes

2 - and although you are as tough as the steel that made us

1 - you have to deconstruct and rebuild if you ever want to
   survive.

   FIRE!

And in one fell swoop, fire raced down her bony sides and with one loud explosion, her towers, like arms, fell out to her sides, and bits of her went flying up through the air in the large, gray plume of smoke that remained. Her metal deck and marred-up sides fell into the Ohio River with an explosive thud and suddenly she was free from the pain of standing firm for so very long.

She was gone.

The bridge called to me relentlessly during this time.

When I was doubtful I could tell my story, she reminded me of the umpteen times I had crossed over her bony back, two sweaty hands on the steering wheel, and how I went on in spite of my fear, sometimes even smiling and singing alongside of fear. When the task at hand overwhelmed me, she told me to keep both hands on the wheel, look straight ahead and not allow myself to be pulled from side to side.

I'd have to travel back over her to a time and place I didn't want to go to, and I had to face it all no matter how painful it was going to be.

"Don't be afraid," she said. "You're tough. Like steel."

So, like her, I set fire to my sides, let my towers, like arms, fall to my sides, and fell with a thud. I had to rebuild myself in order to come back shinier and stronger than ever before.

26256855R00203

Made in the USA
Lexington, KY
22 December 2018